The Rotary Jail

The Rotary Jail

*Escape-Proof Cells
on a Carousel, 1882–1966*

W.C. Madden

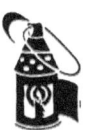

McFarland & Company, Inc., Publishers
Jefferson, North Carolina

LIBRARY OF CONGRESS CATALOGUING-IN-PUBLICATION DATA

Names: Madden, W. C., author.
Title: The rotary jail : escape-proof cells on a carousel, 1882–
   1966 / W.C. Madden.
Description: Jefferson, North Carolina : McFarland & Company,
   Inc., Publishers, 2017 | Includes bibliographical references and
   index.
Identifiers: LCCN 2017018178 | ISBN 9781476666150 (softcover :
   acid free paper) ∞
Subjects: LCSH: Jails—United States—History—19th century. |
   Jails—United States—History—20th century.
Classification: LCC HV8746.U6 .M33 2017 | DDC 365/.34—dc23
LC record available at https://lccn.loc.gov/2017018178

BRITISH LIBRARY CATALOGUING DATA ARE AVAILABLE

ISBN (print) 978-1-4766-6615-0
ISBN (ebook) 978-1-4766-2913-1

Front cover: the old Gallatin County Jail was placed on the National
Register of Historic Places on February 23, 1990 (photograph
by the author); *background* 1881 W.H. Brown & B.F. Haugh patent

Printed in the United States of America

McFarland & Company, Inc., Publishers
   Box 611, Jefferson, North Carolina 28640
   www.mcfarlandpub.com

I dedicate this book to the one I love most, my wife Janice Darlene Madden, who traveled with me to the rotary museums in Crawfordsville, Council Bluffs and Gallatin, and edited the manuscript before it went to the publisher. She helped me so much I was inclined to share the byline with her—but she wouldn't have it.

Table of Contents

Acknowledgments

During the researching of this book, I came across many people who were very helpful in my search for information.

My journey started in Crawfordsville, Indiana, where Matt Salzman gave my tour group an excellent tour of the rotary jail museum. His presentation sparked my interest for more information on the subject. When I found that no book existed, I decided there should be one.

I decided that I had to visit the other two rotary jail museums in Gallatin, Missouri, and Council Bluffs, Iowa. When I arrived at Gallatin, I was greeted by curator Trudi Burton, who was more than helpful in my request for information. She gave an excellent tour of the facility and let me look through a jail log in the museum. The workers at the Gallatin Library were also very helpful in my search for information. They even provided a cup of coffee and tea during our research there.

The same situation held true in Council Bluffs. The two workers there were very helpful with information and one of them provided a complete tour of the museum. We also went to the Council Bluffs Library and workers there were helpful.

When researching information about the Appleton, Wisconsin, rotary jail, I crossed paths with Sgt. Arnold A. Nettekoven and I'm glad I did. He provided a copy of an article from the *Appleton Post* that was very helpful in writing that chapter.

Prudence Doherty, a public services librarian for the University of Vermont Special Collections, pointed me in the right direction for information about the rotary jail in Burlington, Vermont.

Margaret Kelley of the Nodaway County Historical Society was very helpful in providing information about the jail in Marysville, Missouri. Also, Janet Hawley provided some great research material on the Nodaway County Jail.

Somier Mckibbin of the Douglas County Historical Society provided me with a photo of the rotary jail.

Sharon Martin of the DeKalb County Historical Society furnished information and a photo of the rotary jail in Maysville, Missouri.

Mark Slosek provided a paper written by his father, Anthony Slosek, which was helpful in writing about the Oswego County rotary jail. Anthony was the county historian.

Matt Jaeger from the Local and Family History Department at the McCracken County Public Library was helpful in providing some basic information on the McCracken County Jail in Paducah, Kentucky.

Ken Clark of the Pueblo County Historical Society was very helpful in providing the history of the rotary jail there as he sent something he wrote a local publication in May 2009. It was pure luck to speak to him first when I called for information. Then I received the information via email the same day. He may be eighty-four years old, but he's not slowed down. However, he's not computer literate and had to have someone else send it to me. I told him he wasn't too old to learn how to use the computer. Our literacy volunteers once taught a ninety-three-year-old woman how to use the computer.

Although Red Wing, Minnesota, didn't have a rotary jail, it once considered having one. I stopped there while I was in the vicinity visiting my daughter in St. Paul. The people at the library were very friendly and helpful. Sheriff Scott T. McNurlin took time out of his schedule to speak with us for about an hour on the county jails, too.

I contacted the Pauly Jail Building Company about the rotary jails they built, but they no longer have the records for historical projects.

Table of Rotary Jails

Location	Date Opened	Rotary Closed	# of Floors	# of Cells	Company
Paducah, Kentucky	June 10, 1882	1934	2	16	Haugh, Ketchum & Co.
Crawfordsville, Indiana	June 1882	1938	2	16	Haugh, Ketchum & Co.
Maryville, Missouri	1882	1904	2	16	F.C. Allen
Maysville, Missouri	1885	1938	1	8	Haugh, Ketchum & Co.
Council Bluffs, Iowa	Sep. 10, 1885	Dec. 1, 1969	3	24	Haugh, Ketchum & Co.
Omaha, Nebraska	Nov. 1885	1908	3	30	Pauly Jail Building
Williamsport, Indiana	1886	1907	1	8	Pauly Jail Building
Appleton, Wisconsin	June 3, 1887	Nov. 1906	1	8	Patent Rotary Jail
Oswego, New York	1887	1909	2	20	Pauly Jail Building
Sherman, Texas	1887	1912	2	16	Pauly Jail Building
Burlington, Vermont	January 1888	August 1907	1	10	Pauly Jail Building
Salt Lake City, Utah	July 4, 1888	1910	2	20	Pauly Jail Building
Wichita, Kansas	Oct. 1888	Feb. 1919	2	24	Pauly Jail Building
Waxahachie, Texas	Nov. 1888	1929	2	20	Pauly Jail Building
Charleston, W.V.	1888	1922	1	16	Pauly Jail Building
Dover, New Hampshire	1888	1908	2	16	Pauly Jail Building
Gallatin, Missouri	1888	1964	1	8	Pauly Jail Building
Pueblo, Colorado	1889	1966	2	20	Pauly Jail Building

Preface

This book covers the history of one of the most unusual detention facilities ever built—the rotary jail. After researching the subject for a magazine article and not finding much information, I thought it was important to write a book about the concept and the jails that were constructed, so that the information would be preserved for history in one reference.

Most of the information in this book comes from newspaper research using three websites: newspapers.com, newspaperarchives.com and chroniclingamerica.loc.gov. Information about three rotary jails—Council Bluffs, Iowa; Crawfordsville, Indiana; and Gallatin, Missouri—comes from personal visits to the rotary jails that were turned into museums. Other information comes from books and contributions from historical societies.

The book is organized chronologically by the date the rotary jails were built. In some cases, only the year a rotary jail was constructed is known. Some jails continued to be used after the rotary jail section was discontinued, so the date the rotary was closed is indicated in the table on the facing page.

Introduction

Novelist Richard Wright once wrote, "Men simply copied the realities of their hearts when they built prisons."[1]

From the early colonial period through the Civil War, many county jails were poorly constructed of wood or stone and used wrought and cast iron for grating. Many were located by the courthouse for the convenience of the sheriff and the officers of the court. In some cases, they were as simple as somebody's root cellar for an overnight stay. In fact, French writer Alexis de Tocqueville wrote in the early 1800s that the county jails were the worst jails in the world.[2]

However, the years following the Civil War were troublesome times as the nation recovered from the worst war in its history. Crime was on the increase and larger county jails were needed to take care of the prisoners. The development of inexpensive steel in the 1850s contributed to design of better jails.

A few entrepreneurs began developing plans for smaller jails for counties to use. One of those distinctive efforts was the rotary jail design by William H. Brown and Benjamin F. Haugh from Indianapolis, Indiana. How they came up with the concept is not known, but it incorporated several building ideas that were already implemented.

For example, in the latter half of the seventeenth century, Antoine Desgodet designed a hospital with an octagon center and sixteen radiating wards. The center "was to carry a dome which served the purpose of sucking out used air." Another Frenchman, Antoine Petit, created plans for a hospital featuring six long wards running radially within a vast circle. Its dome also served as a ventilator.[3]

There were a couple of other inventors who came up with octagon shaped buildings, while incorporating radial cells.[4] And railroads utilized a giant circular turntable that was rotated manually through the use of gears.

As far as jails are concerned, the idea for a circular jail was first conceived by Jeremy Bentham, who designed an English panopticon prison in 1791. The cells were built on the outside walls and each faced the middle of the circle, so that they could be observed by one person. The idea spread to Richmond, Virginia, where Benjamin H. Latrobe built a circular, castle-like prison in 1800. Then the Western Penitentiary in Pittsburgh, Pennsylvania, was built in 1826 as a panopticon.[5]

All of these building types and plans may have led Brown and Haugh to invent a different type of smaller more secure jails for counties to use. Their design was one of the most unique and drastic changes in jail history in the United States and Europe. It was a one-of-a-kind marvel. The jail was the circular much like a giant metal pie pan. The individual, wedge-shaped cells were separated from one other by solid iron walls, but the cells themselves had neither bars in front nor doors. Instead, the cells rotated within a cylinder of stationary bars, a cage, which contained a single locked door through which prisoners could be admitted, released, or fed. For the sake of efficiency and economy, the whole mechanism could be operated by a solitary jailer, who through an easy turn of crank on any of the floors, could set in a motion a series of gears located in the basement of the jail that rotated the massive, circular block until the desired cell lined up with the door. The cells could even be rotated so that none lined up with the door at all. And because the pointy end of each cell contained a water closet (an innovation for its day), there was no reason why an inmate would ever have to leave his cell until his appointed time. The rotary jail was touted as "escape proof," providing maximum security with a minimal staff.[6]

Throughout its history, the rotary jail was escape proof with the exception of one occasion in Wichita, Kansas, when a prisoner was able to use acid and saws to free the rotary allowing for the escape of seven other prisoners.[7]

Descriptions of the rotary jail noted that it was to rotate continually throughout the night. However, it seems that continual rotation was more of a sales pitch than a reality. Power for turning the drum was to be provided by a water mill or weight-and-spring device. But in reality, the turning of the jail was done by a hand crank. This was not an easy task considering the weight of the massive turntable.[8]

The rotary jail was advertised in the *Indianapolis News* and it caught the attention of counties looking for a better facility and a way to keep their prisoners securely jailed with less manpower. Soon the new design began being built. And within a decade, eighteen were constructed by several different companies. However, the Pauly Jail Building Company constructed the largest number of the radically designed jails. The rotary jail became the premier member of their product line. Their catalog stated "there is perhaps no invention of the present age, connected with the construction of jails and other prisons, which has attracted so much attention among those interested in that subject as the Rotary Jail."[9]

However, many communities experienced buyer's remorse (some within a few short years) after constructing their rotary jail. Their drawbacks were numerous. A jailer could only observe an inmate when the cellblock was in motion. Ground settlement beneath several jails tilted the cellblock out of balance so that it pressed against one side of the circular sleeve and became extremely difficult or completely impossible to operate. Fire marshals and prison inspectors became more and more concerned about the fire hazards the rotary presented because of the slow means of escape if a fire were to break out. And inmates suffered many broken bones and crushed limbs from the rotating giant.[10]

The concept of a rotary jail received some good reviews from different entities. For example, the Somerset County, Pennsylvania, Grand Jury recommended the jail in 1886. However, none was ever built there. Probate Judge Elias A. Smith recommended the jail for Salt Lake City. Eventually, one was built there.

The rotary jails that were eventually built in the United States ended up getting several nicknames: the "Merry-Go-Round Jail," the "Lazy Susan Jail," the "Human Squirrel Cage," and "Carousel of Cells."

The rotary jails were built by several companies over the years. The majority were constructed by the Pauly Jail Building Company, which was first established in 1856 and is still in business.

While eighteen rotary jails were built in the United States, many more were considered. The problem with the rotary jail was that it was much more expensive to build than a regular jail. For example, the Goodhue County commissioners of Red Wing, Minnesota, considered a rotary jail and were given a quote of $14,000 for it from both the Pauly Jail Building Company and the Patent Rotary Jail Company. But the Patent Rotary Jail Company also quoted them a price of $11,000 for a square jail. The commissioners opted for the less expensive square jail and built it instead of a rotary. That jail remained until 1973.[11]

County commissioners were drawn to the rotary jail because it offered a high-tech approach to harboring the criminals at the time, including bank robbers, confidence men, murderers, and others.[12]

Unfortunately, the problems and hazards with the rotary jail led to their demise and by the 1930s, many were either closed or no longer being used as originally intended. The most consistent problem encountered was the locking up of the contraption. Some problems took days to fix because someone from the company would have to come and make needed repairs. With the lack of swift transportation, it might take a repairman a day or more to travel to the jail with the problem. A hazard that occurred often entailed prisoners getting injured when the rotary rotated. Many jailers never informed the prisoners when they were going to move the rotary, so inmates would get body parts caught in the bars as the cylinder rotated. One inmate even got his head crushed from the movement of the rotary, which led to the demise of that rotary jail. Another hazard was fire. Some inmates would purposely put something, such as a shoe or even a pegleg, in the bars to stop the rotary from moving. Although the rotary was sold as a fireproof jail, fires did sometimes occur not from the metal jail but from the contents in the cells, such as mattresses or clothing. One fire in a rotary jail killed a man in his cell, but he wasn't located in the rotary section of the jail.

The last rotary jail in use was located in Gallatin, Missouri, and it was closed in 1975; however, the rotary section was stopped from working in 1964 when the gears and the steel were scrapped. Only three rotary jails have been preserved for history in Council Bluffs, Iowa; Crawfordsville, Indiana; and Gallatin. All of the others have been demolished, except for one that was transformed into an office building.

Most of the jails incorporating the rotary design were three-story brick structures with a two-story rotary jail inside. However, a couple of the rotary jails were only one-story or placed in a basement. Only two rotary jails built contained a three-story rotary jail inside. Those structures were located in Council Bluffs, and across the Missouri River in Omaha, Nebraska.

While the patent showed eight pie-shaped cells on each level, some were actually built with ten or twelve pie-shaped cells on each level. One or two inmates could be housed in a cell. Either beds or hammocks were provided for sleeping. Jails also had additional traditional cells built for female or juvenile inmates. A few had solitary confinement cells that remained separate from the rotary.

In the end, the rotary jail was viewed as failed architecture and as a failure of the idea that technology would always provide a solution that was in the best interests of humankind.[13]

"All prisons that have existed in our society to date put people away as no human being should ever be put away," wrote author Barbara Deming.[14]

1

The Invention

The Industrial Revolution was a time when many inventors came up with new ideas, products, and new ways of doing things. The age set the stage for new inventions coming about in the late 1800s during the Second Industrial Revolution, which is when architect William H. Brown of Indianapolis conceived the rotary jail.

Brown, iron foundry owner Benjamin F. Haugh, and John L. Ketcham applied for United States Patent No. 244,358, on July 12, 1881. The patent read:

> To all whom it may concern: Be it known that we, WILLIAM H. BROWN and BENJAMIN F. HAUGH, both of the city of Indianoplis, [sic] county of Marion, and State of Indiana, have invented certain new and useful Improvements in Jails or Prisons, of which the following is a specification.
>
> The object of our invention is to produce a jail or prison in which prisoners can be controlled without the necessity of personal contact between them and the jailer or guard, and incidentally to provide it with sundry conveniences and advantages not usually found in prisons; and it consists, first, of a circular cell structure of considerable size (inside the usual prison—building) divided into several cells capable of being rotated, and surrounded by a grating in close proximity thereto, which has only such number of openings (usually 20 one) as is necessary for the convenient handling of the prisoners; second, in the combination, with said cell structure, of a system of shafts and gears, or their equivalents, for the purpose of rotating the same; third, in constructing within said circular cell structure a central space for the purposes of ventilation and the disposition of offal, &c.; fourth, in constructing niches in the side of the cells next said central opening to serve as water-closets, and arranging underneath said niches a continuous trough to contain water, to receive and convey away into a sewer with which it is connected all the offal deposited therein by the prisoners in all the cells; fifth, in the combination, with a cell structure, of a central vertical hollow shaft, which will also serve as a smoke-stack; and, sixth, in various details of construction and arrangement, all as will hereinafter be more specifically set forth.[1]

Accompanying drawings detailed a central ventilating space, the water-closet arrangement with valves to the "soil-pipe," a sectional view

(No Model.)   5 Sheets—Sheet 1.

W. H. BROWN & B. F. HAUGH.
JAIL OR PRISON.

No. 244,358.   Patented July 12, 1881.

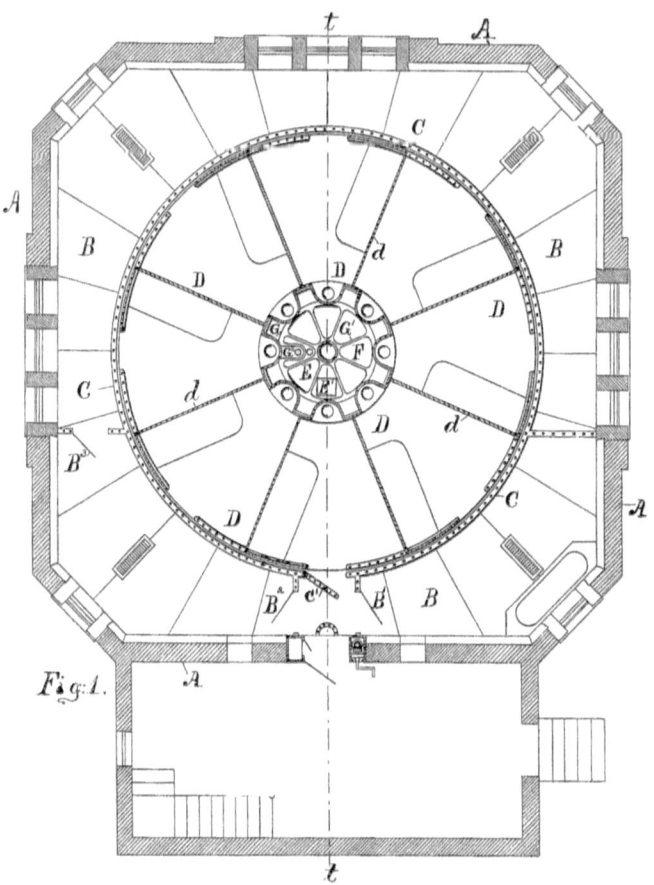

Fig. 1.

WITNESSES.

Arthur Holladay

INVENTOR.
William H. Brown and
Benjamin F. Haugh,
PER
C. Bradford
ATTORNEY.

Horizontal section of jail.

8

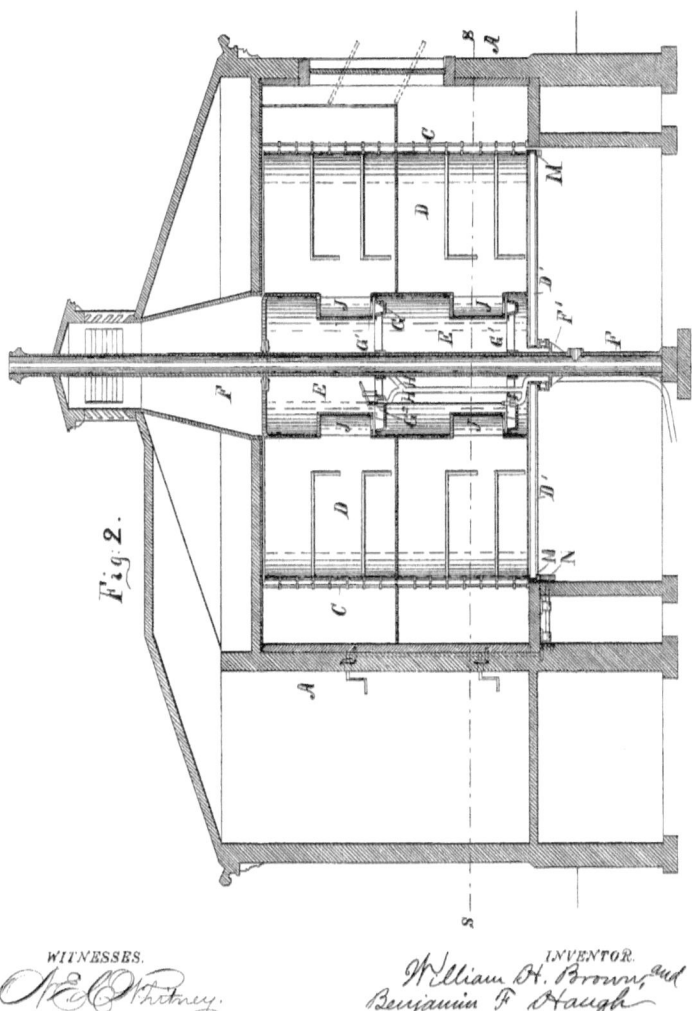

(No Model.)   5 Sheets—Sheet 2.

W. H. BROWN & B. F. HAUGH.
JAIL OR PRISON.

No. 244,358.   Patented July 12, 1881.

Fig. 2.

WITNESSES.

INVENTOR.
William H. Brown, and
Benjamin F. Haugh
PER
C. Bradford
ATTORNEY.

N. PETERS. Photo-Lithographer, Washington, D. C.

Vertical sectional view.

of the mechanism for revolving the cells, and the rollers their superstructure. Between the outer walls and the cell structure, a corridor extended all around a heavy floor-to-ceiling grating that surrounded the cells. In the center, a circular structure, divided into cells by partitions, revolved around a central vertical axis, with a central opening above for ventilation. Niches in the inner walls of the cells provided toilet facilities, each projecting over a trough at the center of the carousel. The cell structure was mounted on low-friction trucks, and was rotated by means of a rack and pinion, operated by a crank or hand wheel through a system of gears. A lock-bolt enabled the cell structure to be locked in one position. The patent described the operation and the advantages of the design.

> The cell structure containing all the cells may be one or more stories in height, (two stories are shown in the drawings,) and rotates bodily on a central vertical shaft within a stationary iron cage or grating. Each cell is provided with a door opening at the center of its front side, but is unprovided with a door, as said opening is closed by the circular stationary cage or grating in front of the same. The cells being entirely closed at all times, except when opposite the general entrance-door, no escape can be effected, except by cutting through the solid grating. As the cells are necessarily frequently moved, and another portion of the grating thereby presented in front of each cell, sufficient time (even if the means were at hand) is never afforded for this purpose, and therefore this jail is much more secure than those of the ordinary construction. Attention is called to the fact, in this connection, that the construction of the cells is such that the prisoners cannot see or communicate with each other in any way, and therefore that any concert of action between them would be extremely difficult.
>
> The prisoners are handled without any possible chance for personal contact with any except the one desired, as the cell structure is rotated until the door-opening of the cell desired is brought opposite the general door opening in the outside grating, and while one cell occupies this position the rest must of necessity be securely closed. This arrangement makes the whole prison as convenient to the keeper as though it consisted of but a single cell, and as safe as if it contained but a single prisoner. When opening and closing the doors leading to the entrance of the cells … the cell structure may be rotated into such a position that not even one door-opening will be open, thus preventing the possibility of an assault upon the keeper at such times. When the door in the outside grating … is closed of course all the cells are closed, whether opposite the general entrance or not.[2]

The ventilation system prevented any offensive odors from remaining in the cells. Hot-air registers in winter or open windows in the outer walls during summer, maintained air movement through the cells to the central ventilating shaft at all times. The central shaft was a large hollow iron casting and housed the smoke stack for the furnace, which prevented the

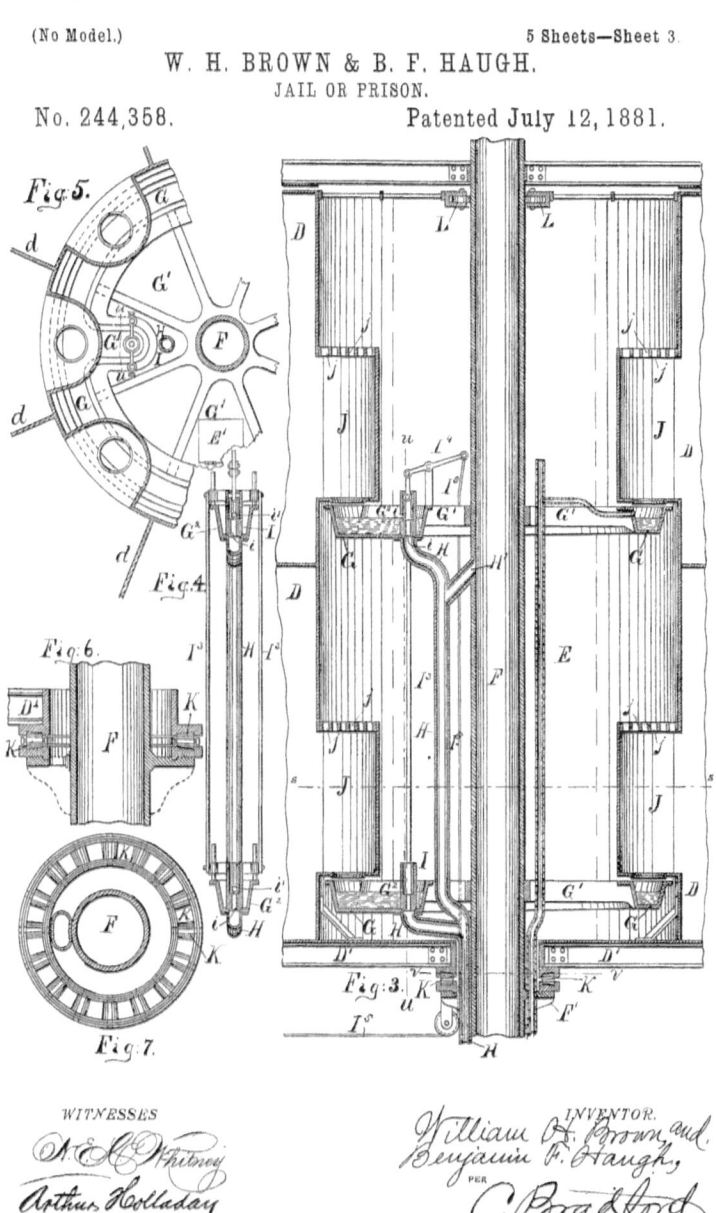

Detail of central shaft.

11

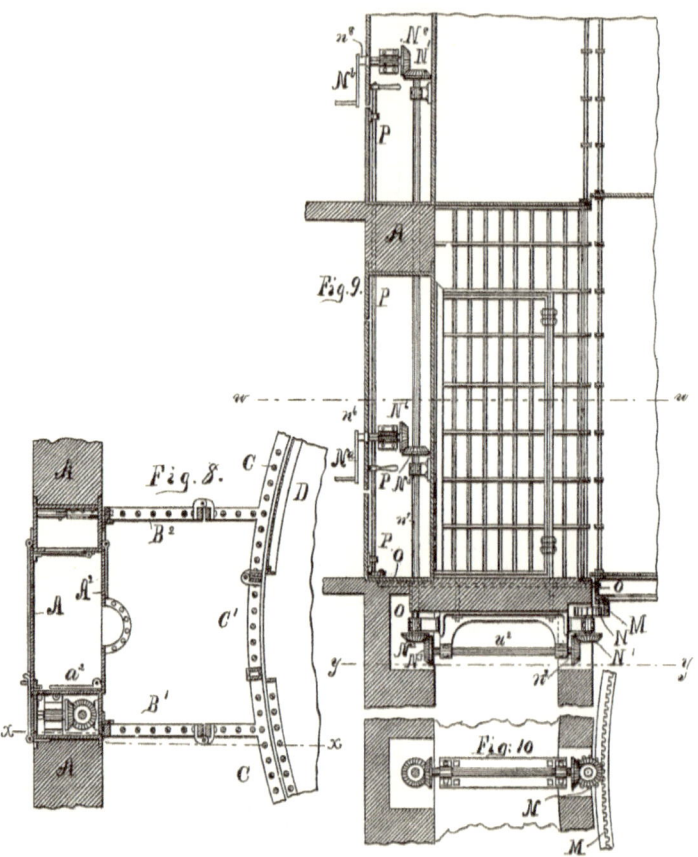

N. PETERS, Photo-Lithographer, Washington, D. C.

Detail of revolving mechanism.

water pipes from freezing in cold weather. An access door in the floor of the ventilating shaft, "through which access may be gained thereto for the purposes of repairs to the water-closet system" offered a bonus function: "If by any means a prisoner should break through into the ventilating-shaft, this trap door would afford a convenient means of recapture, as, said ventilating-shaft being securely closed both at bottom and top, such prisoner could make no further progress toward liberty, but would be securely imprisoned therein." The rotating mechanism was well beyond the reach of the prisoners, and could not be reached even by anyone escaping into ventilating shaft.[3]

Anticipating questions about alternative configurations, the designers explained:

> As it might occur to some to have the cell structure stationary and the surrounding grating movable, we desire to say that we have considered such a construction, and consider it substantially the equivalent of that shown, except that it is lacking in some of the advantages which ours secures. As will be readily seen, for instance, the advantage of bringing any one of the prisoners at any time up to the main entrance could not be so secured.
>
> We have also conceived the idea of keeping the cell structure in continual rotation during the night, or at any other time when the prisoners cannot be conveniently watched, and thus prevent even an attempt on their part to cut their way out at such times. This could be accomplished by ... a heavy weight or spring, the operation of which could be regulated by a clock-work or other similar mechanism.
>
> A large prison constructed in accordance with our plan would consist of a number of separate pavilions arranged around a central building having communication with each of them.... Such a construction at the same time provides for a complete classification of the prisoners. In such a prison the central column would not ordinarily be used as a smoke-stack, but would serve the one purpose of an axis for the cell structure. The rarefication of air in the ventilating-shaft would be effected in such case by a steam-radiator supplied from a boiler located under the central building, or such like method, thus avoiding the necessity of operating a separate heating device in each pavilion.
>
> We have considered the question of constructing each story of the cell structure to rotate separately without regard to the other story or stories; but as this would necessitate an increased number of parts, such as bearing rollers, locking devices, and rotating mechanism, without any advantage which we think sufficient to offset the expense thereof, we have decided that it is not advisable to so construct them.[4]

The submitted design consisted of a two-tier cylindrical cellblock with a central column that served as both support and plumbing for the individual toilets in the cells. Each tier had eight wedge-shaped cells, but the surrounding structure had only one door. When a guard rotated a

(No Model.)   5 Sheets—Sheet 5.

W. H. BROWN & B. F. HAUGH.
JAIL OR PRISON.

No. 244,358.   Patented July 12, 1881.

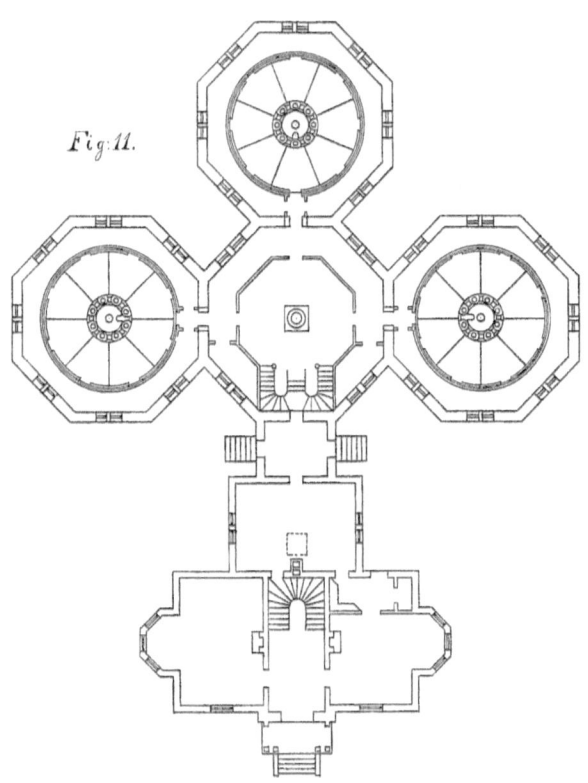

Fig:11.

WITNESSES.

INVENTOR.
William H. Brown, and
Benjamin F. Haugh,
PER
C. Bradford
ATTORNEY.

N. PETERS. Photo-Lithographer. Washington, D.C.

Floor plan for jail complex featuring multiple rotary cellblocks.

hand crank, the cellblock spun, sending the prisoners on a disorienting carousel ride past the lone access point.

The Haugh, Ketcham Company, located in Haughville, Indiana, began running advertisements in the *Indianapolis News* starting in August 1881 stating that the rotary jail was "the only safe and best well ventilated jail made." The new company replaced the Haugh Architectural Iron Works, which had been in business for twenty-five years. The advertisements continued into 1882 on a nearly weekly basis.[5]

The Brown and Haugh patent eventually was purchased by the Pauly Jail Building and Manufacturing Company, St. Louis, Missouri, in 1885. They began selling the "patent rotary jail" and the company built many of the rotary jails throughout the United States. The Pauly Catalog of 1888 offered more than six hundred jail designs from which to choose, including the rotary jail. The company listed ten advantages to building the rotary jail:

First—It is a modern and scientific prison.

Second—It is the latest invention in prisons and the product of a progressive and inventive age.

Third—It is absolutely secure.

Fourth—It is a humane jail, being well lighted, properly ventilated and furnished with all the necessary requirements within reach of the prisoners for cleanliness.

Fifth—Its manner of construction affords separation of prisoners, and avoids herding them together like animals.

Sixth—It is difficult for prisoners to communicate with one another.

Seventh—It, of all systems devised, furnished better protection against the prisoners being able to hold communication.

Eighth—It affords the sheriff absolute protection in handling his prisoners, he never being obliged to come in contact with the inmates of more than one cell at a time. Under this system such a thing as a rush of many prisoners upon the sheriff is unknown.

Ninth—It absolutely prevents such a thing as the organizing of conspiracies among prisoners.

Tenth—Its classification features give the character of a reformatory institution, a detaining institution and a punishing institution, such an institution as every well devised county jail should be.

Problems

The rotary jails had their share of problems. One was getting rid of all the waste the inmates put down their toilets. While the sewage system was state of the art at the time, it resulted in smelly problems. Raw sewage from each cell had to remain in the toilet hopper until the cellblock was rotated, which allowed the pipe from each cell to line up sequentially with a single sewage outlet. This system of holding sewage, combined with the summer heat and poor ventilation in a jail, sometimes resulted in an overpowering stench. Although the companies advertised that the jail was "well ventilated," the jails were later criticized as not being well ventilated or lit.[6]

Prisoners who had any limbs sticking out of their cell during the rotation process had a good chance of getting their arm or foot crushed or amputated. Jailers later announced when the rotating was going to happen to avoid this problem. One man had his head crushed during a rotation and he later died that same day from the injury. As a result, that particular rotary was closed.

In the case of a fire, the rotation process was too slow to help in quickly getting prisoners to safety. A couple of fires in rotary jails illustrated this very problem. Fire marshals closed some of the jails for this very reason.

Another problem that sometimes cropped up was the rotation of the cells became difficult or jammed and the rotary became stuck in position until repairs could be made to fix the problem. As a result of these problems, some rotary jails stopped the rotating process altogether. They made the jail fixed and put individual doors in the cells.

The rotary jail also had its critics. Arthur Hopkins, the leading American prison architect in the early 1900s, once wrote, "I have always felt that the employment of this excess of tool-proof metal to be the most absurd of all our ill-considered prison construction.... To build an entire institution on the basis of its worst possible inmates is nonsense."[7]

The *Wichita Beacon* criticized the rotary jail when it wrote on October 9, 1917: "The county emphatically does *not* need a duplicate of the rotary or any other medieval relic of barbarism."[8]

First Rotary Jail opens
in Paducah, Kentucky

Paducah was named Pekin at first and was settled in 1815. Then the town was laid out in 1827 and renamed Paducah by William Clark of the famed Lewis and Clark Expedition. The community was incorporated in 1830 and became the county seat for McCracken County in 1832.[1]

The first jail in Paducah was built of logs in the 1830s. It was replaced by a brick jail in 1868. By the 1880s, the city needed a larger jail to keep pace with the population and growing number of lawbreakers. By this time, the population of Paducah had risen to more than eight thousand and McCracken County was twice that size, so the county decided in 1881 to go with a two-tiered rotary jail. The stone for the outside walls were delivered in October 1881 from the quarries in Bedford, Indiana.[2]

The construction of the new jail in 1882 was supervised by George Davis of Paducah. The two-tiered rotary section containing sixteen pie-shaped cells was built by Haugh, Ketchum & Company of Indianapolis. The brick work was performed by T.E. Morgan of Paducah.[3]

On June 3, 1882, the jail was officially received from W.M. Brown from Haugh, Ketchum & Company. The building cost the county $19,750. The keys would be placed in the hands of Jailer Edwards and the prisoners would be removed to their quarters in a week.[4]

The first prisoners were moved into the new jail on June 9, 1882, making it the first rotary jail to be opened by two weeks sooner than the one in Crawfordsville, Indiana. The move of the prisoners was made a day earlier than planned because of warm weather. A total of twenty-two prisoners were moved.[5]

The old jail was put up for auction and sold for $100 at the end of June 1882.[6]

The rotary jail at Paducah had its problems. Supposedly, jailers abandoned their posts for days at a time with the keys in their pockets, leaving no way to rotate the cells to provide prisoners with food and water. The inmates had their tricks, too. One incident had prisoners working together to create a rocking motion in order to throw the jail off its gears. Another resourceful inmate was said to stick his peg leg into the stationary bars of the cylinder forcing the entire mechanism to a standstill. However, a particular problem with rotary jails was that they were also easy to break into. With a solitary guard on duty, there wasn't much to stop an unruly crowd from overrunning the jail and releasing whomever they saw fit.[7]

A dungeon was built in the McCracken County Jail in August 1906. Built in the basement of brick with a heavy wooden door, the dungeon would provide a place for Jailer Eaker to put impudent and unruly prisoners. The recalcitrant prisoner would be kept there, existing only on a diet of bread and water.[8]

The grand jury examined the McCracken County Jail in September 1906 and found it to be in excellent condition. They found the prisoners were being properly dieted and receiving kind attention by the jailer.[9]

However, in February 1910, a jail committee inspected McCracken County Jail and recommended a new jail be built to replace the rotary. The committee was dissatisfied with the construction of the jail. They said the rotary was too dark and lacked air flow. They said there was problem with sewage connection as well.[10] As a result of the recommendation, jail officials considered strengthening the walls of the jail by lining it with sheet iron. The county could not afford to build a new jail at this time. Consideration would also be given for prisoners to spend more time out of their cells and in the corridors if these improvements were completed on the walls. The health department had declared the jail as unsanitary.[11]

Not until the 1930s was another jail considered for McCracken County. The rotary jail was discontinued in 1933 and was demolished in 1934.[12]

Before the old rotary jail was taken down, the "Ballad of Paducah Jail" film was filmed there in 1934 and released in October that year. The film was a nineteen-minute comedy starring Irvin S. Cobb, Paul Hurst, and Carl Stockdale. Irvin goes off to hunt for an escaped criminal and is captured himself by a felon.[13]

Nowadays, the McCracken County Jail is located at 700 S. 7th Street in Paducah and has a capacity of five hundred beds. There is a separate facility for juveniles.[14]

Hangings

In the 1800s, several men were hanged in Paducah for their crimes. Some were hanged before they were tried and several were African Americans, referred to as "colored" or "negro" at the time by journalists.

An African American was hanged on January 15, 1890, for the murder of a woman. Jesse Brown met his death for killing his mistress, "Babe" Laurie.[15]

Another black man was hanged by a lynch mob of two hundred men

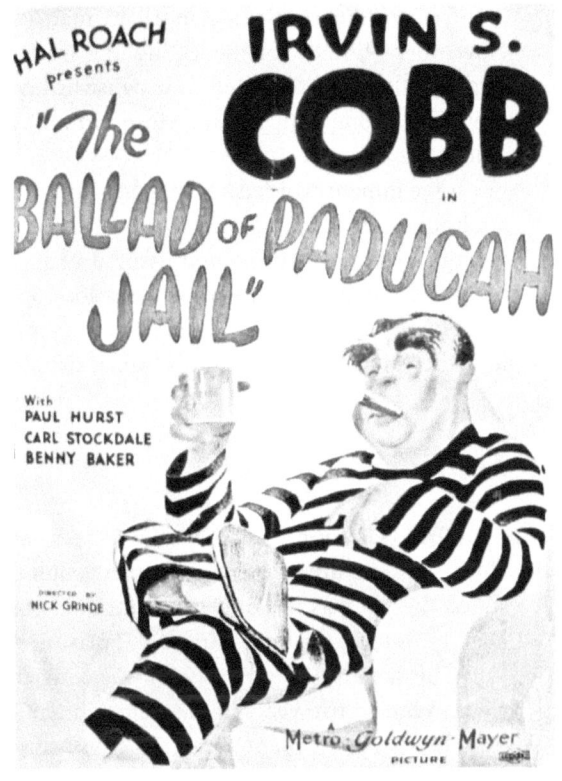

Movie poster for "The Ballad of Paducah Jail," filmed in the old rotary jail in Paducah before it was demolished in 1934.

from a tree on the courthouse square after being forcibly removed from the McCracken County Jail on June 10, 1892. Charles Hill had escaped from a chain gang and gone to a farm house where he had brutally assaulted a young woman. The nineteen-year-old Miss Starr fought him off, but he overpowered her and beat her with his fist and a knife. His attack was interrupted when a lad of the house came in and frightened him away. Hill escaped to Cairo, Illinois, where he was captured and returned to Paducah. An angry mob forced the jailer to turn over the keys to the jail and then strung up the black man. About five hundred witnesses and half the police force did nothing to intercede with the hanging. Hill begged for his life at the jail to no avail before he was seized and taken to the tree for hanging.[16]

19

Yet another African American man was hanged the morning of November 19, 1897, for the killing of a woman. "Devil" George Winston said he killed Vina Stubblefield because he loved her. About fifty witnesses saw the hanging which lasted eleven minutes before thirty-two-year-old Winston finally succumbed.[17]

One inmate avoided hanging by committing suicide in his cell thirty-six hours before his appointment with the hangman in October 1909. George Freeman had been convicted of murder and was sentenced to hang. He killed himself with an overdose of drugs that somehow ended up in his cell. The drugs belonged to another inmate named Hiram Smedley, who said someone took his box of drugs from his cell.[18]

Murderers

Tom Hammon was convicted of manslaughter for killing Will Hall. He was given a nine-year sentence on September 23, 1898. The grand jury stated the jail was in good condition and commended Jailer Miller and Deputy Bonnin for their care of the prisoners.[19]

The sentence of a man who was convicted of murder was cut from eleven years to two years in the state penitentiary by the appellate court in 1910. Lewis Futrell spent about six months in the McCracken County Jail waiting for his appeal. Young Futrell and his father had come to Paducah with a shipment of tobacco and they were staying at the boarding house of Horace Osburn. On the night of February 25, 1909, Osburn accused the men of drinking and ordered them from the house. An argument ensued and the young Futrell shot and killed Osburn. The defense claimed that Osburn attacked the father and Lewis shot Osburn in defense.[20]

A man was moved from the McCracken County Jail on February 5, 1930, after the man he was accused of shooting died. Roy Springer, forty, was removed to Caldwell County Jail after Frank Barrett, sixty-two, died from a pistol wound to the lung. When Fulton's Chief of Police Bailey Huddleston arrested the tramp for stealing cigars at Barrett's store, Springer slashed him in the throat with a knife. Then Springer stole the chief's pistol and shot Barrett with it. The police chief survived the attack. Springer had escaped from an insane asylum in Jackson, Mississippi, on September 7, 1928.[21] Springer was convicted of the murder on May 15, 1930, in Fulton, Kentucky, and he was given a life sentence.[22]

An itinerant berry picker was fatally shot and his wife seriously wounded by the woman's half-brother on May 15, 1932, in Paducah. Anderson B. Williams turned himself into the Kevil town marshal later for killing Charles Dorener and wounding his wife, Elvina. The shooting followed an argument at the breakfast table. A twelve-year-old girl was also the victim of a stray shot from Williams' shotgun. Williams was put in the McCracken County Jail.[23]

Escapes

Over the years many escapes were made from the McCracken County Jail, but the rotary section was not the cause of the deliveries as they were called back then. The worst jail delivery occurred on July 10, 1909, when thirteen prisoners made their way out of the jail. They spent the night in the rotary and were let out of it to the corridor in the morning for meals and exercise. The inmates used an iron bar about two feet in length and a half-inch thick to create a hole about a foot high and eighteen inches wide in the north wall of the jail. Because the hole was about fourteen feet from the ground, the men used a blanket to slide their way to the ground, although some men went down headfirst, striking their heads on the ground. The men then escaped from the enclosure of the concrete wall by dashing through the doorway of the engine room and ran south in the alley between Fifth and Sixth streets. Jonas Smith, an African American, was the first prisoner captured. He was being held on a murder charge and was the worst criminal who escaped.[24]

Two men escaped from the McCracken County Jail on October 12, 1899. Tom Hollihan and Pete Griffin escaped at 3 a.m. in the morning by digging through the south wall of the jail, crawling through the aperture and swinging down to the ground by the bars on the second floor. They used a hammer, case knife and spoon to help them dig through the wall. They were in jail for grand larceny. A reward of $50 per person was posted.[25]

William Childers, an African American who broke jail from McCracken County Jail in February 1906, was captured in Louisville on March 17. Childers was known as "Yellow Boy" to police and was a trustee of the jail when he walked away from the jail. He had been jailed for housebreaking.[26]

Will Bolin, alias "Billy Bow Legs," broke jail from Paducah in 1906 and was captured by police in Louisville on December 1, 1906. He was in the Paducah jail originally for stealing Sunday dinner from Chief of Police James Collins' table.[27]

Two men, who made their escape from the McCracken County Jail in the summer of 1909, made their escape from another jail as well after their capture. Robert Craig and Dave Slaggle were captured in New Madrid, Missouri, but they also got away from that jail as well in January 1910. They were going to be sent back to Paducah for trial on charges of stealing brass from the Illinois Central Railroad.[28]

Four prisoners broke out of the McCracken County Jail on May 28, 1919. They dug their way out of the jail. On June 1, one of the prisoners, Daniel Blackwell, was later shot and killed in Grantsburg, Illinois. Another of the escapees, W.H. Gerk, was traveling with him and was captured. The other two prisoners who escaped were African Americans and were not recaptured. They were Arthur Price and Ed Perkins. Perkins was awaiting a new trial on a murder charge.[29]

A man leaped to his death on April 4, 1926, rather than returning to his cell at the McCracken County Jail where he was being held for murder. Raymond Philley had escaped from the jail at midnight, but he was recaptured in the morning. Then he broke away from officers and jumped into the Tennessee River at Owens Island to his death. "I won't go back to that jail," he told a farmer who had given him breakfast on the island. "If I'm caught, I'll stab myself or jump in the river." He jumped in the river. Philley had broken the lock on his cell door using a bolt. Then he dug a hole through the brick wall and descended to the ground from the second floor using a rope made out of blankets.[30]

Four prisoners who escaped the jail were recaptured on the roof of the prison on April 1, 1933. They used the handle of an ice teaspoon to pry loose a twenty-inch iron bolt which protected a sheet of steel. Then they dug a hole in the south wall of the building and swung to the roof of the one-story kitchen with the aid of a rope made from blankets. The four men were surprised on the kitchen roof by Jailer Roscoe Houser and Deputy Jailer Lurid Thompson, who fired shots to dissuade the prisoners from going any farther.[31]

Six prisoners locked the jailer in a cell and fled the McCracken County Jail on February 26, 1934. When Deputy Jailer Cliff Martin and Trusty Joseph Lindsey started to lock up the prisoners for the night, one of the inmates uncovered a pistol. "Don't move, old man," said James Henley, "or I'll have to shoot you." The prisoners then took Martin's keys and locked them up in a cell. They cut the telephone wires, ransacked the office and left by the front door.[32] The six prisoners were captured the next day when their automobile broke down in Graves County.[33]

Other Criminals

The case of John Sager was a miscarriage of justice as it lacked being a speedy trial. Sager served two years in jail for stealing a mule before his case was heard. The charges were then dismissed by the judge as he proved the mule was his own.[34]

A former county court clerk was convicted of altering and publishing forged checks for the second time and given a five-year sentence in the penitentiary on April 29, 1910. Hiram Smedley had already been convicted of publishing forged warrants and given a sentence of six years in the penitentiary the previous fall. He spent some time in the McCracken County Jail before he was tried the first time. Then he faced the second charge for the July term of the court.[35]

President Woodrow Wilson commuted the sentence of a Confederate veteran who was in the McCracken County Jail for making a false claim that he was a Union soldier. George W. Nunley was sent to jail in November 1912, but physicians reported he would die soon. So the President of the United States commuted his sentence on July 24, 1913.[36]

The McCracken County Jail was overflowing with prisoners after a crusade against violators of Prohibition laws on July 20, 1924. Fifty-six prisoners were checked in at breakfast and are sleeping ten to twelve to a cell.[37]

Three Illinois sheriffs were arrested on federal charges of possessing liquor on November 3, 1932. The three officers arrived in Paducah to take custody of a bank robber who was in the McCracken County Jail, but were then arrested for possession of liquor they had brought and intended to give to the McCracken County sheriff for capturing the bank robber. Arrested were Sheriff Lester Tiffany and Deputy Sheriffs Clayton Tiffany and Tom Dolin. They had two bottles of Canadian whisky twenty-nine bottles of beer. The Illinois officers were denied prisoner, Floyd Fulbright, 42, because Louisiana had posted a larger bond as Fulbright was wanted there on murder charges. Fulbright had been picked up in Kentucky on minor charges. While in jail, he confessed to robbing banks in six Illinois cities and one Wisconsin bank. The Illinois sheriffs were sent back home empty handed.[38]

Safekeeping

Several inmates were brought to the McCracken County rotary jail when it existed because it was a safer facility than most jails in the area.

Because the Cadiz jail was unsafe, Laurence Willis of Golden Pond was brought to the McCracken County Jail in May 1905. He was charged with killing his uncle, Lieutenant W.B. Johnstone at Canton two years previously. He was tried and given a life sentence, but was granted a new trial and the second jury was unable to agree, so he was released on bond.[39]

Jim Kimbrough, an African American from Fulton County, was brought to the McCracken County Jail for safekeeping on July 31, 1906. He had been charged with attempting to assault a girl named Harrington. At first, he was taken to Mayfield, but a lynch mob formed there so he was brought to Paducah.[40]

Another man who was transferred to Paducah for safekeeping was Homer Bridges, an African American, who was threatened in Murray in August 1910. He was accused of shooting Ernest Lowery, a white boy, from a car window at Hazel, Calloway County.[41] Bridges was later sentenced to life imprisonment in November 1910 for the murder of the young white farmer. Bridges had been kept in the Paducah jail until his trial in Murray, where the feelings against him had subsided.[42]

An African American from Louisville was brought from Fulton to the McCracken County Jail for safekeeping in November 1910. Harry Shaver, nineteen, confessed to shooting Henry Cherry, but said it was in self-defense. The charge of malicious shooting against Shaver was changed to murder. The shooting occurred after Cherry ordered Shaver to remove ashes from the firebox of the steamer and Shaver refused. Cherry turned on him with an open knife and Shaver shot him to death.[43]

A prisoner from Fulton was transferred to the McCracken County Jail because the jail in Fulton was considered unsafe on May 26, 1911. Lee Carter, the former Chief of Police in Fulton, shot and killed Frank Baucomb, the son of a Seattle millionaire. Carter was later given a life sentence.[44]

An African American was brought to the Paducah Jail for safekeeping after he shot and killed two white men in his home in Hickman on Christmas night in 1912. Frank and Louis Ramsey together with another white man, Raymond Wallace, and an African American named Gish went to the home of Barfield. When Barfield and his wife returned from church, the men forced their way into his home and shot him in the side. Barfield retaliated shooting them dead with a shotgun. What had caused the incident was friction between the blacks and the white men, who didn't want them working on bottom plantations. Notices like the following had been posted on trees: "Mr. Land Owner, we will advise you that you cannot work niggers in 1912. Try it old nigger. What would you think if you was to go asleep some night and never wake up. Better let this stay here." Wallace and Gish were later arrested and taken to the Hickman jail.[45]

A deputy killed the sheriff in Mayfield and was taken to the McCracken County Jail for safekeeping on March 6, 1922. Deputy Sheriff Sam Galloway shot and killed Sheriff John T. Roach over a salary dispute. Galloway shot the sheriff three times and he died in two minutes. Galloway then turned his gun on unarmed Deputy Sheriff Arthur Roach, but he didn't shoot him. Instead, he turned the gun over to the deputy and surrendered to him. He was whisked away from the jail in Mayfield and brought to Paducah.[46]

Mrs. Lillian Walters was brought to the Paducah county jail for safekeeping without bond after she was arrested on a charge of accessory to murder on October 23, 1923. She was accused of assisting in the Eddyville Prison mutiny that resulted in the murder of three guards and three prisoners. She was ready to plead guilty to the charge of supplying arms to the convicts and to take her punishment.[47]

A Marshall County man was brought to the McCracken County Jail for safekeeping after a mob of masked men forced him to tell them where he had taken a five-year-old boy on March 13 in Benton. Solon Dowdy had kidnapped the child and taken him to Joplin, Missouri. He confessed to the mob, who decided not to lynch him. He was then brought to Paducah until trial on six felony counts.[48]

Four African Americans were brought to the McCracken County Jail for safekeeping after admitting slaying a man on October 30, 1928, in Hickman. Cleveland Allen, Charlie Perkins, Thomas Jackson, and Charlie Hampton were arrested by Sheriff John Thompson and confessed to killing Dee Plant with an ax. The sheriff brought them to Paducah by car.[49] The four men pleaded guilty on May 13, 1929, in Hickman and threw themselves on the mercy of the court.[50]

25

A farmer who was severely beaten by a masked mob that took him from his cell in Smithland was brought to the McCracken County Jail for safekeeping on October 17, 1933. Richard Edmonds was a mass of cuts and bruises after the mob beat him. Because the mob said they were going to beat some other men, Circuit Judge C.H. Wilson ordered the three others to Paducah as well: George Lee, twenty; Boyd Champion, twenty-three; and Roy Farmer, thirty-three, all of Livingston County. Five masked men had invaded the jail and forced the jailer to turn over the keys at the point of a shotgun. The "regulators" had been operating in the county for almost a year. In late August, they took Louis Skinner and hanged him from a tree for several minutes and beat him. The judge has reported the problems to the governor.[51]

Married in Jail

A marriage was conducted in the Paducah jail in April 1915. L.O. Mills was being held in jail for bigamy when he married Verna McDonald, age 16. He had married the McDonald girl under the impression he was divorced. So the first marriage to the McDonald girl was declared invalid. However, his first wife did finally obtain a divorce a few days before Mills and McDonald married again.[52]

Baptized in jail

An inmate of the McCracken County Jail was baptized in the little river in back of the jail by a reverend on July 26, 1923. Mrs. Henrietta Wagner, who was being held in connection with the explosion that killed Mrs. Rosetta Warren and her unborn child, had professed religion.[53] Wagner was later convicted of murdering Mrs. Warren by using ten sticks of dynamite to blow up the house. She was given a life sentence.[54]

The McCracken County Jail was empty for a few hours on July 23, 1932, for the first time in nearly eighteen years. However, new inmates occupied cells after the Police Court let out for the night.[55]

3

Second Rotary Jail opens in Crawfordsville, Indiana

County jails in Indiana were first established in 1792 under laws of the Northwest Territory. They continued under the laws of Indiana Territory and state constitutions of 1815 and 1851.[1] In December 1880, Indianapolis architect Benjamin F. Haugh showed up at a meeting of the Montgomery County commissioners in Crawfordsville, a mere forty-two miles from the capitol city. The commissioners reviewed his specifications and decided upon his invention of the rotary jail for their new jail the following spring.[2]

Construction of the jail began in the spring and was scheduled to be completed by January 1, 1882, according to Matt Salzman, the executive director of the Rotary Jail Museum. The sheriff's house was to be attached and sat in front of the jail. Sometime during the construction, the commissioners decided that the room for the kitchen and dining room in the sheriff's house was too small, so another room was added to serve as a kitchen. This addition to the original plans cost another $4,000 in addition to the $18,000 budgeted for the project, Salzman explained. This also delayed the completion date until June 1892. In fact, the sheriff moved into the jail on June 22, making the Crawfordsville rotary jail the second rotary jail to open in the country. The rotary jail in Paducah, Kentucky, opened on June 9.[3]

When the jail was completed, it created quite a backlash, because many homes lacked the indoor plumbing that this facility contained. The county commissioners were so proud of their "uncrackable" jail that they had their names inscribed in stone above the front door. These same commissioners were soon voted out of office for the cost overruns they created. The "complete scientific system of water supply and sewer drainage" ran through a hollow cast-iron shaft that was eight feet in diameter and ran through the center of each circular platform. The waste all drained into a trough in the basement and the entire sewage system could be flushed at one time. The shaft also served as the vent for the boiler in the basement. This dual use of the central core for smoke ventilation and plumbing created the advantage of preventing the pipes inside the stack from freezing in the winter.[4]

Built by the Haugh, Ketcham & Company Iron Works of Indianapolis, the two-story rotary jail had 16 cells and could accommodate thirty-two prisoners. Two additional cells were built on the second floor for women and difficult prisoners. The cell for women could hold four inmates. The solitary confinement cell held only one inmate who was considered dangerous. An infirmary was housed on the third floor with three cells, allowing additional inmates to be "crammed in" if necessary, explained Salzman. The rotary weighed some thirty-two tons, according to Salzman.

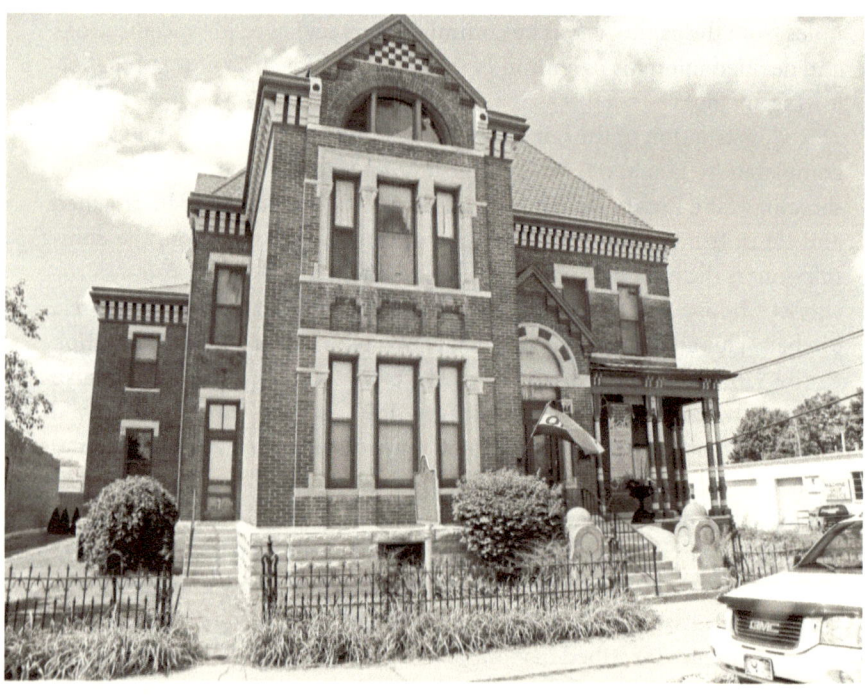

The former Montgomery County Jail was placed on the National Register of Historic Places in 1975 and is now a tourist spot in Crawfordsville (author photograph).

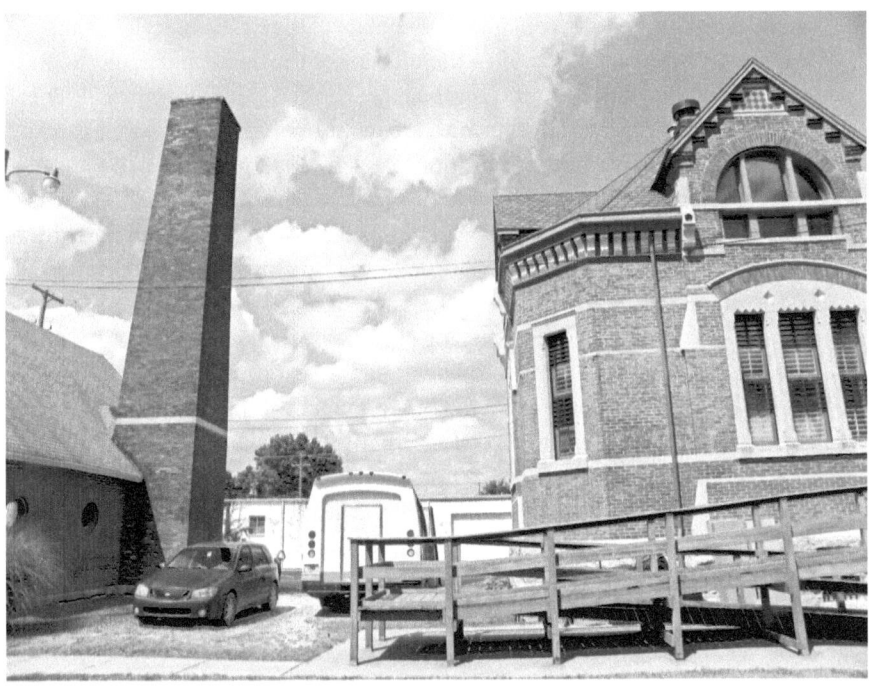

A heating plant (left building) was built behind the old Montgomery County Jail to provide steam heat to the structure (author photograph).

The red brick and limestone Rotary Jail and Sheriff's Residence doesn't easily fit into one classifiable architectural style. It's more of a combination of Italianate, Queen Anne/Eastlake, and Romanesque Revival. The exterior of the Sheriff's Residence highlights multiple elements of Italianate Style particularly the large brackets along the cornice line, the hipped and gabled roof design, and the partial-one storied porch. Many of the windows present in the house are tall and narrow and form groups of three. Additionally, the single windows feature simple rectangular hoods, while the grouped windows showcase more elaborate framed crowns including columns and decorative shapes. Queen Anne houses, very common in Crawfordsville during the late nineteenth century, often featured different types of wall texture. Variations in wall texture were often achieved through elaborate brick work. Brick patterns can be seen above the first floor windows facing Washington Street and the zigzag pattern found over the front door and under the main gable. Additional decorative patterns of yellow and red tile can be found under the front gable. Elements of the Eastlake style, a subset of Queen Anne, can be found in the interior of the home, particularly the beveled notched design found on the hand-carved wooden staircase. The same design is repeated in the concrete windows in the jail as well as the wooden doors in the house. Additionally, a grooved pattern can be found in the perpendicular door and window frames. The arches found over the door are elements of Romanesque Revival style, sometimes called Richardson Romanesque. The attic level windows and third-floor jail windows also form arches. The interior of the home features many original architectural features. However, exterior chimneys, pocket doors, and a few other things have been removed. The design was not adequately tested and refined before its execution, and the Montgomery County Jail went through numerous modifications to its cell mechanism and heating arrangements. A coal boiler furnace was first used in the jail for heat, but it was too small to heat both the house and the jail, so all the heat was diverted to the house resulting in inmates sometimes getting frostbite. Five years later a steam plant was built behind the jail and steam provided adequate heat for the jail, sheriff's home and the courthouse.[5]

Gas lighting was used for the first for nine years before electrical wiring was installed into the home, according to Salzman. The lights had been designed for gas or electric use and were easily converted to electricity. "This house was lit with electric lights before the White House was," the director said.

The rotary jail had its issues in Crawfordsville. Besides inmates getting their limbs amputated on occasion, some inmates would purposely stop the device from rotating. Such was the case of an inmate called "Pegleg." He had the habit of wedging his wooden limb between the fixed out bars and the inner bars of the rotating cellblock. The sheriff got tired of buying replacement limbs for those shattered when the block was set in motion, so he eventually required Pegleg to surrender his prosthetic leg before being locked up.[6]

The Montgomery County Jail had inmates for the most part all of the time. On May 5, 1915, the jail did remain empty for nine hours for the first time in many years. All of its doors were allowed to stand open and the rotary didn't have to move. As a result, all of the jail employees had a chance to attend a circus that had come to town. Just before supper a man was arrested on arriving in the city from Indianapolis and the doors had to be closed again.[7]

Although the rotary jail was advertised as fire proof, fire was a concern in the establishment as getting prisoners out of the jail took time if a fire occurred. A fire did occur at the Montgomery County Jail in October 1918. Roland Stout, age twenty, had been placed in solitary confinement because he was mentally deranged. A few hours after he had been removed from his home and put in his cell, he lit fire to the mattress in his cell on the second floor of the structure that was separate from the rotary section of the jail. The jailer thought the smoke might be coming from the attached sheriff's residence, so he ran there first. Not finding any smoke or fire coming from there, he returned to the jail and went upstairs to find the smoke pouring out of the solitary confinement cell. By this time, Stout was dead from smoke inhalation.[8]

The rotary broke down in December 1928 and all of the prisoners in the jail had to be transferred to the Boone County Jail for a short time until repairs could be made.[9]

In 1930, the Indiana State Board of Charities' investigators noted: "This structure of brick and steel is old, insecure, unsafe ... natural light and ventilation are poor. The revolving cellblock offers dark, unsanitary cells for the sixteen men it accommodates."[10]

Because of the evaluation and the fire threat that the jail posed, the rotary was finally stopped in 1938 and the cells were opened to the corridor. Many injuries had also occurred over the years because of the rotary. "A lot of people had their arms and legs amputated or crushed because of the rotary," said Salzman.

In August 1938, the State Welfare Department advised Montgomery County that their "Merry-Go-Round" Jail should be torn down and federal aid used to rebuild it. Furthermore, they declared the jail a fire hazard. They also noted the jail should not be used as a juvenile detention home either.[11]

Instead of tearing the jail down and building a new one, the rotary was fixed in place and the jail was reconfigured, Salzman explained. One area was turned into a drunk tank. In another area, the cells were left open into a corridor so it created one large cell instead of the small individual cells inside the rotary. A catwalk was added to the second floor rotary section to allow inmates access from their cells and to the outer door.

The jail did keep long-time prisoners clean. "If you stayed more than a week, you got a bath," said Salzman.

31

The jail served the county until it was closed in 1973 and a new county jail was built. The following sheriffs served the county and maintained the jail during its ninety-one year existence[12]:

1881–1883: James Q Wilhite	1916–1920: Fred H. Brown
1883–1886: Alexander Harper	1921–1924: Ira Luddington
1886–1888: E.P. McClaskey	1925–1928: Thomas Rice
1888–1890: John P. Bible	1929–1931: William F. Hitch
1890–1892: C.E. Davis	1932–1936: Verner Lee Bowers
1892–1894: John P. Bible	1937–1940: Merle Remley
1894–1896: C.E. Davis	1941–1944: Harold Roth
1896–1900: David Canine	1945–1949: Harold Zeller
1900–1902: C.M. McCullough	1949–1951: Roy Hardaker
1902–1908: John H. Mount	1951–1962: Merle Remley
1908–1912: Edward Lawrence	1963–1970: Clarence Demoret
1912–1916: James F. Wren	1970–1973: Robert R. Shull

Museum

In 1975, the Montgomery County Cultural Foundation, a not-for-profit corporation, took control over the jail and turned it into the Rotary Jail Museum. Also, the building was listed in the National Register of Historic Places on May 1, 1975.

The museum holds a number of fundraisers during the year. In late October, the museum holds a Haunted Jail tour for two nights. People purchase tickets to tour the decorated jail full of scary creatures. Tales of the jail are told by tour guides while the costumed characters jump out to scare the visitors. On February 7, 2016, "Marriage, Murder & Mayhem at Mardi Gras!" was held at the jail to raise money. It is also a popular stop with paranormal investigators. The museum also allows for these investigations to be held by the research groups for a donation.

A visit to the museum includes a tour of the rotary jail and sheriff's residence. The gift shop has exclusive T-shirts, postcards and gift items. The museum also houses interesting exhibits of local and Indiana history that have been donated by local citizens.

The Present Jail

The Montgomery County Jail is located at 600 Memorial Drive in Crawfordsville, Indiana. The new facility was opened in June 2006. It has

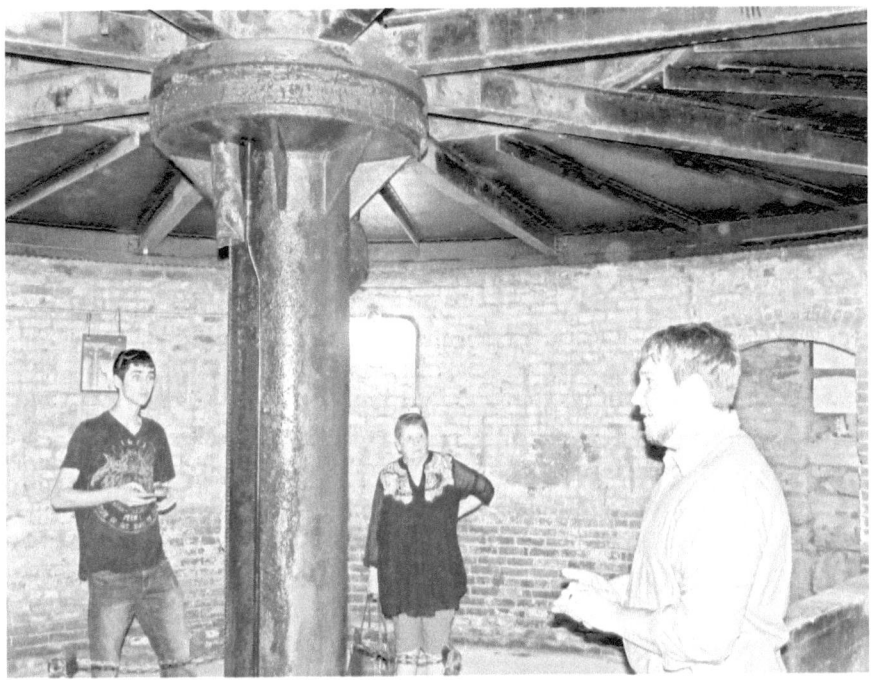

Executive Director Matt Salzman explains to visitors how the rotary jail operated in the basement of the Rotary Jail Museum (author photograph).

a capacity of two hundred and twenty-four beds: one hundred and thirty male beds, forty female beds, twelve temporary beds, two padded beds and forty beds for work release prisoners.[13]

Hangings

During the time of the rotary jail, two hangings were conducted on the grounds. The first came in 1885. James McMullen and his wife were killed the night of January 7, 1885. John W.C. Coffee was an ignorant farm hand and who lived near the victims. According to his first confession, he went to the house of McMullen. After chatting a while with him, he beat out the old man's brains. He then made the old woman tell where her money was kept, and after taking her out of doors, he killed her. He then threw the body back into the house and set fire to the building. He also implicated James Davis in the murder. Davis was convicted and sentenced to death, but he appealed and was not convicted. After nine months with no solution to the murder, citizens were getting uneasy, according to Salzman. Since Coffee confessed three times to the murder, it was easy for a jury to convict him for the murder. The execution was terribly bungled. On the first attempt, the rope broke and Coffee was sent to the ground slightly injured. He was carried up the scaffold groaning terribly. The trap was sprung again. Again the rope broke. Coffee fell to the ground a second time with blood spurting from his nose. On the third attempt, a thicker rope was passed over the crossbeam and he was sent to his death a third time. While his neck did not snap, he was slowly strangled to death. It took a full eight minutes before he died. A total of two hundred tickets were sold to the public to witness the hanging, said Salzman.[14]

The following year John C. Henning was convicted for the cowardly and brutal murder of Mrs. Lottie Volmer. Because of the popularity of the first hanging the year before, Sheriff Alexander Harper sent out invitations for the Henning execution. Tickets were in demand and sold from two to five dollars, according to the Rotary Jail Museum records. Newspaper reporters even had trouble getting tickets to cover the event. At least three hundred and fifty attended the event, including sheriffs from several counties, according to museum records. He was hanged on May 27, 1886. The divorced man had fallen in love with Volmer and wanted to marry her, and the couple secured a marriage license; however, she changed her mind and refused to marry him without giving any excuse for her refusal. "Jack the Tinker," as he was called, became desperate and began drinking harder than ever before. In vain he pleaded for a reconciliation with her. On the night of October 24, 1885, he visited her home. She had a visitor, Miss Emma Oliver. After talking pleasantly to them for a few minutes, he asked Volmer to go out walking with him. She refused. Then he requested she go upstairs with him. She again refused his request. He then drew a revolver on her. She retreated to the street with him shooting her as she fled. She died on the street with four pistol balls in her body. Henning went out the back door and escaped in the tall weeds. He was captured an hour later and thrown into the Rockville Jail until the following night when Sheriff Musser was advised of an approaching mob. He took the prisoner to Brazil. Then he was taken to Terre Haute and back to Rockville later for trial. His attorney asked for a change of venue and it was granted, so he was tried in Crawfordsville. The trial lasted four days and the jury found him guilty. Judge Snyder overruled a motion for a new trial and sentenced him to be hanged. An appeal was made to the Indiana Supreme Court and it was refused as well as a request to Governor Isaac P. Gray for commutation to imprisonment for life. Henning spoke for fifteen minutes on the scaffold before he was dropped to his death at 1:40 p.m.[15]

Murderers

Mrs. James Nelson was placed in the Montgomery County Jail on May 18, 1895, after admitting she killed her child. She gave officials the indication that her child had been kidnapped, but the murdered body was found concealed in her bedroom. She asserted that she was ill and the child's crying so affected her nerves that she arose and deliberately choked the tot to death.[16]

Philip Hawk for arrested for causing the death of one of his students, Miss Grace McClomrock, on February 20, 1896. Hawk confessed and implicated Dr. Stout in the case. A grand jury convened, but no indictment was handed down as Stout had relatives and friends on the jury. Stout escaped custody, but Hawk was caught and interred in the Montgomery County Jail because mob violence was feared.[17]

Otto Walker was given a life sentence for murdering his wife on March 5, 1908. He had been imprisoned in the Montgomery County Jail and was to be transferred to the State Penitentiary at Michigan City. Thirty-four ballots were required before a verdict was reached. Walker expressed regret that he would not be hanged for his crime.[18]

A Crawfordsville man was arrested, charged with murder and tossed into the Montgomery County Jail on October 15, 1916, until he could be moved to Indianapolis. George Farlow, thirty-five, was accused of killing William Walter Johnson, twenty-three, in Lover's Lane on the bank of the White River in Indianapolis.[19] Farlow was later convicted of first-degree murder and was given a life sentence in a Shelbyville Circuit Court.[20]

A Lafayette man was found guilty of murdering a taxicab driver in December 1917 and sentenced to spend the rest of his life in jail. William Ashby murdered Thomas E. Sense, a taxicab driver, on the night of June 3 west of Lafayette. He was arrested and confined in a rotary cell in the Montgomery County Jail until his trial. After his trial, he was sent to the state penitentiary.[21]

On the other hand, a woman was arrested and put in the Montgomery County Jail on April 24, 1918, accused of helping a taxicab driver murder a man. She was charged with first-degree murder in the case of Peter Mataxas, who was killed in October 1917 while with a group of persons on a joy ride in Lafayette.[22]

A man in the Montgomery County Jail claimed he didn't kill a woman on August 30, 1932. Morris Green, age twenty-two, said that he got in a scuffle with Miss Lila Jones, age thirty-three, and struck her over the head with a hatchet he had in his pocket. However, a total of four hatchet wounds were found on her body. He then dragged her body to the porch to summon a physician. She died without ever regaining consciousness.[23] Green was later found guilty of murder and he was sentenced to life in jail for her murder. The jury took only a half hour to consider him guilty. Green's defense of insanity failed.[24]

Escapes

Five prisoners broke out of the jail from the inside corridor in September 1883. They crawled up through a small space by the window to the room above. Finding that door unlocked, they opened it, jumped down into the main corridor, and with a heavy bar of iron burst the iron register in the floor and slid through it into the cellar and escaped. All were being held for petty larceny.[25]

James Miller, who tied together bed quilts to make his escape from the third story of the Montgomery County Jail, was captured in Tippecanoe County and returned to jail in April 1885. He was charged with forgery.[26]

Prisoners in the rotary section were allowed some freedom in the inside corridor, but were locked into the rotary at 9 a.m. every morning. On the morning of May 18, 1892, while the Sheriff John P. Bible was in court, his wife thought she heard men working on the bars of the jail. She rushed into the corridor and saw one of the prisoner's attorneys taking to him through the grating and thought everything was all right. A couple of minutes later, four prisoners escaped from the jail. The deputy sheriff discovered the delivery and burst into the courtroom yelling that the four inmates had just escaped. Fleeing were a white man named Frank Clark and three black men: Tom Lyons, Lewis Miller and John Miller. They had used acid and saws to break through the bars in the corridor.[27]

A prisoner made a daring escape from the Montgomery County Jail in May 1900. David Taylor convinced the turnkey that he was sick and needed some fresh air, so the jailer took him out of the steel rotary section and up to the third story. When the turnkey turned his back, Taylor crashed through one of the windows, which was not barred, and into the limbs of a shade tree twenty feet below. Taylor caught the limbs safely, dropped to the ground and ran off unhurt. He then swam the river and made good his escape. He was jailed for swindling banks out of nearly a thousand dollars.[28]

Two men made their escape from the Montgomery County Jail in August 1909. Harry Morgan, of St. Louis, and William Powell, an African America, were in the corridor while Sheriff Ed Lawrence and Turnkey O'Connor were working in the rear of the jail. The prisoners made a dash through the corridor and out the front entrance.[29]

A horse thief escaped from the Montgomery County Jail in November 1913. Arthur Gasaway was arrested for stealing a horse and buggy from a livery barn in Crawfordsville and put in the jail. However, he soon escaped

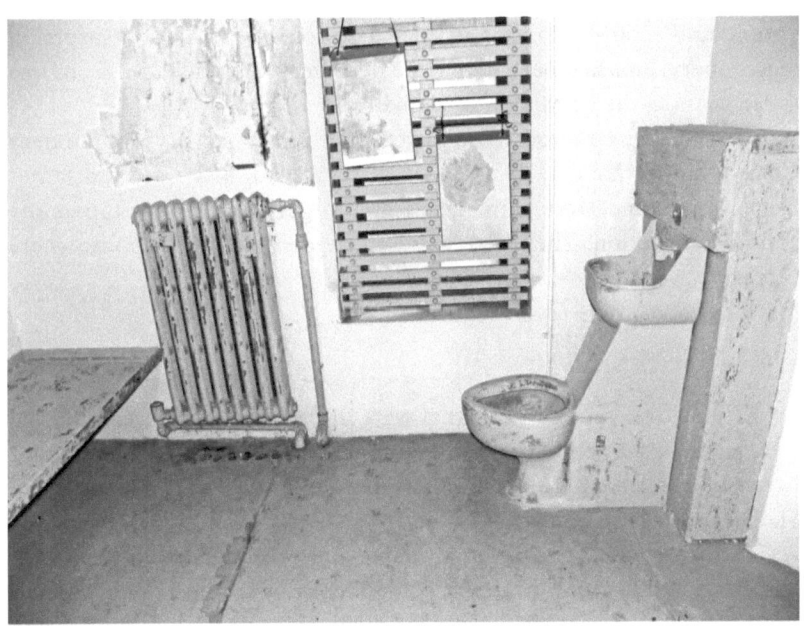

Besides the rotary jail section, the old Montgomery County Jail had other cells like this for women or juveniles (author photograph).

somehow. His case came before the grand jury who returned a verdict of horse stealing and larceny against him. He would have likely been convicted and sent to the penitentiary. Gasaway had served time in the Kansas State Prison and a prison in Pennsylvania. It was thought he had escaped from the prison in Pennsylvania where he was serving time for deserting from the army.[30]

Four prisoners sawed through bars in a cell on the first floor of the Montgomery County Jail on March 17, 1928. Those escaping were Leslie Johnson, nineteen, Indianapolis; Fayette Hiner, twenty-four, Indianapolis; Warren H. Spooner, twenty-five; and John M. Watson, forty-seven. Johnson and Hiner had just been sentenced to five-to-twenty-one years on a charge of auto banditry. Spooner was recaptured as he was walking along the highway. Watson was being held on a charge of stealing a herd of cattle.[31] Johnson turned himself into Indianapolis police two days later, saying he had been forced to join the three others in the escape.[32]

Two men sawed through the bars of a cell window on the third floor of the Montgomery County Jail on May 13, 1930. Harry Smith, twenty-seven, and William Ellis, twenty-three, then jumped twenty feet to the ground and escaped. Smith had been arrested days earlier on suspicion of a robbery. Ellis had been convicted of forgery and sentenced from two to ten years in the Pendleton Reformatory.[33]

Two suspected forgers also sawed their way out of the Montgomery County Jail on January 29, 1932. Fred Birchfield, fifty-one, and James Delph, forty-nine, were both arrested on forgery charges but apparently had no connection. They were believed headed for Indianapolis, where Birchfield was from.[34]

Other Criminals

The "clover-seed thieves" that were in the Montgomery County Jail were taken to the penitentiary in March 1886. Charles Baxter was sent for five years and fined $25. James Tomason went for two years and was fined $1. The case against Calvin Bails was dismissed.[35]

A man confessed to being a firebug and was confined in the Montgomery County Jail in April 1909. John Shehan talked freely of his crimes and was willing to pay the penalty for them. He attributed his downfall to drink. On March 15, he set fire to four different barns. One belonged to the mayor of Crawfordsville. The perpetrator then watched as the barns burned.[36]

38

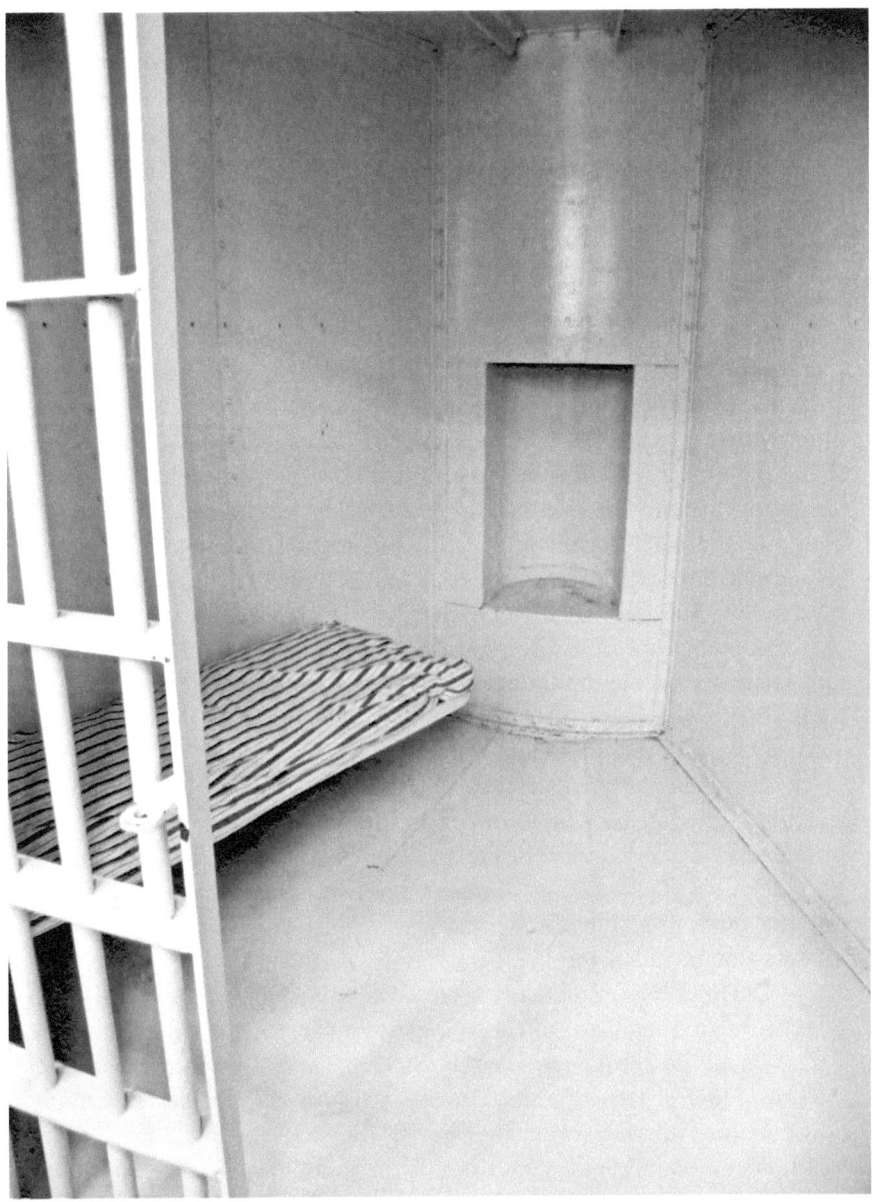

The cells at the Rotary Jail Museum have been painted to make them look nicer than they did when it was used as a jail (author photograph).

Prisoners in the Montgomery County Jail petitioned the sheriff to compel one of the prisoners to be quiet. Isaac Zook of Fresno, California, formerly a Methodist minister, was spending a great deal of his time reading out loud from the Bible to the other inmates in the jail. He had been sentenced to jail after his wife found him living in California with another woman.[37]

Usually the military takes care of their own and they have their own facilities for those who break the military law, but in 1918 a soldier was given a twenty-five day sentence in the Montgomery County Jail. Private Layton Wolfe refused to obey his superior officer and left the armory without permission. He was placed under arrest by two sergeants, tried by the regimental summary court and the sentence was approved by Colonel Payne. Several other men in local batteries were also tried under the sixty-first article of war and under the National Defense Act of 1916.[38]

An African American motor delivery driver for the George W. Graham department store was arrested and placed in the Montgomery County Jail on August 31, 1920, for the systematic thefts of goods from the store. Ralph Caldwell, age forty-five, confessed to police that he took goods valued between $5,000 and $6,000 over two years there. He also stole groceries from the W.F. Robb Grocery across the alley from the department store.[39] Caldwell was sentenced to a term of one to fourteen years in the State Prison in Michigan City on October 6, 1920, by Judge West. His wife was also placed in the county jail for being an accomplice and in default of bond.[40]

Two stepsisters landed in the Montgomery County Jail on September 15, 1927, after stealing $1,000 worth of dresses and coats displayed at a style show at the Grand Theater in Crawfordsville. Lucile McCormick, eighteen, and Evelyn Apple, sixteen, as well as their mother, Mrs. Magge Apple, thirty-five, were thrown into the jail. Mrs. Apple was charged with possession of stolen goods.[41]

During Prohibition many arrests were made for alcohol possession and rum running. Two of the youngest rumrunners every arrested in Crawfordsville were caught on May 22, 1930. Dean Brown, nineteen, and Clyde Moore, sixteen, of Arcola, Illinois, were arrested in a local restaurant by the Crawfordsville Police. They were placed in the Montgomery County Jail. The two admitted to rum running for about four months. They possessed a dozen pints of whisky. Federal prohibition officers took over the case from there.[42]

4

Nodaway County Jail— Maryville, Missouri

Maryville was laid out in 1845 as the seat of the newly organized Nodaway County. Up until 1858, Nodaway County had no regular jail for confinement of prisoners. During the October 1857 term of the county court, $3,000 was appropriated for a county jail to be built in Maryville. William O. Howard was appointed as the superintendent of the jail. In February 1858, Howard was replaced by James Ray and the bid for the jail was advertised. In the May term, it was ordered that the jail be built on the public square, thirty feet north of the clerk's office. The jail was built and it lasted until 1880 when a grand jury condemned it for being unfit and unsanitary for the further keeping of prisoners. If a prisoner was charged with a grave crime, the sheriff was to provide a guard over the premises.[1]

Work began the following year on a modern rotary jail on East Fourth Street at a cost of $19,400. The brick building was forty-by-eighty feet and two stories high in the front where the jailer's house was located. The rotary jail section was one level and contained eight cells, and sat in the rear of the building. An outer grating extending from the floor to the ceiling was constructed of chrome steel and was hardened to such a degree that it was saw and file proof. The grating had no door except for the door opposite the main entrance door. The revolving turntable was operated from outside the entrance door. And this apparatus could only be operated from the guard room, where the jailer could stand and bring his prisoners out one by one without coming in contact with them.[2]

The new Nodaway County Jail was constructed by the firm of F.C. Allen under the directions of architect Eckel & Mann of St. Joseph, Missouri. The Haugh, Ketcham & Company Iron Works of Indianapolis supplied the steel and iron work. Work was completed in 1882 and the jail put in use.[3]

41

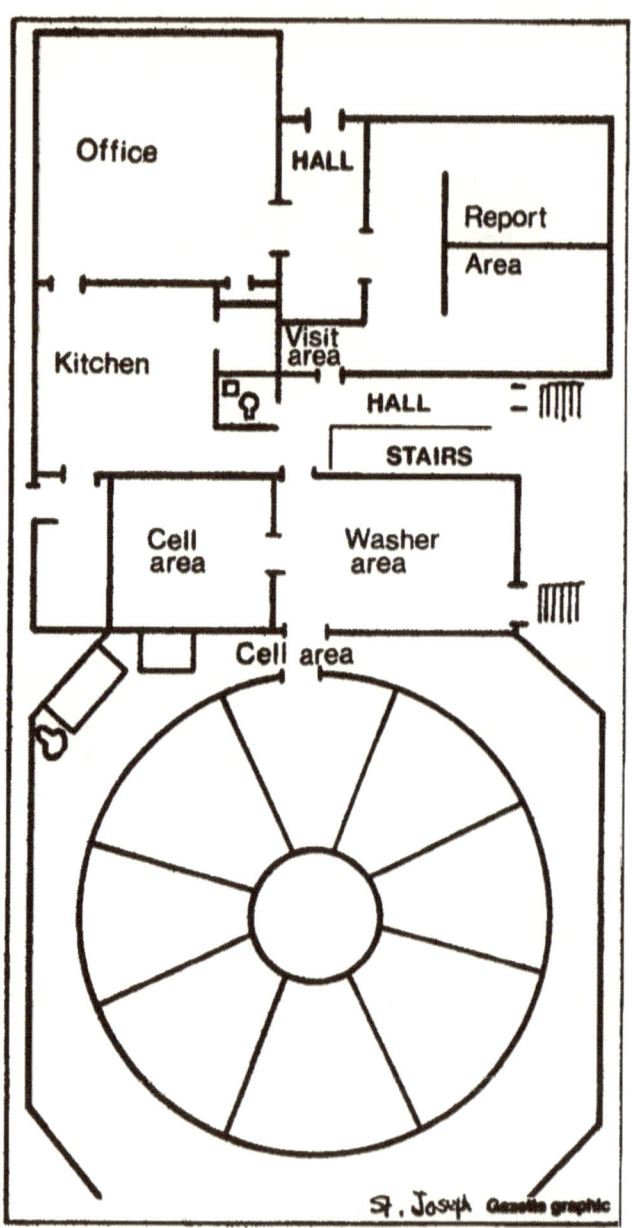

Diagram of the Nodaway County Jail (*Journal of the Society of Architectural Historians*).

Soon after completion of the jail, the inmates caused problems with the rotary mechanism when they "rocked" the inner cylinder making it impossible to revolve the huge cylinder.[4] The problems with the rotary jail literally came to a head in 1904 when a prisoner was killed during a rotation. About 7 a.m. on June 28, the cells of the Nodaway County Jail were being slowly turned as it was customary for them to do when someone let out a loud groan. On investigation prison officials found the body of Charles W. Fry in his cell with his head badly crushed and blood streaming over the floor in great profusion. He was removed to the Hotel Ream and his family in Hopkins was called to his side. He never regained consciousness and died about 7 p.m. the same day. It was thought he stooped over to pick something up from the floor of his cell and miscalculated the distance so that his head was caught between the door opening and the revolving cell. The marks on the side of the door and cage indicated that his head was only about a foot from the floor when he caught, so that he must have been bending very low when the accident occurred.[5] The death of Fry resulted in the rotary being discontinued. The inner cylinder was frozen to the base and doorways were cut into the outer shell. The second level was enclosed leaving but one deck for sixteen prisoners, two to each of the eight cells.[6]

Four prisoners were burned severely when a can of disinfectant exploded on December 11, 1927. Harry W. Nies, age twenty, was admitted to St. Francis Hospital and died there. The other men survived the explosion. They were Jack Hawkins, Herschel Fite and Joseph Maxwell.[7]

The Nodaway County Jail had no jail facilities for women in 1949 pointed out Prosecuting Attorney Emmett Bartram at a hearing.[8]

During 1954 the Nodaway County Jail held a total of three hundred and forty-seven prisoners. A dozen of those prisoners committed major felonies and went on to serve more time in the Missouri State Penitentiary. Sheriff Earl Anderson was in charge of the jail at the time.[9]

In 1957 the entire jail was renovated with modern plumbing and heating systems. Various attempts had been made to raze the building.[10]

By 1977 the old jail was not in very good condition and the inmates hated it. There was one separate cell, designed for females or juveniles, which could be used as a holding tank. If it was occupied, there was only one large area for the men. "There's no way it's adequate," Nodaway County Sheriff Roger Cronk explained. "You can't lock prisoners separate from each other, even for their own protection."[11]

A prisoner in the "Crowbar Hotel" complained about nothing to do. Another one wanted an intercom system between the jail and the sheriff's residence. "If someone got sick here, or if a fire started in one of these mattresses, all you can do is beat on the wall, and hope they hear you," an inmate said.[12]

The prisoners complained that they couldn't get any fresh air. One man complained about the unbearable heat in the summer with no ventilation or air conditioning. One of the prisoners, an expert in such matters, once said, "It's the worst jail I've ever been in, except for the treatment you get, and I've been in about 15."[13]

In 1978, a professor at Sterling College in Kansas urged the county to save the Nodaway County Jail as a historic landmark with the U.S. government. Professor Earl Bruce White wrote, "Too much history is destroyed in the United States as it is, and something as unique as the rotary jail should be saved. Hoping you will heed my plea and keep your rotary jail intact for future generations to see." The county failed to act on the request.[14]

The old jailhouse had its legends, and it was not long after Susan Cronk moved in that she learned about its "haunted" nature. The stories, though mere fabrications by inmates for the purpose of frightening little children, gained an element of truth whenever the old boiler in the basement fired up, or the radiators rattled, or the wind blew the old window glass sitting loosely within the window panes.[15] After unsuccessful efforts to save the jail, the rotary jail building was razed in January 1985.

The Jail Today

The present Nodaway County Jail is located at 404 North Vine Street and was constructed in 1985. It has an average daily inmate population count of nineteen. The jail's stated inmate capacity is forty. Darren White is the sheriff.[16]

Murderers

An inmate who was pardoned by the governor committed another murder and was hanged by a mob in Maryville in 1885. Charlie Stevenson had been pardoned by Governor Thomas Theodore Crittenden after serving seven years of a twelve-year sentence for second-degree murder. Stevenson returned to Maryville and shot a young German man. When it was thought the man would not live, an angry mob entered the Nodaway County Jail, removed Stevenson and hanged him within a hundred yards of the present Missouri governor's home.[17]

Ezra Rasco, a 16-year-old boy, murdered Mrs. Baumley and then confessed to the killing. He was initially taken to the Nodaway County Jail until officials decided to move him to St. Joseph on October 8, 1896, for safekeeping until his trial.[18]

A murder occurred on the corner of the public square in Maryville on December 21, 1897. John Joyce shot R.C. Montgomery in the back twice at noon in front of the courthouse. Montgomery died instantly and Joyce surrendered to police officers a couple of minutes later. The wealthy farmer killed Montgomery because he traveled to Omaha on the same train as Mrs. Joyce to Omaha. Joyce was put in the Nodaway County Jail until his trial in April when he was acquitted for a jury on April 20.[19]

George Vance, a Clearmont grain dealer, was arrested for the murder of his daughter on January 4, 1899, in Clearmont, Missouri. He was hustled out of town and kept concealed to prevent him from being lynched. Then he was put in the Nodaway County Jail. When Gertrude Vance became violently ill, she told the doctor that her father had assaulted her under the threat of death. She later died, so he was arrested.[20]

C.G. Jesse was convicted of killing editor Frank Griffin and was put in the Nodaway County Jail in March 1900 until he was transferred to the prison in Jefferson City to serve two years. Griffin was the editor and publisher of the *Maryville Daily Review*.[21]

A father pled guilty at the third trial for second-degree murder of his son on October 15, 1935. Emmett Bartley, fifty-seven, had been convicted of the murdering his son on January 16, 1933, in Atchison County. However, a new trial was granted and a change of venue was made to Nodaway County. He was again convicted and sentenced to thirty years. On appeal, the case was remanded for a third trial.[22]

Only one inmate, Fred McQuinn, was in the Nodaway County Jail on May 27, 1949, and he was wanted on a first-degree murder charge in Albany.[23]

Escapes

Many escapes occurred at the old Nodaway County Jail during its existence; however, not so many when it was a rotary jail.

Three prisoners escaped from the Nodaway County Jail on December 14, 1887, but one was shot and recaptured during the attempt. As the sheriff stepped in the corridor where the prisoners were eating supper, he was seized and thrown to the floor by Hamilton Logan. Isaac Wright and Hardin Halpin then took the keys and made their way out. Logan locked up the sheriff but forgot to disarm him, so the sheriff shot him as he tried to escape.[24]

Four prisoners escaped through the wall of the Nodaway County Jail in April 1909. Two of the inmates, George Gibbs and "Red" Henderson were captured at Burlington Junction the day after the break, but John and Charles Thompson continued to elude police. The men had removed bricks to the outside wall of the jail to make their escape possible.[25]

Eleven prisoners nearly escaped from the Nodaway County Jail in 1911; however, a guard discovered the plot and stopped the game. He found two sticks of dynamite, three caps, four feet of fuse, a saw, a file and an iron bar four feet in length.[26]

A man with a record of jailbreaking escaped from the Nodaway County Jail on September 25, 1920, while awaiting trial on burglary and larceny charges. Irwin Swearingen, thirty-seven, was captured in Kansas City on October 23, 1921, and was taken to the penitentiary in Jefferson City to finish out his sentence.[27]

A man escaped the Nodaway County Jail by sawing a hole in his cell and walking out the basement door on September 21, 1931. William Helpley was captured in November in Milwaukee, Wisconsin, using the alias of William Holmes. Helpley was originally in the county jail for felonious assault with intent to kill and burglary. Breaking jail was added to his sentence prior to his extradition back to Missouri.[28]

Two men sawed their way out of the Nodaway County Jail on June 24, 1935. The escaped prisoners were Raymond Marks, twenty-five, wanted for bank robbery, and Stephen Slyker, twenty-three, accused of forgery. Five other prisoners in the same cellblock wisely chose to remain behind.[29]

A man escaped from the Nodaway County Jail on June 26, 1937, by chiseling and prying a hole through the ceiling of the cellblock. Then L.R. Seals, 38, tied three blankets and quilts together to lower himself from the second floor window. Seals had been transferred from the jail in St. Joseph after completing a year's sentence there. He was to serve another six months in jail for passing a bad check.[30]

Three men escaped from the Nodaway County Jail after sawing through two sets of bars with a hacksaw on September 26, 1950. The three were Floyd Sargent, Gene Matson and Lester Jones. Sargent and Matson were apprehended in Independence about four hours later, but Jones was still at large.[31]

A man escaped from the Nodaway County Jail by digging a hole in the floor on March 11, 1953. Harold Ray Abbott, thirty-eight, was captured later the same day near Stanberry by the sheriff and highway patrol officers.[32]

A man squeezed his way out of the Nodaway County Jail on May 20, 1959, only to be captured twenty-four days later in Seneca, Kansas. Clyde Harrington, thirty-four, was given a two-year sentence in a Missouri penitentiary for jailbreak and a no-account check. He escaped the jail by prying a steel floor plate loose in his cell, dropping into the basement, and cutting a small hole in the basement wall.[33]

Two inmates cut away bars and jumped down fourteen feet to gain freedom from the Nodaway County Jail on April 18, 1960. It was the second breakout at the facility in less than a year. Arthur Partridge, being held on a second-degree burglary charge, and Clifford Lewis, being held on a bogus check charge, were the escapees. "This is hardly a maximum security jail," said Sheriff James E. Tucker. "We have no way of keeping the prisoners apart at night and in places the bars are so rusted and wood so rotted they could almost kick their way out."[34]

Three men escaped from the Nodaway County Jail the morning of July 27, 1964. One of the escapees was Earl Emery and he turned himself in at the Iowa border two days later. Emery admitted to officers that Gene Mullins, forty, had a hacksaw blade in his shoe and sawed through the bars, so that he and Jerry Burdick could break out. The other two men escaped authorities.[35]

Three men escaped from the Nodaway County Jail on September 28, 1973, and two were captured in Nebraska a short time later. David Eris Hamilton, seventeen, and Jackie Dean Jackson, nineteen, were caught, but Jerry Lee Kelly remained at large. The men escaped by sawing a bar away and kicking some steel mesh out of the way.[36]

Unusual Prisoners

A negro preacher who resisted being taken to the Nodaway County Jail was killed by police officer John Wallace on August 31, 1899. The Reverend William Johnston was convicted of making indecent proposals to a white woman, Mrs. Alice Barton, and given a nine-month sentence in the county jail. When Wallace came to get the preacher, Johnston drew a pistol from his pocket. Wallace fired at him immediately as did Constable Jennings and the preacher fell dead.[37]

An eight-year-old boy was sentenced to thirty days in the Nodaway County Jail for petit larceny in November 1891.[38]

Two judges from St. Clair County were sent to the Nodaway County Jail for contempt of Federal Court. Back in 1876, St. Clair County voted $250,000 for the building of a railroad. The road was never built, but the bonds were sold by the promoters. The county taxpayers refused to pay the interest or the principal, amounting to about $1.5 million by 1901. The Federal Court ordered the county judges to levy taxes to take up the bonds. The judges refused and were held in contempt. As a result, they were jailed. Judge Neville and Judge Samuel C. Peden ended up in the Nodaway County Jail. Peden was finally released from jail on October 30, 1902.[39] Judge Neville was eventually released from jail on December 22, 1902, to go home for Christmas. Neville was released after giving his word of honor that he would not attempt to hold court if he returned home. The judge didn't suffer much while he was in jail as he sometimes acted as the jailer and on occasion as a special policeman. He also worked as a telephone lineman drawing $2 a day for work.[40]

Like the saying, "Like father, like son," a son joined his father in the Nodaway County Jail on August 9, 1938. Bert Davis, Jr., was placed in the jail on a charge of selling liquor without a license. His father was in the jail already after committing the same crime at the Hillside dance pavilion.[41]

A married couple spent their honeymoon in the Nodaway County Jail on February 9, 1940. Cecil H. Ross and Lois Wooten were married in the sheriff's office. Following the ceremony, the couple was taken to the jail to spend the night in a cell. Blankets were hung in the cell to give them some privacy. The ceremony was held two hours after Ross had been sentenced to the state penitentiary for obtaining money under false pretenses.[42]

Other Criminals

Chauncey Robbins was arrested after a desperate struggle with Sheriff Thomas Perle for the violation of a ten-year-old girl in Calhoun County. The sheriff brought him to the Nodaway County Jail and held him until he was transferred to Calhoun County.[43]

The largest fine ever levied in the Nodaway Circuit Court was handed down by Judge W.C. Ellison against William Nicola of Hopkins on February 28, 1907. Nicola was ordered to pay $4,800 for violating the liquor laws. He could spend up to eight years in jail if he didn't pay the fine. The grand jury indicted him on twenty-four counts. Nicola pleaded guilty and was fined $200 on each count.[44]

Suicides

Just about every jail has had a suicide, which is why they now put suicide watches on some prisoners. The Nodaway County Jail was no exception. A man committed suicide at the jail on May 12, 1904. George W. Nyet came to Maryville from Pickering and acted strangely as he wandered the streets. He went into Crow's photograph gallery and by his actions appeared to be demented, so Sheriff Enis was called to arrest him. He was imprisoned in the Nodaway County Jail. About 4 p.m. he was found to be unconscious in his cell and it was discovered that he had attempted to hang himself with a chest protector. The string had broken allowing him to fall and resulting in him striking the iron door of the cell with his head. The head injury along with his excessive use of morphine were noted as the cause of his death. He had traveled with his wife and this left her in a destitute condition. His remains were sent home to Mansfield, Ohio.[45]

The former sheriff of Nodaway County, who cared for the jail from 1892–1897, committed suicide at his home by taking carbolic acid. Ed Barton had been drinking heavily all day and had brandished a revolver in a saloon until he was arrested and fined. He paid the fine and then went home and ended his life. Since his term as sheriff, he had made a fortune in real estate.[46]

DeKalb County Jail— Maysville, Missouri

DeKalb County was created from part of Clinton County on May 25, 1845. It was named in honor of Baron Johann De Kalb, the major general who was the right hand of the famed Marquis de Lafayette, who fought for the Americans during the War of Independence. The county commissioners decided a town in the center of the county was necessary as the county seat, so Maysville founded as that town on August 18, 1845.[1]

The Governor appointed Charles Allen as the first sheriff of the county on April 8, 1845. He refused to serve but was elected to the post in 1847. He had no jail at first, so he had to improvise. Once after an early August session, the court found a man guilty of quarreling and fined him. He couldn't pay the fine, so the court ordered him imprisoned. The sheriff knew that William H. Ritchie had a cellar in his grocery store, so the man was placed in the cellar overnight. The prisoner was said to have found whisky casks in the cellar treated himself to it. He is believed to be the happiest prisoner ever incarcerated in any jail, according to the sheriff's history.[2]

The first jail erected in DeKalb County came in 1858. Andrew Sherard built the jail on the northwest corner of the square. It had a deep cellar that was called the dungeon, which was walled with stone and had dirt floor. The only entrance was through a trap door in the floor. The jail itself was constructed of wooden logs that were hewn and squared to fifteen inches. The logs were securely fastened together with heavy iron bolts placed about ten inches apart. The jail served the county until it was condemned and sold by the court in 1873. Prisoners were then incarcerated in jails in neighboring counties.[3]

On Christmas night 1878, a fire destroyed the courthouse. The proposal to build a new courthouse was submitted in 1880, but it was defeated by the southern portion of the county who wanted the courthouse in Stewartsville. The following year the proposition was again submitted and did not pass again. The proposal was again floated in 1882 and was defeated for the third time. Finally, the Court House Proposition was put to a vote on November 4, 1884, and it passed. The courthouse would also include a jail. The architects estimated the cost of the new jail attached to the courthouse would be no more than $40,000. The jail was to be constructed with eight iron-latticed cells on a turntable, a guard room, and other convenient rooms. The architects for the jail were Haugh, Ketchum & Company Iron Works. The jail cost $32,000 for the jail and living quarters for the sheriff. Besides the rotary, there were two other cells to house female prisoners. Above the cells were two rooms for a doctor to provide to the medical needs of the inmates.[4] The jail was completed in 1885.

The courthouse was struck by lightning at 10:30 p.m. the night of June 21, 1905. A fire ignited from the strike and burned the cupola off of the tower. As a precaution, the sheriff took three prisoners from the rotary jail in the back of the courthouse to Yeater & Johnson's drug store until the fire was extinguished.[5]

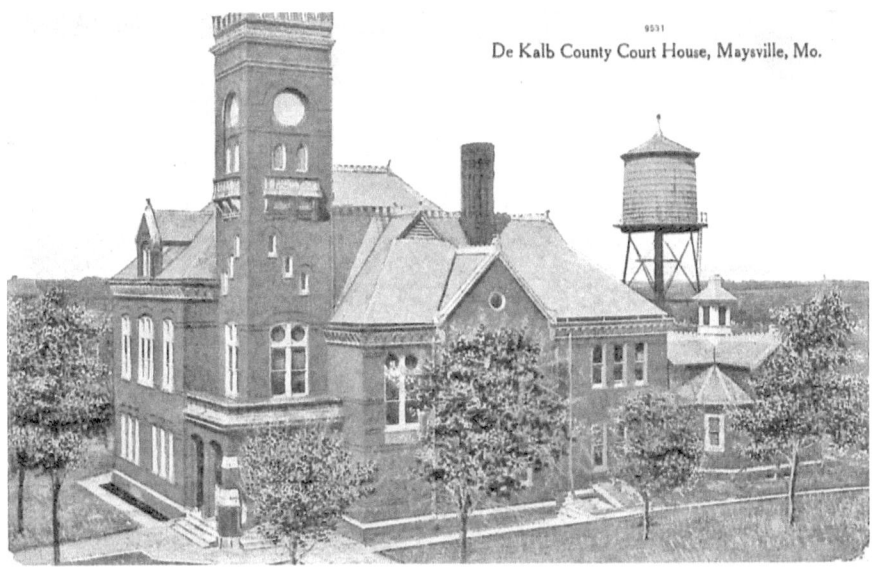

De Kalb County Court House, Maysville, Mo.

The rotary jail in Maysville, Missouri, was located behind the DeKalb County Courthouse as shown in this postcard from the era.

The rotary jail remained in use until 1938. In August 1938, voters approved a $55,000 bond, which was to be matched by a $45,000 government bond to construct another courthouse. The jail and sheriff's quarters were located on the third floor and it was dedicated on October 20, 1939. The old rotary jail was torn down in October, too.[6]

Murderers

Martin Paulsgrove was found guilty of murder in the first degree on October 16, 1905. He had killed his sweetheart, Mary Newman, a school teacher in Andrew County. He was transported to the DeKalb County Jail in Maysville to wait until his trial there. His defense attorney thought he wouldn't get a fair trial and impartial jury in Andrew County, so he asked for and received a change of venue. Paulsgrove shot his sweetheart to death on January 18, 1904. The farmer had just returned from the Philippines, where he had served as a soldier. He was given a death sentence by the court.[7] Two years later, Dr. W.J. Clark declared Paulsgrove insane after he ripped apart his cell in a rage in the DeKalb County Jail.[8] Later the prisoner was adjudged as sane and sent to the state penitentiary. However, Paulsgrove was then was declared insane and sent to the lunatic asylum in Fulton, Missouri. In 1921, he escaped from the asylum and remained at large for four years until he was captured again and sent to the penitentiary.

A jury found a man not guilty of murder on the grounds of insanity on October 17, 1925, in DeKalb County Circuit Court. Elze Meek, who was grading a road, killed his overseer, William Culley, on a highway near the Meek home on September 18. Immediately after killing Culley, Meek disappeared. A posse led by county officers scoured the weeded sections of the county for miles around in an effort to find the road overseer's slayer. Bloodhounds were also brought in from Chillicothe, but they were unable to follow the trail of the crazed man because of rain. The manhunt continued for a week when Meek was discovered at the farm house half-starved and dirty. He surrendered to a posse member at the farm and was interred in solitary confinement at the DeKalb County Jail until trial. Meek was bound in a straightjacket and remained quiet throughout the trial. He was removed to the asylum after the trial. In the crowded courtroom, Dr. Glen D. Johnson and Dr. H. T. Yeater, Maysville physicians, testified that Meek was insane and not responsible for the crime.[9]

Prohibition Problems

Probably the most famous sheriff in DeKalb County's history during the time of the rotary jail was Frank Smith. And he was famous for good and bad reasons and both involved liquor. Prohibition began in 1920 while Smith was the sheriff of the county.

On the good side, Sheriff Smith went after some moonshiners on October 21, 1921. He was joined by the prosecuting attorney, Covell Hewitt, and they went to investigate the report of liquor being manufactured at the Heimbaugh home. They found the still, a large amount of mash and a pitcher of liquor, so the sheriff arrested Harrison Heimbaugh. As they escorted him back to the sheriff's automobile to take him back to the DeKalb County Jail, they were ambushed by his son, Claude. Harrison threw himself on the ground just as two shots were fired. The sheriff was hit in the head by buckshot and injured severely. The prosecutor hustled him back to the car and drove him back to Maysville to seek medical help. One of sheriff's teeth was knocked out by the shotgun blast. The other pellets proved to be painful but not life threatening. The prosecutor returned to the Heimbaugh house with a posse, arrested the two men, and brought them back to the jail. Claude Heimbaugh was indicted by a grand jury for assault with intent to kill. Both Heimbaughs were charged with keeping an illicit still.[10]

On the bad side, the sheriff allowed an inmate in the DeKalb County Jail to run a still and a bar in the jail. Clarence "Nick" Leard was serving a six-month federal sentence for bootlegging. Sheriff Smith basically gave him the run of the jail and allowed him to make liquor in his cell and sell it to customers. Allegedly, Leard used the jail as a bar and operated a daily booze route, picking up the empties and leaving filled bottles of booze like a milkman. On February 9, 1923, as a result of this activity, the federal government issued a government warrant and arraigned him before Commissioner George D. Beardsley, charging him with maintaining a bootlegging nuisance in the county jail. Sheriff Smith was released under a $2,000 bond, pending his appearance in a federal court at St. Joseph. Byron H. Coon, special United States assistant district attorney announced that he would file additional charges. The federal agents also arrested Leard's three brothers and sister-in-law when they found them with a quantity of liquor. The raids created intense excitement in the community and the street near the jail was soon crowded with spectators. The sheriff was taken to the courthouse until he could be transported to Kansas City.[11]

Leard received a two-year sentence in a federal penitentiary on October 1, 1923, and was ordered to pay a fine of $1,000 by Judge A.L. Reeves after a jury found him guilty of selling liquor. Sheriff Smith and Deputy Sheriff D.F. Riggs were censured by the federal judge in the case. Judge Reeves said:

> I am entirely in sympathy with the verdict of the jury. I think it would have been amiss if any other verdict had been returned. This is the most reprehensible thing that has come before this court; where the sheriff permits a prison or anyone else to keep a gallon of whisky in his possession in the jail. The testimony was that this man was at liberty and permitted to go and come while he was supposed to be confined in jail and there was nothing to contradict that. There has been a very apparent disregard and disrespect of the law in Maysville.

Leard was given the keys to the jail and courthouse, which allowed him to come and go when he pleased. The government investigated Leard by sending two youths on two different occasions to purchase whisky from Leard. A few days later a party of government officers from Kansas City made a raid on the jail and discovered a gallon jug of corn whisky in the jail. At the time of the raid, the jail was locked and no one was in it. Leard was uptown on his delivery route and was taken back to the jail.[12]

A Suicide

Joseph Jump committed suicide in the DeKalb County Jail and the jail was said to be haunted after that, according to a newspaper report in 1889.[13]

Escapes

The largest escape known is when five prisoners got free from the DeKalb County Jail in February 1901. Charged with robbery in Clarksdale, the men pulled a clever ruse on the sheriff to escape. They were in the corridor of the jail when they asked Sheriff William Duncan for a drink of water. As he opened the door to hand it to them, one of them grabbed him and began choking him. Another joined in and soon the five overpowered the sheriff. They locked him in a cage and walked out. No trace of the men could be found by deputies.[14]

Other Criminals

A man was sentenced to the DeKalb County Jail for six months for passing a $5 Confederate bill during a voting contest at a church festival in May 1897. Earl Bell was convicted by a jury in a federal court. He claimed the bill was handed to him and he didn't realize it was Confederate money. The girl he voted for ended up becoming the most popular woman at the festival. The court told Bell that his offense merited a more severe penalty, but the chivalry he evidenced commended itself.[15] Allen Sick was also given six months by the U.S. Court in the DeKalb County Jail for passing counterfeit money in January 1901.[16]

Sheriff Porter Meek arrested five DeKalb County men under charges of complicity in election fraud during the local election in November 1907. He arrested Hugh Flood, Mike O. Laughlin, Charles Dale, Clyde Sampson, and J.G. Jones. The men were incarcerated in the DeKalb County Jail. Flood, Jones and Dale were bartenders in Cameron.[17]

Sheriff Vernon Campbell arrested Walter "Buck" Wagers, twenty-five, as being a suspect in the robbery of two banks on December 29, 1930, and placed him in the DeKalb County Jail. He also placed Coval Stephens and Carl Ellis of Amity, Missouri, in the jail on charges of participating in the two robberies.[18]

The Jail Today

Daviess and DeKalb counties joined forces to open the Daviess/ DeKalb County Regional Jail, which is located in Pattonsburg, Missouri. It has two buildings that have a capacity of more than two hundred inmates. Sheriff Wes Raines was in charge of the jail in 2016.[19]

Sheriffs

The following sheriffs operated the county jail when it contained a rotary[20]:

1882–1886: Edward J. Smith	1894–1898: B.F. Channel
1886–1890: James Gibson	1898–1902: William Duncan
1890–1894: Robert Rogers	1902–1904: Frank Brant

1904–1906: J.B. Means

1907–1912: Porter Meek

1913–1916: Ollie Sherard

1917–1918: Sextus C. Lynch

1919–1920: Floyd Leard

1921–1924: Frank Smith

1925–1928: Druery W. McMillan

1929–1932: Vernon D. Campbell

1933–1936: Robert P. Daniels

1937–1938: Coulson Sherard

6

Pottawattami County Jail— Council Bluffs, Iowa

Pottawattami County was established on February 24, 1847. The county's name was derived from the Native American tribe that once existed and lived within the Iowa Territory.[1] County commissioners ordered Sheriff John D. Parker to build a county jail in Kanesville on May 23, 1849. Chester Loveland was awarded $300 on October 2, 1849, to build the structure. Designed by Judge Frank Street, Loveland completed the first jail on April 11, 1850, at what is now 220 South First Street in Council Bluffs. The structure was built with "three inch plank, doubled so as to break joints, and filled so full of spikes that it would be impossible for a prisoner to saw out."[2]

Three years later on January 19, 1853, Kanesville was renamed Council Bluffs. The first jail was used until Marshall Turley was given $750 to build a new jail on the same location as the first jail on February 8, 1854. The jail was constructed using cottonwood and became known as the "old Cottonwood Jail." On April 14, 1860, Sheriff S.H. Craig reported the county jail was "unsafe and insufficient to confine a prisoner without any degree of security and is necessary to remove prisoner." The prisoner was taken to Fremont County. Subsequent prisoners were sent to other counties to be held. On April 7, 1862, the county sold the old Cottonwood Jail to the city of Council Bluffs for $100. On November 29, 1866, the cottonwood jail caught fire with Ashton Palling housed in it. He had been arrested for drunkenness. His cries were heard by a nearby neighbor, but they thought nothing of it. Needless to say, the laborer was burnt to a crisp. Palling was a harmless man and his fiery demise was a shock to the entire community.[3]

By the 1880s, Pottawattami County needed a new jail. The board examined the plans for a rotary jail provided by the Eckel & Mann Company of St. Joseph, Missouri, at a meeting on June 9, 1882. The drawings were agreeable to the board in every respect, according to minutes. The architectural firm already had experience building a rotary jail in 1882 in Maysville, Missouri. Local officials paid a visit to the jail there and were impressed by the design of the structure. Then in February 1884, the board met with the architect from Eckel & Mann and delegates from various townships to take action on building of a new jail since the old Cotton-wood Jail had been condemned. The board accepted the plans "as being in their opinion the best adapted for the use of the county."[4]

The county passed a bond issue in early 1885 for the new jail and it would more grandeur than the single story, eight-cell prototype that they saw in Maryville. The structure would be four stories in height with the rotary jail taking up the first three stories of the interior and weighing about 90,000 pounds. The outside of the jail was completed in a Victorian style with detailed brickwork, Romanesque arched windows, and limestone trim to make it a grand structure that looked nothing like a plain, old jail. The rotary section would contain twenty-four cells, eight on each level.[5]

Bids for the county jail were opened on April 9, 1885. The Wickham Brothers had the lowest bid for the cost of the exterior building at $7,350. Haugh, Ketcham & Company Iron Works of Indianapolis submitted the lowest bid for the interior rotary jail inside the building at $21,000. Local contractors were hired to handle work on the exterior of the building, including John Epeneter, B. Terwillinger, and G.S. Lawson.[6]

The completed rotary jail section would have eight cells on three floors, so it could hold up to forty-eight inmates in the rotary. The women or juvenile section on the second floor could house another five prisoners. This area would be equipped with a bathtub and other necessaries along with a hospital cell-room. Each floor had two exercise rooms where pris-oners could be allowed to eat, wash, and exercise at the discretion of the jailer. A solitary confinement cell was located off of the sheriff's office that could hold one inmate standing up. Prisoners usually stood for an hour in confinement, but the record was ten days, according to a museum offi-cial. It was used up until 1960. The jail also had another solitary confine-ment area in the corridor that could hold up to dozen prisoners. Violent criminals were put on the third floor of the rotary.[7]

The sheriff had a kitchen on the first floor across from the sheriff's office. Initially it had an iron stove that would heat up pieces of coal to put in the cells to warm up the jail for the inmates. Twenty years later,

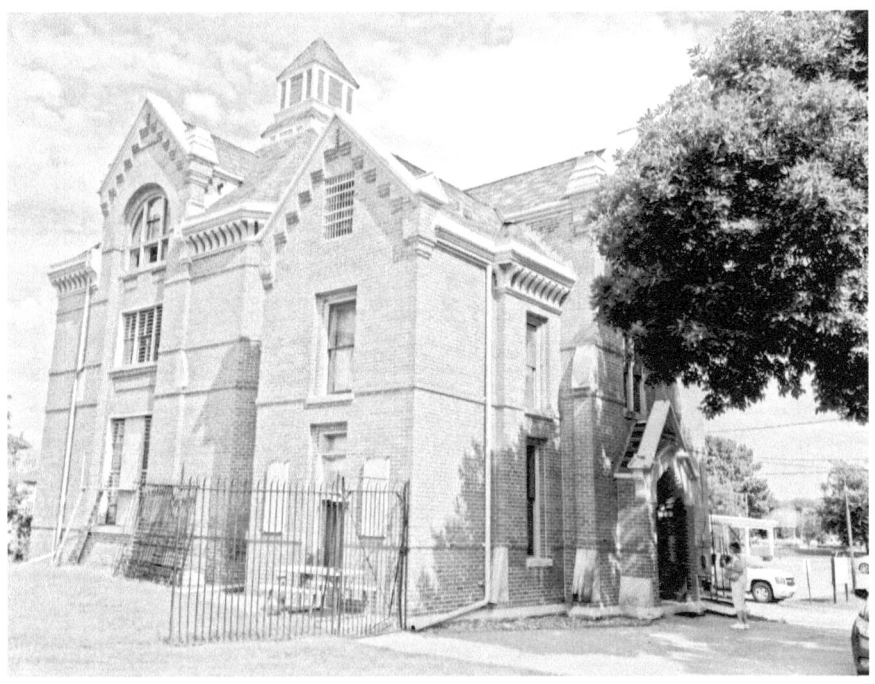

The Squirrel Cage Jail is a major attraction in Council Bluffs and is open three days a week for visitors (author photograph).

radiators were installed in the jail and steam was pumped in from the courthouse, according to a Squirrel Cage Jail of Pottawattamie County officials. The fourth floor of the jail was designed to provide living quarters for the sheriff and his family; however, the smell from the septic system drove them to the second floor and women inmates and storage were moved into the fourth floor. The sewer smell was supposed to go up and out through the center of the jail, but apparently it didn't function properly, explained museum officials.

Construction began in March 1885 and was completed in six months. The new building was opened on September 10, 1885, and the fifteen prisoners in the old Cottonwood Jail were transferred to the new rotary jail. Among them were murderer Cuff Johnson, horse thief Miles Mullen, forger Frank Scofield, confidence man Ed Rankin, and revenuer John Gordon. Also, the Brock family was doing time for larceny. The rotary section of the jail weighed 90,000 pounds.[8]

County residents gave Sheriff Theodore Guittar much grief after it was built and called it "Hotel Guittar," because they thought it was too plush since each cell had its own toilet, which was more than many residents could afford. Most still had outhouses. The forty-five ton rotary jail was reputedly powered by a water wheel, which could keep the platform in motion all night when the jailer went to bed.[9]

The rotary jail almost immediately proved hazardous for prisoners as they received broken arms or legs as they had their hands or feet caught between the bars during the revolving of the cylinder. Also, the rotary mechanism was prone to mechanical problems. Nine months after the rotary jail opened, the *Omaha Bee* wrote that the jail had numerous defects with the most recent one being that "the great iron cylinder is settling somewhat, and in doing so there is a decided inclination to settle more on one side than the other." Sure enough the rotary jail became jammed on November 10, 1888, and no prisoners could be taken out or admitted. Some disarrangement of the machinery caused the problem.[10]

Two years after construction the local newspaper, the *Globe*, reported that the jail was a failure. "The great revolving cylinder which contains most of the cells in the building does not work on its axis with satisfaction." The

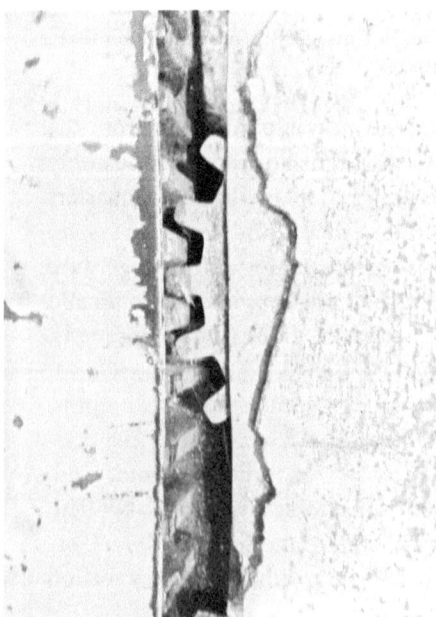

article went on to say that it should be taken down and removed from the jail. Prisoners caused many of the problems in the rotary. They would stick a shoe in the bars of the rotary to stop it from rotating. They also clogged up their toilets, so the fire department was called in to fix the problem, according to museum officials. Prisoners would throw items from their cells onto the platforms or into the corridor below. There was no way to determine who the guilty

The gears of the rotary are evident at the entrance to the cells at the Squirrel Cage Jail in Council Bluffs (author photograph).

party was because the cells were revolved frequently and there were three levels.[11]

The rotary jail continued to receive criticism from local officials. In 1910, grand juries and fire marshals complained about the jail being a fire hazard. The Pottawattamie County Board of Supervisors unanimously passed a resolution in 1910 to ask voters for $75,000 to build a new county jail. A site was selected just west of the courthouse and plans made to include residence apartments for the sheriff and his family. Editorials decried the unsafe conditions of the old structure and its nonexistent ventilation, saying "rotary cells of the present jail not only are a farce, they are dangerous to the lives of the prisoners." The voters didn't buy into the argument.[12]

Around 1940, the jail finally had electricity installed and county officials put in a shower for inmates, according to museum officials. The prisoners showered with their clothes on in cold water. They wore the clothes they came in with or were provided later by guests as the county provided no clothing. So the shower also served as a laundry for the prisoners.[13]

In 1960 the city fire marshal stopped the squirrel cage from rotating and declared it a fire hazard, according to museum officials. A fire exit was installed on the second floor and a spiral staircase was replaced with a regular metal staircase. The number of usable cells was therefore reduced from thirty to eighteen, since the jail could no longer be rotated.[14]

The State of Iowa decided in 1969 that it was time to close a number of old jails in the state, including the Pottawattami County Jail in Council Bluffs. State Jail Inspector William Swassing commented that the prisoners at the jail were "mingled together" and an officer entering the jail had to mingle with the inmates. Apparently, the rotary cells were not being used all of the time.[15]

The State Department of Social Services ordered the Pottawattamie County Jail to be closed by December 1, 1969. The Pottawattamie County Board of Supervisors further ordered the transfer of prisoners from the county jail to the Page County Jail at Clarinda. The sheriff complied with the order and moved the prisoners before the deadline.[16]

The last sheriff who was in charge of the jail was Roy O. Wichael. He was recognized for modernizing the Sheriff's Office by employing twenty-two deputies and eighteen special deputies during his fifteen years as sheriff between 1960 and 1975. He died while he was in office on June 30, 1975.[17]

Squirrel Cage Jail Museum

The old jail was purchased by the Council Bluffs Park Board for preservation in 1971. One of the first things the Park Board did was to put the building on the National Register of Historic Places in 1971, saving from the wrecking ball as municipalities don't like tearing down buildings on the register. In 1977, the Historical Society of Pottawattamie County raised the funds needed to save and renovate the building for future generations. They purchased the building in 1979 and turned it into a museum. The cell section remains much as it did in 1969 when the rotary was stopped by the county. The signatures and dates of many of its' infamous prisoners remain scratched in the cell walls and ceilings. It remains a well restored snapshot of an interesting era. The museum is open Thursday through Sunday for tours and at other times with special permission. An admission is charged, which helps pay for the maintenance of the old building. Special events are planned during the course of the year as well, such as a flashlight tour at night. Ghost hunting groups have also rented the jail at night to research the presence of spirits may inhibit the old building.[18]

The Jail Today

Nowadays, the current Pottawattamie County Jail is located at 1400 Big Lake Rd, Council Bluffs, Iowa, opened in 1999 with a bed design capacity of two hundred and eighty-eight. The jail houses inmates of all security levels, from maximum to minimum and includes work release inmates. The facility was designed to be expandable. The City of Council Bluffs also has a jail located at 227 South Sixth Street.[19]

Murderers

Many individuals charged with murder spent some time in the Pottawattami County Jail over the years before they were tried and sent to the penitentiary if they were found guilty. While very secure, the rotary jail was no place for serious offenders.

The most famous murderer to spend some time in the Pottawattami County Jail was a serial killer named Jake Bird, according to museum officials. The African American was born in Louisiana and when he grew up he became a manual laborer and railroad worker, so he traveled through-

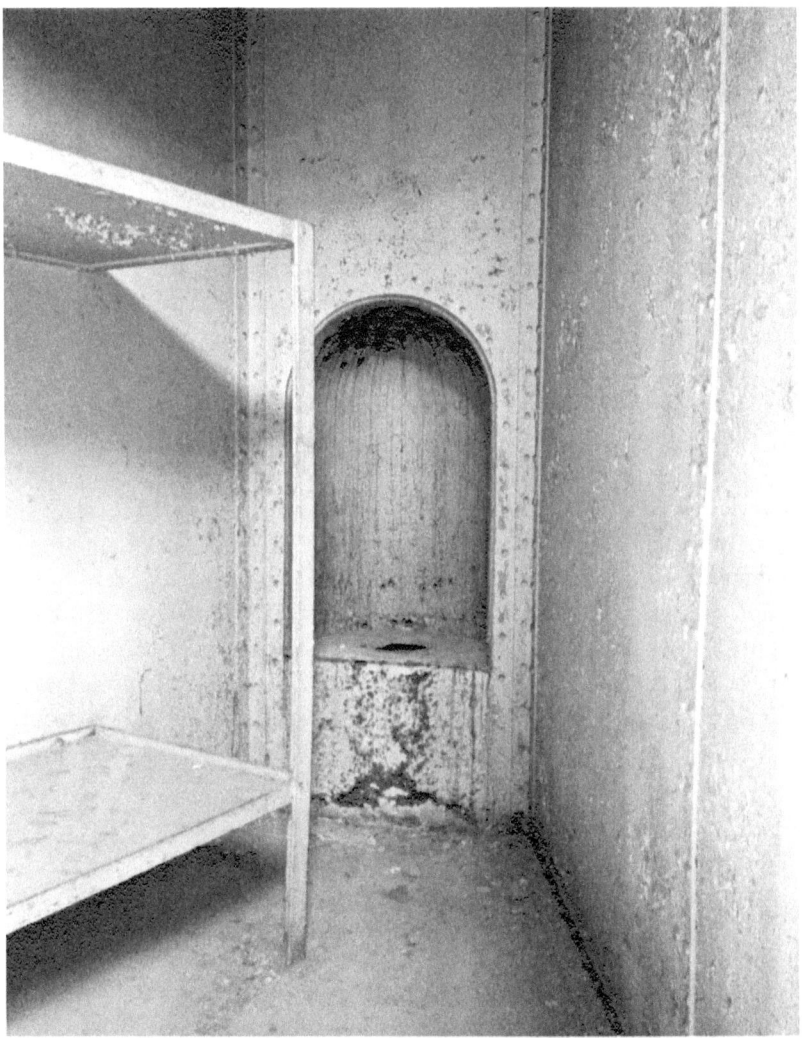

The cells in the Squirrel Cage have been left alone to show visitors exactly their condition at the time the Pottawattami County Jail was in use (author photograph).

out the United States. He was finally convicted of the murder of two people in Tacoma, Washington, in November 1947. He was scheduled to be executed, but Bird claimed he had committed forty-four other murders which he was willing to help police solve, so Washington Governor Monrad C. Wallgren granted him a sixty-day reprieve. Police from other states interviewed Bird and eleven other murders were substantiated. For the others that he claimed, he was considered a prime suspect. He had killed white women in Iowa as well as ten other states. The forty-five year old was hanged on July 15, 1949, at 12:20 a.m. before more than a hundred witnesses.[20]

Elmer Newell was placed in the Pottawattami County Jail and charged with murder of Lee Addison of Oakland. Newell claimed that Addison committed suicide, but the circumstances surrounding the case did not warrant that belief. A grand jury indicted him for the crime. Newell was later found guilty and sentenced to sixteen years in the penitentiary. The murder resulted after the two had quarreled in a saloon.[21]

Two Minneapolis men spent some time in the Pottawattami County jail before they were convicted of murdering Alvin Koehrsen, fifty-four, of Walnut, on February 22, 1961, in Council Bluffs. Charles Noel Brown, twenty-nine, and Charles Edward Kelly were both sentenced to death by District Court Judge Leroy Johnson for the crime after a jury found them guilty on May 18, 1961. The twenty-nine-year-old Brown was sent to the gallows on July 24, 1962.[22] Kelly was executed on September 9 for the crime. He was also the second youngest person to be ever hanged in the state at the youthful age of twenty-one. Both men were among the last to be hanged in Iowa. Both admitted to killing two other men and wounding three others.[23]

Escapes

Three years after completion of the jail, eleven prisoners walked out the front door and escaped, but it had nothing to do with the rotary section of the jail. The prisoners escaped by filing the lock on the door leading from the exercise room to the back corridor. Then they climbed the grating to the third floor where they found the doors unlocked. The last one, a man by the name of Hallman, was captured by the jailer Mulligan at the front door of the jail. Captain L.B. Cousins captured two others, Johnson and Diamond, who he saw running by the park. Sheriff O'Neill was criticized for the "grossest negligence."[24]

Eight men sawed their way out of the Pottawattami County Jail on April 28, 1937. By June 8, all of the inmates had been captured and faced charges of jailbreaking. Jack Rhoades, twenty-two, surrendered to Sheriff Joe F. Perry on June 8. He was serving a year's sentence for receiving stolen property.[25]

Two other men sawed their way out of the Pottawattami County Jail in September 1942. Ernest Birt, twenty-six, of Council Bluffs, and Fred Threlkeld, 23, of Mountain View, California, got out successfully and police were after the pair.[26]

Three men knocked down the jailer and escaped from the Pottawattamie County Jail on October 21, 1948, but one was captured a short time later. Jailer C.E. Anthony said two of the men knocked him down when he took them a supply of soap about 6:30 p.m. The three then left the jail. W.H. Gill, sixty, of Council Bluffs was captured by Council Bluffs police on a downtown street. The other two inmates—Harold Hall, nineteen, of Emerson, and Ben Romsberg, twenty, of Rich Hill, Missouri—got away.[27]

Two inmates escaped the Pottawattami County Jail on July 17, 1949, during a church service. Then they robbed two filling stations the next day in Council Bluffs. The escapees were Leon Ross, twenty-one, and Floyd Peterson, twenty-three, both of Council Bluffs. At the time of the robbery, they were armed with .22-caliber rifles.[28]

Four Pottawattami County prisoners broke out of the jail on December 8, 1958. The four tied up the night jailer and stole $80. Those who escaped were Orval Gitchell of Omaha, thirty-three; John Bartlett, eighteen; Donald Stahl, twenty-four, and Albert Tague, twenty-five, all of Council Bluffs. Deputy Sheriff Wayne Moser said the men jumped jailer Arthur Schuelzky when he checked the bullpen at 8:15 p.m.[29]

Escaping from the Pottawattami County Jail was becoming so easy—except for the rotary jail portion—that prisoners were escaping with ease by 1969. Four prisoners escaped on January 1 by knocking a hole in the jail wall. According to the *Harvey Tribune*, March 9, 1969, they left a note behind: "I sincerely hope that this escape will help you get a new jail because you need one. I knocked out the wall in an hour. Sincerely yours, Mike and Bill." Three inmates were picked up a few hours later by police in Omaha, Nebraska. The other prisoners, William F. Bond, nine-

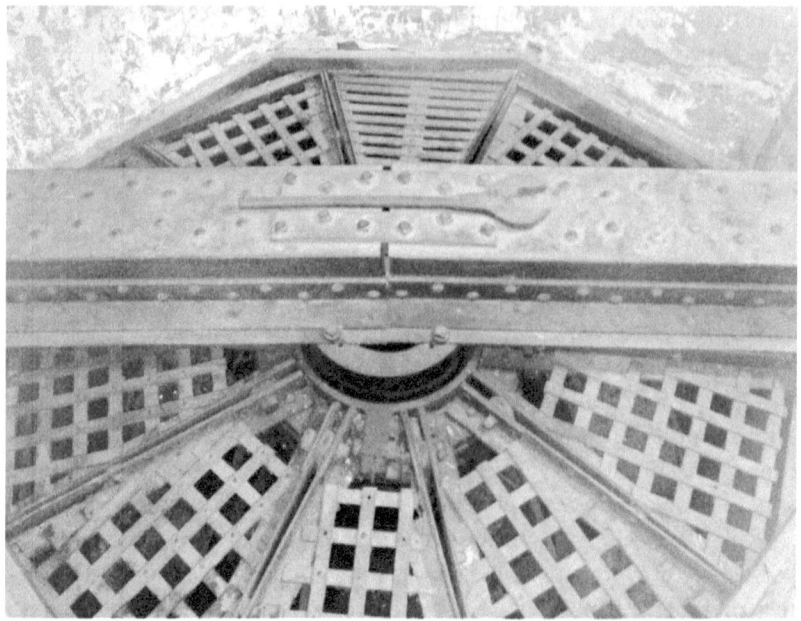

A huge wrench sits on top of the rotary at the Squirrel Cage Jail. The rotary was shut down in 1960 by the Council Bluffs fire marshal (author photograph).

teen, gave himself up the next night. "Nab Last of 4 Council Bluffs Jail Escapees," reported the *Waterloo Daily Courier*, January 3, 1969. The jail was closed after the escape to make repairs on it, according to the *Cedar Rapids Gazette*, January 6, 1969.

Other Criminals

A congressman was credited with the saving of two African Americans from a lynch mob at the Pottawattami County Jail on December 28, 1903. The commotion began when two men had been arrested for assaulting two women and were placed in the jail. A crowd of about a thousand stormed the jail after midnight on December 28. The crowd was armed with a steel railroad rail and smashed through the wooden door of the jail. Then Congressman Walter I. Smith appeared at the nick of time and persuaded the mob to let the law take care of the matter. Smith mounted the courthouse steps and asked the citizens to abide by the law and let the courts decide their fates. The woman had been brutally assaulted and the feeling was strong among the crowd to seek revenge for the attack. When the two men were arraigned in court, several hundred people showed up but no demonstration was held. The men could not make bond and were sent to jail. The mob's attitude boiled over and that night they decided to do something about it. Nearly the entire city police force was there as well as the sheriff and his deputies to stop the mob.[30]

A man from Michigan was sentenced to ninety days in the Pottawattami County Jail after he pleaded guilty to lascivious acts with a child on August 22, 1944. Bill Boadway was given the sentence by Judge Charles Roe. He was arrested on August 19 in his room at a local hotel. The complaint was filed by a 16-year-old youth employed at the hotel.[31]

Governor William S. Beardsley pardoned a fifteen-year-old youth who was housed in the Pottawattami County Jail on the charge of breaking and entering. Thomas Lee Benson had given his age as eighteen when he was arrested after a break in by three men at a grocery store on May 3, 1952. When his parents received a letter about his fate, they drove from Long Beach, California, to speak to the governor, who granted the pardon. Benson had run away from home on March 25 and met up with two other young men who broke in the store with him. They were four years older than he was. Lyle E. McElroy, nineteen, received a four-month sentence, while Albert Leroy Tague, nineteen, was sentenced to ten years in prison.[32]

Safekeeping

The "escape proof" rotary jail was a good place to hold prisoners for safekeeping. One of those held there for that purpose was Leonard Huseman, 33, of Yorktown. He was indicted in 1943 for the first-degree murder in the shooting of Sheriff Cecil M. Crawford of Page County. A Page County posse captured Huseman in 1943 and he was shuffled from the Atlantic and Pottawattami County jails for safekeeping. Then he was found to be insane and was released. However, in July 1949, he was returned to the Page County Jail as the murder case was reopened.[33]

Unusual Prisoners

Over the years, the rotary jail had its fair share of unusual inmates and prisoners it didn't know what to do with. Early on in the history of the jail there was a thirteen-year-old African American girl who was arrested for strolling about the streets late at night with white men. Ada May Monroe gave Omaha has her home and claimed her mother had thrown her out of the house; however, a letter received from the mother that said "she has been unable to do anything with the girl, and as soon as she would get back home, she would run away again." Mrs. Monroe suggested sending her to a reform school.[34]

The jail also became a place for some crazy people before they found their way to the mental asylum. In early 1887, the *Omaha Bee* reported that Council Bluffs police picked up five women for vagrancy one night and one was called "Swede Mary." The woman was reportedly

> chasing snakes up Broadway. After being placed inside the (police) station she objected to the police allowing a man to stay in her cell who had no head on him. She insisted he was there, and that he was a horrible looking fellow. Then she jumped onto a chair, and tried to get out of the way of the snakes who formed the legs of the chair. Then she wanted a gossamer to keep her from getting wet, there being a lot of snakes over her head who kept spitting on her. She had a horrible night and when brought before Judge Aylesworth ... she told a fearful take of the horror of the place.

The judge "sympathized with her, told her that it was no fit place to keep a lady, for there had been so many drunks locked up there that the air was full of snakes and other frightfuls. He would let her go to a nice boarding house for ten days" and sent the woman to the rotary jail.[35]

Died During Imprisonment

Over the history of the jail, three inmates died during their imprisonment. One inmate died of a heart attack. Another committed suicide by hanging. The third died after falling from the third level of the jail cage—a height of twenty-eight feet from the floor—when he was trying to write his name on the ceiling. A fourth death followed an accident in which an officer shot himself in the confusion of fortifying the facility

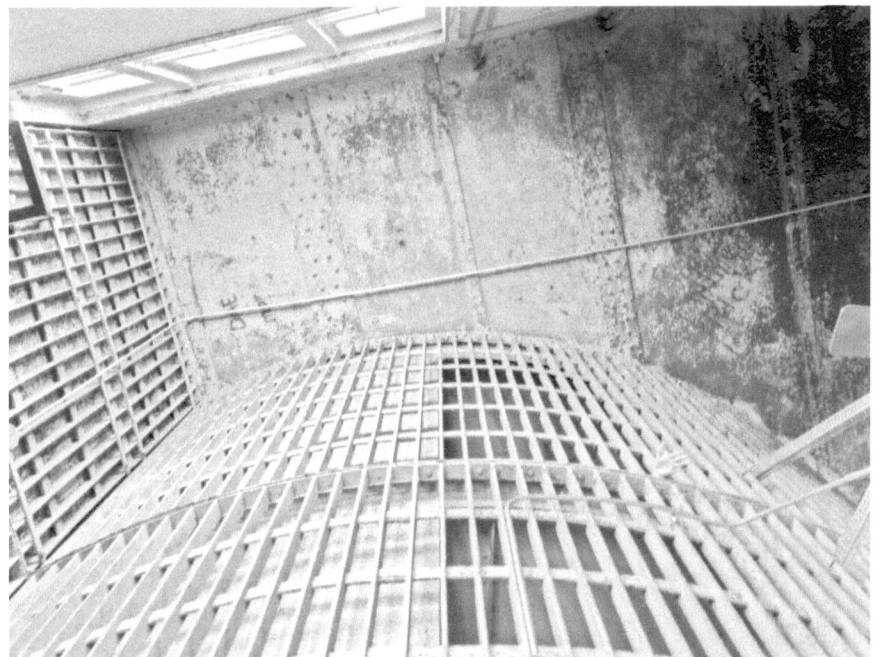

Inmates used to climb up the bars to the ceiling of the three-story rotary jail from the corridor. One prisoner fell twenty-seven feet to his death (author photograph).

from an angry mob that was threatening to storm the jail during the Farmer's Holiday Strike of 1932.[36]

Haunted Jail

In the late 1950s, when Bill Foster became the new jail superintendent, he experienced enough paranormal activity to realize that the former occupants in the fourth floor apartment still existed there despite being dead. He chose a bunk on the second floor, "because of the strange goings-on up there." One of the spirits may have been the first superintendent, J.M. Carter, who believed by some as being restless. The intense spirit may have never given up his position, so he hung around checking up on jailers and prisoners over the years. Also, a full body apparition of Otto Gudath, the superintendent from 1949 to 1958, was seen by witnesses on the fourth floor. Though deemed to be friendly and cordial, these presences are still supervising the museum staff, perhaps looking over the shoulders of the staff to see their progress in their activities in running the museum. Doors have opened and closed by themselves as they go about their business. Cabinet doors have also opened by themselves. The feelings of being watched or followed have been most frequently noted on the third and fourth floors though the voice of a little girl has been picked up in various locations throughout the building, as has the presence of two ghost cats.[37]

The Paranormal Research & Investigation Society of the Midwest conducted a daytime investigation on June 8, 2005, and an overnight investigation on July 1, 2005. They were able to record some scientific evidence which suggests that although the rotary jail closed its doors long ago,

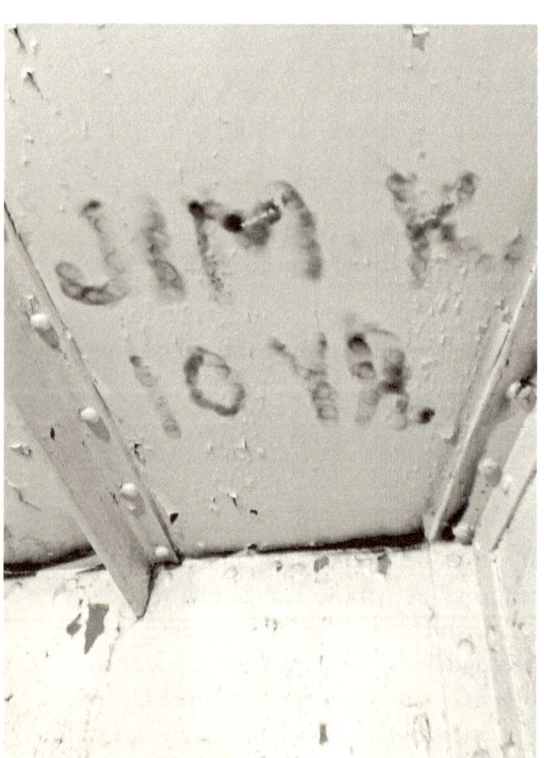

A Squirrel Cage inmate left his mark in candle smoke (author photograph).

some inmates and jailers are still there, unable to let go. A PRISM investigator caught the picture of a male apparition on film from outside a window on the fourth floor where the superintendent lived. They noticed odd light balls there as well. They captured on film a cabinet door opening by itself three times. Several electromagnetic spikes were recorded on special meters and infrared thermometers noted abnormal temperature fluctuations. More importantly, the team was able to correlate these readings with orbs (tiny balls of light) recorded on video.[38]

The Carroll Area

Paranormal Team did a preliminary investigation of the rotary jail museum in 2008 and came to the conclusion that there was enough evidence to suggest that the building is haunted. The group members, all specialists with trained eyes toward signs of potential paranormal activity, noted unexplained light upon occasion in the infirmary as well as unusual sounds.[39]

There have been some manifestations of spirits at the rotary jail. A woman was working on a project in the building and was startled to see an entity of a sad little girl dressed in gray sitting in one of the cells. Visitors to the jail have reported that they have felt an unseen presence tugging on their clothes like a child would do.[40]

Douglas County Jail— Omaha, Nebraska

By the 1880s, the population of Douglas County, Nebraska, had grown to more than 38,000 and a new jail was needed to handle the growing number of criminals in the county seat of Omaha, which means "Dwellers on the bluff." The rotary jail in Omaha was completed in November 1885 at a cost of $30,000 by the Pauly Jail Building Company. The rotary section was three stories high with ten cells on each floor. It weighed forty-five tons and was hung from above on a turning track instead of rotating from below. At first it was moved with a crank, but a little water motor in the basement was planned so that it could be rotated simply by moving a lever. The entrance on each floor was guarded by two doors. In this manner, the guard could swing the cylinder around until the cell appears and then open the inner door to let the prisoner out, while the other prisoners remained in their cells. This design eliminated the chance for the other prisoners to rush the guard. The rotary cylinder could be kept moving slowly all night, so that prisoners would not remain in one place long enough to do any mischief.[1]

In December 1886, Jailer O'Neil decided to keep the prisoners in their cells during the session of court as several were convicted or were about to be convicted. At other times, he allowed them access to the corridor.[2]

In August 1908, plans were drawn up for a new jail by architect John Latenser because the Douglas County Jail was no longer large enough to hold all the prisoners. At one time during the year, the jail held one hundred and fifty-two inmates as follows: twenty-eight in the African American quarters, fifteen white bound overs, eighty-seven in the bullpen, and twenty-two in the matron's quarters. The daily average was ninety prisoners. Mayor Dahlman had issued one hundred and fifteen pardons, of which forty-three were black prisoners and seventy-two white prisoners.[3]

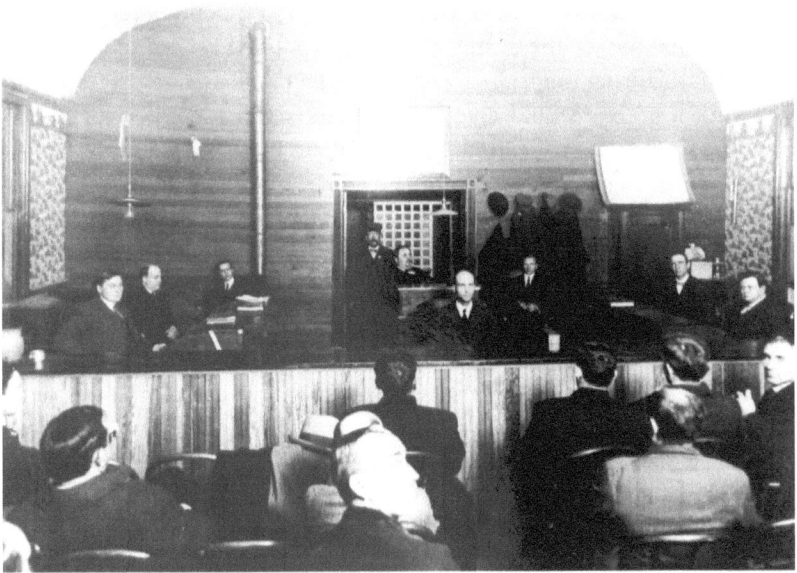

During a 1911 Omaha City Council meeting, Mayor Charles Tracy, City Clerk Ed Steiger, and Marshal Maney stand by the jail door of the old Rotary Jail (Douglas County Historical Society).

Hangings

When the new rotary jail was built, the architect designed its main hall to be used for executions, but the county authorities did not intend to use it. Judge Neville considered it "unadapted" to the purpose and suggested that the execution be held in the jail yard. A tall plank enclosure was to be built enclosing the scaffold and only a limited number of spectators would be admitted. The last hanging in Omaha had been on St. Valentine's Day in 1868. Ottway G. Baker was hanged on February 14 for murdering Woolsey D. Higgins on November 21, 1866. Baker was hanged on Capitol Hill in the presence of thousands of spectators.[4]

Thomas Ballard was convicted of first-degree murder and sentenced to be hanged on January 29, 1886. Ballard shot and killed Henry M. Verpoorten in the St. James Hotel in Omaha on March 15, 1885. The Nebraska Supreme Court later decided that Ballard would not be executed.[5]

The first hanging at the new jail occurred 1891 when Ed Neal was sentenced to death for a double killing of Allen and Dorothy Jones on a farm in Pinney in March 1890. Neal was captured in Kansas City, Kansas, and returned to face the crime. He never expressed a word of sympathy at the trial. During the trial, a woman by the name of "Joe" Clark fell in love with him. She would give him a bright smile and when he smiled back she wept. A kind-hearted jailer left them unattended at times. Neal asked a priest to marry them before he was hanged. The priest consented if the woman would relinquish her mode of life and become a member of the Catholic Church. When she refused, the wedding never occurred. He was hanged on October 9.[6]

A lynch mob formed after Edward McKenna died from a gunshot he received from Bernard McGinn on July 31, 1893. Sheriff Bennett armed his deputies and swore in several special deputies. The group dispersed a crowd at the Saratoga school yards. Omaha Police Chief Seavey with seventy men dispersed crowds forming at the courthouse. When the prisoners in the Douglas County Jail were informed of the possibility of a lynching they were excited, except for McGinn. He was cool and maintained a stoic demeanor. There were three murderers and four prisoners charged with criminal assault confined in the county jail at the time. The prisoners had a sleepless night and police officers slept in their uniforms ready for any emergency. McGinn and Dodrill were later transferred to Lincoln.[7]

Loris Higgins was confined in the Douglas County Jail after he was arrested for murdering Mr. and Mrs. W.L. Copple, farmers from Rosaline on May 12, 1907. In September, Sheriff Sid Young and his deputy took Higgins to Bancroft for his trial, but the train was met by a mob of twenty masked men. The masked men brushed the sheriff and his deputy to the side and threw a rope around Higgin's neck. They placed him in a wagon and hauled him to the Logan Bridge. They tied the rope to the highest beam on the bridge. Higgins was given a chance to say his last words. He vowed his faith in the religion he had found through the help of church women of Omaha who came to his cell. Then they threw him into the air. He reached the end of the rope and snapped his neck and died instantaneously. Finally, the mob made sure he was dead by firing forty bullets into his body.[8]

A large crowd of men gathered at the Douglas County Jail just before midnight on June 27, 1908, intent on lynching Charles Bond, who was sentenced to life imprisonment for killing John Wrede, a South Omaha saloon keeper. More policemen were sent to the jail to prevent the lynching and the crowd was dispersed.[9]

Murderers

A man was convicted in February 1898 for murdering a police officer in June 1897. August Kastner shot and killed Officer Dan Tiedeman in the early morning hours of June 9 at Nelson's Saloon in Omaha. After the reading of the verdict, Kastner was hauled away to the Douglas County Jail for safe keeping until sentencing. He would be held in the rotary jail until going to the penitentiary to serve out his sentence.[10]

A divine healer was indicted by the grand jury of Pottawattami County for the death of Miss Ethel Yates of Council Bluffs. Silas J. James was caught by Deputy Sheriff Roach and lodged in the Douglas County Jail on January 30, 1900. James had been called to prescribe for Miss Yates at the beginning of her illness. Instead of improving, she steadily grew worse and soon died. After the indictment, James found a hiding place in South Omaha. The healer said he had nothing to fear from a fair trial as the treatment he prescribed for Miss Yates was proper. Results of his trial are unknown.[11]

The killing of a police officer caused a riot in South Omaha on February 21, 1909. John Masuredes, a Greek man, was arrested for the murder of Policeman Edward Lowery on February 19. Two nights later in the Greek neighborhood, people rioted and more than thirty buildings were burned, wrecked, or badly damaged. Several Greek citizens were injured in the fracas as well, but no deaths were reported. Masuredes had been locked up in the Douglas County Jail, but was moved to the penitentiary in Lincoln because of the rioting. Fifteen people were arrested during the riot and incarcerated in the Douglas County Jail.[12]

Escapes

While escape from the rotary was nearly impossible, other escapes occurred from other parts of the jail over the years. One of the largest escapes soon after the rotary was built came in 1893 when four prisoners got away. Sheriff Bennett was out in the country hunting ducks and his brother, the head jailer, was away giving residents in South Omaha some points on how to run an election. Only Jailer Ernest and Deputy Sheriff Lewis remained at the Douglas County Jail watching over the inmates.

During the afternoon, some inmates were given the task of shoveling hard coal in the bins in front of the furnace. During the detail, they decided to escape from the jail via the coal bin. Escaping were John Rice, John Ferguson, Ed Fitzgerald, and Henry Smith.[13]

Other Criminals

Strangely enough, the entire municipal government of Lincoln was incarcerated in the Douglas County Jail for a week in the fall of 1887. The incident began when A.J. Sawyer was elected mayor on an independent reform ticket in opposition to the regular republican nominee, E.P. Roggen. The city had been "wide open" and wild for some time, and a Law and Order League had been formed to settle things down and purge the city of gamblers and other criminals. Mr. Sawyer was the president of this organization. When Roggen was named by the regular Republican convention, a large number of most influential citizens bolted and called a rump convention, nominating Sawyer. The latter was found to have a majority of five hundred and thirty-seven when the votes were counted.

Sawyer promptly declared war against the gamblers. As a result of his operations, charges were preferred against Albert F. Parsons, the police judge, the reformers alleging that he was guilty of malfeasance in office since he had not turned over money collected in fines as provided by law. A committee of the council was appointed to investigate the charges. After listening to the testimony, the committee reported that the police judge was guilty as charged and recommended that he be removed and the office declared vacant. The ordinance in force relating to the removal of city officers required that the trial be conducted by the entire council. The ordinance was amended and the report of the committee was again filed.

But while the resolution declaring the office vacant was pending, Parsons showed up, accompanied by his attorney, L.C. Burr. The police judge requested the trial be held before the entire council on a certain day, and if all the members concurred he would be satisfied with the result. The mayor and council agreed.

Then Parsons attempted to organize a plan against the city officials. His attorney went before Judge Brewer of the United States Circuit

Court and obtained an order restraining the mayor and the council from taking any further action in the matter until the whole case could be reviewed in his court. This interpretation of the law was very distasteful to the municipal officers. They regarded the order as a direct blow at local government, and, after consultation with several prominent attorneys, chose to ignore the mandate of Judge Brewer. The mayor declared the office of the police judge vacant. The council confirmed this action.

No time was lost by the opposition in calling attention to the circuit court to this opposing action and then the trouble began. Judge Brewer directed the city officials to appear before him and show why they should not be fined for contempt of court. They appeared and presented their reasons for disregarding the order of the court stating that the court had no right to issue it.

Judge Brewer overruled. As an eye opener, he sentenced Mayor Sawyer, and Councilmen Briscoe, Burks, Cooper, Pace, and Dean to pay a fine of $50. Councilman Billingsley, Graham, Hovey, Ensign, Fraas, and Dailey were asked to donate $600 each. The city officials declared that they would rather suffer imprisonment than pay the fine so the United States marshal quietly gathered them together and took them to comfortably furnished quarters in the Douglas County Jail. Here the obdurate prisoners were wined and dined by everybody while G.M. Labertson hurried to Washington to file an application for a writ of habeas corpus with the United States Supreme Court. The writ was granted, the prisoners released. In the following January, the stand taken by the mayor and councilmen was vindicated by a decision of the Supreme Court. In Lincoln there was great rejoicing over the result and all the imprisoned officials were looked upon as heroes.[14]

The Douglas County Jail was used by United States marshals to house convicts for the selling of liquor without a license. Deputy United States Marshal Heffinger arrested a couple of Richardson County bootleggers in April 1891 and put them in the jail. One was George W. Baker and he was expected to be fined $25 or $50 besides costs. The marshal indicated other arrests in Omaha in the future.[15]

Selling liquor to the Native Americans was a problem that law enforcement addressed from time to time in Omaha. In August 1898, two men were indicted for selling liquor to the Indians. An Indian woman by the name of Se-gah-hu-ne-ga was also confined to the Douglas County

Jail after she failed to post bond after a federal grand jury indicted her for selling liquor.[16]

Governor James E. Boyd pardoned an adulterer confined to the Douglas County Jail on June 30, 1892. Ed Hudderd, the telegraph operator and station agent at Portal, had been given an eleven-month sentence for adultery, but he only had to serve three months thanks to the pardon. He had eloped with the wife of a farmer. The couple headed west when Hudderd was arrested and brought back. He pleaded guilty to the crime and was sentenced to eleven months in jail. Mrs. Peterson was still at large.[17]

Two Omaha evening newspapers criticized the Douglas County Jail for allowing a prisoner, "Bank Wrecker Mosher," free rein in the jail in October 1893. Sheriff Bennett was allowing liquor to be furnished to him in the jail. Before Judge Dundy sentenced Mosher to the penitentiary, he was given the freedom of the city. He was taken to theatres and places of amusement. He was also allowed to see women at a brothel. Mosher was also allowed to go across the street from the jail to eat meals in a restaurant.[18]

Ex-State Treasurer Joseph S. Bartley was arrested and incarcerated in the Douglas County Jail on June 24, 1897. He was convicted of embezzling $150,000 from the state and sentenced to twenty years imprisonment in the penitentiary as well as a fine of $303,768 on June 27, 1897, in Omaha.[19] He decided to appeal the decision and remained in the county jail because he couldn't make bond for more than a year until the Nebraska Supreme Court affirmed his sentence on July 6, 1898. Then he was sent to the state penitentiary to serve out his sentence. Governor Ezra P. Savage commuted the sentence and Bartley was set free after five years of a twenty-year sentence on January 2, 1902.[20]

Four men, two of them millionaires, had to spend a little time in the Douglas County Jail as they were convicted of land fraud in western Nebraska in 1906. However, they were exonerated when they appealed the sentence; however, the United States Court of Appeals upheld the conviction in 1910. Millionaires Bartlett Richards and William G. Comstock were fined $1,500 each and only had to serve a year in the rotary jail, while Charles Jameson and Acquilla Triplett were fined $500 each and had to serve eight months in jail.[21]

Then in 1907, Ansley Walker, a Native American, was charged with introducing liquor on his reservation by Deputy United States Marshal John Sides and interred in the Douglas County Jail. When Walker was discovered with a jug of whisky in his wagon, he broke the jug over the wagon wheel thinking he destroyed the evidence, but the smell was enough to convince authorities he was guilty.[22]

Judge Munger ordered the deportation of two Chinese men, Liu Hop and Leo Lung On. They were lodged in the Douglas County Jail until they could be sent to San Francisco. The case against some ten other Chinese was dismissed.[23]

Insane Prisoners

A half a dozen insane women were housed in the Douglas County Jail in May 1889. The legislature was dealing with the problem of adding more insane asylums or housing the insane in jail. It was a problem of dollar and cents.[24]

A man was held in the Douglas County Jail for four months without being charged for a crime. It seems police wanted John McPherson of Friend to confess to some knowledge of the murder of a man by the name of Jones. They finally released him and when he came home he was dirty and covered with vermin. Another newspaper, *World Herald*, reported: "John McPherson, a young man who has been held in the county jail for some time as an insane person, has been discharged as cured and left for his home in Friend." Friends of his claim he has never been insane and the matter is being investigated. A damage suit may follow. McPherson was a Russian exile.[25]

The Jail Today

The City of Omaha and Douglas County combined their jails together and nowadays have a modern facility called the Douglas County Corrections Center. It has two hundred and forty-one double occupancy cells, sixteen handicap cells, a central control area, a courtroom, a laundry and kitchen area as well as medical and dental areas.[26]

Warren County Jail— Williamsport, Indiana

Williamsport was founded and platted in 1828 by William Harrison (not to be confused with President William Henry Harrison). Located in the southeast corner of Warren County near the Wabash River, it became the county seat in June 1829. The first post office in the county began there on September 28, 1829.[1]

The first jail in the county was constructed of stone. The one-room jail had an oak floor and a ceiling made of boiler iron. On the east side of the room was an iron cell about eight-feet square with two berths in it. One berth was two feet above the floor and the upper bunk was about four feet from the floor. During the day, the prisoners could walk around the jail corridor, but at night they were locked up in the iron cell.[2]

In 1886, the second Warren County Courthouse was torn down and a third courthouse was built in the new area of the town that had developed in the proximity of the railroad. It was decided at that time to add a rotary jail in the basement of the new courthouse, which was highlighted by a one hundred and fifty-five foot tower.[3]

The specifics of the new rotary jail were revealed to public in an article in the *Warren Republican*. The entrance door to the prison would be made with a frame of one-half inch plate iron with a hollow box on one side containing the rotating mechanism. The door would be made of one-quarter inch iron and have a strong Yale lock. The walls would also be made of one-quarter inch jail plate, firmly riveted together and well anchored to the walls. The exercise room was to have a three-sixteenth-inch plate iron ceiling. The circular grating around the cell structure was to be made of five-ply iron and steel bars. The doors leading to the vestibules and the exercise room would have the best quality Scandinavian locks. The center column on which the cells rotated was to be made of cast iron and thoroughly braced at the top. At the upper end it carried a set of conical steel rollers from which the cells were suspended and rotated. The floor of cells was to be made of one-quarter inch jail plate and riveted to suitable bars. Partitions between cells and the front of cells were to be made of three-sixteenth inch jail plate and all firmly bound together with angle irons and three-eighths inch rivets. The top of cells were formed of steel bar lattice gratings and well secured to partitions of cells. Two bunks of one-eighth inch sheet iron bound with angle iron were riveted to the walls of each cell. The closet to be formed in the rear of each cell is to receive the night pail. The wrought iron night pail will have a lid and handle. The rotating mechanism is to be a crank to be connected to a vertical shaft in the hollow door jamb. Under the floor lay a system of cogs with the main rock which extends around the base of the cells. All was to be the best materials and workmanship equal in every respect to the corresponding parts on the new Patent Rotary Jail that was built in Crawfordsville, Indiana, by the Pauly Jail Building Company.[4]

The corridor around the rotary extended only about one-third of the way around it. By 1889 the jail was considered neither strong or sanitary, according to a report by Alexander Johnson of the Board of State Charities of Indiana. The cell water closets were unusable. The water closet in the corridor flushed poorly. Sewage had no proper fall and was getting clogged. Windows were located on one side of the jail making for poor ventilation. There was a bathtub, but it wasn't being used because there was no hot water. There was a separate cell for women, but it was rarely used and tramps were often housed there instead. Bedding was unsanitary and washed only once every two months. One of the heaters for the courthouse was located just outside the door of the jail and coal dust and ashes sifted into the jail.[5]

Secretary Johnson inspected the jail in October 1891 and found it in "bad condition." He thought the rotary was "quite unsuitable" as it was located in a crowded corner of the basement of the courthouse. At the time of his inspection the rotary was not working, so only one cell could be used properly. He stated that it was not clean and ventilation was "very poor." He recommended the county build a suitable facility and move the rotary into it. He also recommended the cells be repaired so the rotary could be rotated as it was intended.[6]

Warren County grand juries also inspected the jail and found it less that satisfactory not to their liking. The October 1891 grand jury found the jail to be in "bad" condition as to sanitary purposes. They condemned it and said the place was "unfit for the incarceration of prisoners."[7]

The grand jury for the March term of 1897 examined the Warren County Jail and reported: "We find that the jail is cold and damp, that the ventilation is very poor, and that the sanitary condition is bad."[8]

In October 1897, the grand jury commented that it was impossible for jailers to handle prisoners with either convenience or safety, or keep the sanitary conditions of the jail up to the current standards. It suggested that the commissioners would be justified in building a new jail to remedy the present unsanitary conditions.[9]

The following year the March grand jury made a careful examination of the County Jail and found the sanitary condition to be fair. They found that the location of the jail was not to be commendable.[10]

The Secretary of the Indiana Board of Charities Amos W. Butler visited the Warren County Jail in September 1900 and did not like what he saw. He stated that the conditions were not sanitary and the jail was not safe. He wrote that "it is a disgrace to the county and State." He found that half of the rotary jail cells were away from the light and against a damp wall. Light and ventilation was only provided by basement windows. Two men were located in each cell. Women slept on cots. There was a pump for water. The men had a water closet, but the women had to use buckets in their compartment. He did credit the sheriff for keeping the quarters "tolerably clean." An old iron bath tub was provided for use by the inmates. The only bedding was old, dirty and lacking comfort. The bedding was thrown away when it got too foul. No occupation or activity was provided for inmates. In the winter, tramps were often imprisoned with the city prisoners. He noted that every grand jury in recent years had condemned the jail and recommended a new jail. He noted that the county had grounds for a new jail. A total of one hundred and thirty-eight prisoners were kept in the rotary cells during 1899.[11]

At times, the small Warren County Jail was empty. At other times, the jail was nearly filled to capacity. It could hold up to twenty prisoners—sixteen in the rotary section and four in the other cells. One week in November 1901 saw the jail full of different criminals. William Smith and Joe Price, an African American, were in jail for being drunk. James Macey and Burt Hogue were captured by the Horse Company and lodged in jail on the charge of stealing. Almond Francis was brought from West

Lebanon on the charge of adultery. Lon Ham and Charles Travis were imported from Marion, Indiana, for assuming a false name and for obtaining goods under false pretense, respectively. Sheriff Williams had as many as ten inmates for breakfast.[12]

The Warren County Courthouse was gutted by fire and only the heavy brick outer walls were left standing on January 22, 1907. A high

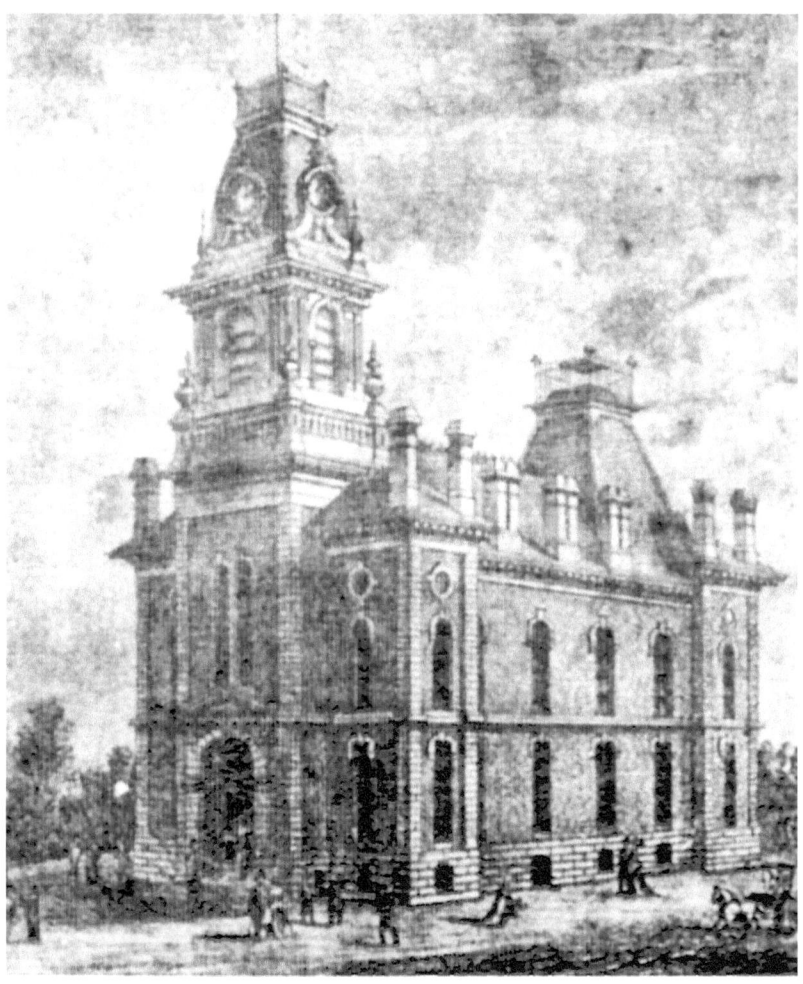

The Warren County Courthouse was gutted by fire on January 22, 1907, which spelled the end for the rotary jail in the basement (Williamsport-Washington Township Public Library).

wind blowing prevented of the firemen from saving the building. The estimated loss to the $80,000 structure was $50,000 with $25,000 being covered by insurance.[13] Sheriff Dan Tague transported his prisoners to the jail at Fowler, Indiana, for safekeeping as the Williamsport jail was also damaged by the fire.[14]

With the fire destroying the old courthouse and jail, new plans were made for a jail to be a separate structure at the corner of Second and Monroe Street. The reconstruction of the courthouse and a separate jail was estimated at $80,000.[15]

The present Warren County Jail is a maximum security facility. Because the inmates in this jail range from low-level offenders to those being held for violent crimes such as armed robbery, rape and murder, the security level is as high as it is in any maximum security state prison. Some of the security features in the facility include security cameras, electronic detection and reinforced fencing topped with razor wire. Inmates include those who have been sentenced to a year or less. Those sentenced to additional time are sent to the Indiana Department of Corrections or Federal prison system.[16]

A Murderer

Only one suspected murderer was ever placed in the Warren County Jail. Wash Welch was suspected of killing Charles E. Crosson and throwing his body in the Wabash River. He was interred in the Warren County Jail awaiting trial for murder in August 1897. Welch was accused of tearing off the man's clothing and beating him with a club until he was nearly unconscious. It was thought that Welch, a former inmate of the Joliet Prison, had accomplices in the murder and they were in the Jeffersonville Prison serving time for "sandbagging" a farmer near Williamsport. The Wabash was dredged yet no body was ever found. Results of the case are unknown.[17]

Escapes

Before the new courthouse was built and the new jail put in its basement, escapes were quite common in the old county jail. Prisoners could dig their way out of the old jail like three did in November 1871. Those three inmates easily pulled up the oak flooring as the boards were old and rotted badly in the joints. They then dug their way through the dirt under the stone wall.[18]

Four prisoners who were headed to the state penitentiary attempted to break out of the Williamsport Jail in March 1893. However, the tool they were using to cut through the wall broke and they gave up on their attempt.[19]

Three inmates did succeed in escaping from the inside corridor of the rotary jail by sawing off the padlocks and climbing atop the cage and making their way to a window on the south side of the building in November 1893. Then they crawled over the rotary. The men were Charles Stewart, Osro Gray, and Fred Smith. Stewart and Gray had been charged with horse stealing and had been granted a change of venue for their case. They were to have been removed to Covington soon. Smith was serving out a thirty-day sentence for house breaking and had about twenty days left to serve. Sheriff Powell offered a reward of $50 for the recovery of Stewart and Gray.[20]

Two men who escaped from the Williamsport Jail were captured at Terre Haute in December 1893. Charles Steward and Henry Gray were brought to Covington and confined there.[21]

Other Cases

One of the most sensational cases during the time of the rotary jail in Warren County was the embezzlement case against the former treasurer of Warren County. The treasurer stole money from the county and fled the state in January 1893. A grand jury indicted Augustus Cronkhite in March 1893 for embezzlement. A warrant was sworn out for his arrest. On March 24, 1894, Cronkhite was captured in Los Angeles, California, and he was returned to the Warren County Jail until his trial. He was first elected treasurer of Warren County in November 1888 and took office on January 1 the following year. When he entered office, he was heavily in debt. There was a mortgage on his farm of $15,000. He wiped out this mortgage by borrowing from the county. Additionally, he made many improvements to his farm using county money. He also borrowed another $44,000 to pay off his old debts.[22] Cronkhite was fined $10 and given a three-year sentence in Michigan State Prison on June 7, 1894. The total amount of his embezzlement was set at $65,000.[23] Cronkhite served two and half years in the Michigan City Prison and was released on December 11, 1896.[24]

A class leader and Sunday school superintendent landed in the Williamsport jail after he approached young men and boys along the road and told them he had a warrant for their arrest. His object was to scare them into giving him money to avoid being arrested. A.B. Britten was put in jail as he couldn't pay the $300 bond put on him by Esquire Fisher. His wife and home were located in State Line.[25]

Three boys were put in the Warren County Jail after they disturbed a religious meeting at Indiana Mineral Springs in April 1898. James Rhodes, Frank Leary and another boy were arrested and tossed in jail, but only Leary was able to make bail by using his pay as a bellboy at one of the Lafayette hotels.[26]

Alcohol offenders were frequent visitors to the Warren County Jail. One such inmate, S.P. Hunter, wrote a letter to the editor of the local newspaper after his incarceration there in March 1898. He stated that he was picked up two hours after paying a fine for the same offense and thrown back in the jail. He complained of being "crammed in the county jail wheel of fortune, only to be tortured by bed-bugs and gray-backs" for a term of eighty-seven hours. He was fed only two thin slices of bread, a dab of dough, gravy and a few spoons of soup beans. He was given water in a rusty tin cup and had to sleep on an iron shelf with one dirty wad of covering."[27]

Outagamie County Jail— Appleton, Wisconsin

Outagamie County was created in 1851 and a jail was first considered. After the first county courthouse was built in Appleton, the county seat, the basement of the facility was used as the first jail. In February 1852, a separate structure for the jail was finally agreed upon. During the building of the first county jail in Appleton, prisoners were held at a jail in DePere.[1]

The first Outagamie County Jail was regarded as antiquated by 1885 and the county supervisors decided a new jail was needed. By this time, the population of the county was more than 28,000 and the city had more than 8,000 residents.[2]

The building committee of the Board of Supervisors of Outagamie County visited jails Rockford, Freeport, and Elkhorn in 1885 to determine what type of new jail was needed. They "highly recommended" a rotary jail. The two-story building would be of brick with a stone foundation and a roof of tin and iron containing sixteen ordinary cells, two dark cells, and four separate cells for females and juveniles or hospital use as may be needed, making a total of twenty-two cells, built to accommodate from sixty to eighty prisoners. The remodeling of the old jail would cost nearly as much as a new jail and still not be totally satisfactory when completed. The committee estimated the rotary-type jail like the one in Crawfordsville would cost $25,000–30,000.[3]

A committee appointed to consider building a county jail reported favorably in April 1886, the cost was to be about $25,000; the present jail was insecure and continually needed repair. Their recommendation was to the construct a new jail to cost that sum, to be paid for by the sale of county bonds. There was a minority report against this improvement. The majority report was adopted by the vote of seventeen to fourteen.[4]

Following considerable discussion, they decided on the rotary jail and contracted with the Patent Rotary Jail Company of Chicago for $14,500.06 for an eight-cell jail. The work was to be completed December 1, 1886, but was delayed until March 1, 1887.[5]

On July 22, 1886, the county contracted with Henry Paepke of Neenah to build the residence attached to the jail for $8,835. Later the contractor agreed to build the third story for $500. In November 1886, the contract for the steam heating apparatus at $723 was signed. These various contracts were changed somewhat and prices were altered to correspond.[6]

On June 2, 1887, the last prisoner in the old county jail was discharged and for the first time in many years that institution was empty. The new jail was completed on June 3, 1887. However, there were no inmates in the old jail to transfer to the new one, so it remained empty until June 8 when Deputy Marshal Marshall arrested a man accused of selling liquor on the Oneida Reservation. The first inmate was Silas Webster, a resident of Brown County.[7]

Sheriff James Golden was able to move into the new residence attached to the jail building on June 3, 1887.[8] Electrical wiring was installed to the Outagamie County Jail in September 1891.[9]

On the strange side, a farmer, John Joers, was blowing out the gas in the jail when he was almost asphyxiated in September 1898.[10]

In 1898 the county board decided the prisoners were living too soft just sitting in a cell in the Outagamie County Jail and wanted them out working. The rotary cells were considered no longer safe as well. This led to the establishment of a county workhouse.[11]

In 1905 the Outagamie County Jail in was declared unfit by grand jury. However, the sheriff's residence connected to the jail was still good enough and it was kept. In November 1905, the county board voted to tear down the existing jail and erect a new one; five supervisors voted against this step.[12]

Contracts for the new jail had been let by the end of 1905, but construction wouldn't begin until March 1906. The new jail would look like the county jail in Oshkosh and would cost in the neighborhood of $16,000. The new jail was completed by November 1906 at a final cost of about $19,000.[13]

The rotary jail was torn down to make way for the new jail building. The removal of the rotary jail was put up for bids and Manitowoc Iron & Metal Company secured the purchase of the jail with a bid of $325 (about $8,830 value in today's money)[14] in April 1906. It was the highest of four bids made. The company would ship out the iron and steel within a few days after it was torn down.[15]

A man claimed the new Outagamie County Jail, which replaced the rotary jail, was a waste of public money because of faulty construction. A man named Koch claimed that the cement floor had cracked, that putty had been used in place of iron rivets, that the plumbing was defective, and the heating apparatus was poorly placed.[16]

Nowadays, the Outagamie County Jail has a total of 556 beds and has a diverse population that includes both male and female adults. The jail ranks seventh largest in Wisconsin in prisoner capacity. The Outagamie County Jail booked a total of 6,050 in 2014. The Outagamie County sheriff in 2016 was Bradley G. Gehring.[17]

Escapes

Four prisoners escaped from the county jail by sawing off three bars of a cell window in the corridor and not the rotary section.[18]

Two men made a bold attempt at escaping from the Outagamie County Jail in October 1891. While exercising in the corridor, M.H. Burton and Albert White seized the turnkey and bound and gagged him. Then they took an axe and started to dig. When discovered they had completed a hole a foot deep, they crawled under in the wall.[19]

Martin Gagen cut the chain from his legs and scaled a fence to escape from the Outagamie County Jail in January 1892.[20]

Tramps confined to the Outagamie County Jail attempted to dig their way out of the jail corridor the day after Christmas by removing bricks under the window on the north side of the facility. Their attempts were heard by a short-term prisoner upstairs, and he notified the sheriff. The four tramps were then caught as they forced two bricks out of the outer wall. The work was done with knives and forks stolen when meals were served. When captured all of the tools were worn out except for half of an iron spoon.[21]

Frank Reiebel, who was jailed for abusing his wife, escaped from the Outagamie County Jail on February 2, 1896, but in April he was back behind bars, according to *The Weekly Wisconsin*, April 25, 1896.

Adolph Elkey of Seymour, who was in jail for stealing wheat from an elevator, tried to escape by digging out of the jail, but his two Native American cellmates informed the sheriff before he succeeded. Elkey used an old knife to remove some bricks from the wall in March 1898.[22]

Frank Foster escaped from the rotary jail on November 4, 1901. The prisoners were being locked in their rotary cells for the night when Foster pushed aside the turnkey and bolted. Since the door to the outside was unlocked, he went through the outer office and into the street. He successfully evaded capture. Authorities believed he secured a hat and some clothing from friends before leaving town. Foster had been in the jail since June after being convicted of stealing a horse and buggy.[23]

William Bruce escaped from the Outagamie County Jail in August 1904. He sawed the bars of his cell to make his escape. How he secured the saw was a mystery. It was the second time in a two months that Bruce had escaped from the jail.[24]

Three men broke out of the Outagamie County Jail on August 30, 1904. Frank Schnadt, Alex Seymour, and Tobin Alberts sawed a hole through the floor and made their escape through a basement window. The men then went to the county barn and harnessed up Sheriff Mitchell's best team of horses and drove to the north end of the city. There Alberts and Seymour went into a saloon and soon became intoxicated. They were captured at the saloon the next morning. Schnadt was awaiting trial on a state prison charge and was not recaptured.[25]

Joseph Steidl, a member of a highwaymen gang, broke out of the rotary jail on January 13, 1905. Somehow he got his hands on a rope and used it to get out of his cell. He cut a hole in the corrugated iron ceiling and used the rope to assist him in his escape. After getting into the cell above his, it was easy sailing after that. However, he was spotted by a private detective who alerted police. A squad of officers was promptly detailed and they rounded him up and returned him to jail. Steidl was facing a state prison sentence for burglary at Welcome.[26]

Another highway robber who escaped from the jail was Alberts. He fled in early 1905. By April he was rearrested in Green Bay after a careful three week search by police.[27]

Three prisoners escaped from the Outagamie County Jail in August 1905. Louis Tagge, one of the escapees, was arrested in March 1906 for impersonating a sewing machine agent in Danville, Illinois.[28]

James Manning made an attempt to escape the Appleton jail by tearing down part of a brick wall in October 1891.[29]

An Injury from the Rotary

Several inmates were injured over the years by the rotary when they didn't get out of the way as the jail was rotated. One of them was Charles Brady. The tramp fell in the door of his cell while it was being rotated. His arm was caught and broken near the shoulder. In fact, the bone was protruding through the skin after the incident. Had the rotary not been stopped, his arm would have been severed.[30]

Native American Prisoners

Because there were nearby Native American reservations, some Indians ended up serving time in the Outagamie County Jail. In 1891, three Oneida tribe members were found guilty of killing a farmer's cow. Because the cow wandered onto the reservation, the Oneidas claimed they had a right to kill and eat the animals. The court thought differently. Jacob Smith and Adam Christjohn were sentenced to sixty days in the rotary jail, while Wm. John was given a lesser stay of fifty days.[31]

Three men were convicted of taking liquor to the Oneida Reservation on June 13, 1900. Dixon Schenadore, Enos Koeck, and James Schenadore were sentenced to sixty days each in the Outagamie County Jail. Aaron House pleaded guilty to taking liquor to the reservation, but his sentence was suspended. August Wauters also pleaded guilty to a similar charge and he only received a reprimand from the court since it was his first offense.[32]

In August 1900, nearly a dozen Indians were confined in the county jail—three from Seymour charged with burglary and the others United States prisoners; they spent most of their time in jail playing euchre. They were religious men and became model prisoners. The *Post* called the jail, "An Indian Camp."[33]

Some men were convicted of taking liquor to the Indians in June 1903 and sentenced to the rotary jail. Joseph Beaupre was found guilty of providing liquor to the Keshna reservation and sentenced to sixty days in jail. Richard Skenadore and Elijah Anton were also found guilty of taking liquor onto the Oneida reservation and given sixty days in jail as well as a $100 fine. The court criticized the Oshkosh saloonkeepers for selling liquor to the Indians.[34]

Famous Criminals

The rotary jail in Appleton held some famous criminals during its eighteen-year history. One was murderer Porter Ross of Kaukauna. He was found guilty of the murder of his wife and her sister, Katie Duprey, at a resort on March 8, 1896. Ross was in put in the Outagamie County Jail on two occasions as he stood trial twice. He tried to show he was insane by holding almost nightly communications with the spirits of his murdered wife and sister-in-law. He was loud and awoke inmates and jail attendants, thus assuring himself of an audience in May 1897. This ploy did not work as he was convicted for his wife's murder in June 1897 and received a two-year sentence, which he served in Waupun.[35] Then Ross was returned to the rotary jail in March 1899, to await trial for the murder of his wife's sister. Her younger sister died from gun-shot wounds three weeks after he killed his wife. Ross created a sensation in the county jail while awaiting the second trial when he ate pieces of wire and broken glass in an attempt to show he was crazy.[36] Ross was acquitted on the charge. The grounds given by the jurors were that the defense attorney had satisfactorily shown that Ross shot the woman while scuffling with one of the men who had accompanied the two women to the resort.[37]

1886 saw four or five murder cases on the docket. Mrs. Girkie was tried for the murder of Peter Armstrong; she shot him while he was trying to enter her house; and she was convicted of murder in the second degree. About the same time, Hugh Boyle was tried for murder in the death of Theodore Endter at a trial in Dartford. Anton Helmrod shot John Bauer and was tried for his murder. This was about the time when numerous river, canal, water power and riparian rights (rights for allocating water) cases were first instituted. The local bar became one of the most conspicuous and one of the ablest in the West.[38]

Wenzel Kabat, an Appleton man charged with murder, was supposed to remain in the Winnebago County Jail until trial in 1905, but that didn't go as planned. He spent this time waiting in the rotary section of the Outagamie County Jail until his trial in the circuit court in Outagamie in March 1906. He was charged with murdering Michael McCarthy, a Kaukauna farmer, but no body was found. An unknown source told police that McCarthy was alive and was being held for a $2,000 ransom. However, McCarthy's brother believed the information as without foundation. Furthermore, Kabat also denied the allegation. McCarthy may have been cremated in some woods. Bones, a bloody ax and a saw were found hidden in a mass of dense underbrush near the scene of the supposed crime.[39] Kabat may have disposed of a farm McCarthy owned in Nebraska valued at $3,200. Unable to file on murder charges, the prosecutor filed forgery charges against Kabat. He was convicted of forgery and sent to the reformatory at Green Bay in 1902.[40]

William Maas spent ninety days in the Outagamie County Jail before he went onto the Outagamie County Asylum. He had been found guilty of clubbing his wife to death. The state was evaluating him in 1897 to decide his disposition.[41]

Two members of the notorious Walch gang were apprehended and tossed into the county rotary jail on October 22, 1903. One of those captured was Frank Lepton, who had shot a police officer in the scalp at the base of his skull during a robbery. The other was David Walch, who a store owner had wrestled a gun away from as Lepton struck him with a root beer bottle. For over a year the two men had been hunted like wild beasts, but they had eluded officers and traps set for them. Lepton was also wanted by the Appleton police for a fight two weeks before.[42]

J.G. Benateau committed suicide in the county jail on June 16, 1894. He fired two shots into his chest and two through his head with a 22-calibre revolver. Benateau had been put in jail pending a trial after making threats to his girlfriend. The man was madly in love with Nettie Feldhoven, but when she turned down his proposal of marriage, Benateau got angry, drew a revolver and threatened to shoot her and himself. After appearing before the judge, he was searched by an officer and no weapon was found. However, the prisoner shot and killed himself in the jail later that day.[43]

Other Inmates

Samuel Roby was put in the rotary jail for thirty days for assaulting his own lawyer, P.R. Barnes, in April 1890. He had been incarcerated since autumn.[44]

In 1901, an attorney complained about his client getting sentenced in the county rotary jail. Frank Witt of Appleton tried to use a cancelled two-cent stamp for mailing and was found guilty of the infraction by the United States Court and given a $100 fine or 30 days in jail. Witt chose the latter and was assigned to the rotary jail to serve out his sentence. His lawyer, Henry Fitzgibbon of Menasha complained, "It is pretty hard, when we have to go to jail and when we can't have our choice of jails."[45]

A man who murdered his wife in Chippewa Falls confessed to the crime in August 1902, while he was incarcerated in the Outagamie County Jail for another crime. George Wolf gave jealousy as his motive.[46]

During the last winter for the rotary jail in 1906, one of the inmates was held seventeen-year-old horse thief, Martin Verhagen. He was sent to the state reformatory in Green Bay.[47]

A man who severely beat a thirteen-year-old girl on September 13, 1906, was put in the Outagamie County Jail for the second time within two years for the same offense—criminal assault. Paul Wenzel's attack allegedly left the girl in critical condition. Nearly every stitch of her clothes had been torn off as well in her desperation to escape him. Helena Kloehn's screams were heard by Ernst Wendland, who lived not far from the scene. The girl was carrying dinner to her father at the Outagamie paper mill when she was attacked. Wenzel had recently been paroled from the state reformatory, where he spent eight months of a three-year sentence on the same charge made to a younger girl. He was held on a $300 bond.[48]

One of the last inmates at the rotary jail was a Japanese man who had been thrown in jail for no apparent reason. United States Marshal T.B. Reid said he had orders to take Yung Ley to Chicago. From there he would be taken to New Orleans and then sent by rail to San Francisco, where he would be shipped to Hong Kong as part of the Chinese exclusion act. Ley had been running a laundry in Appleton for the last couple of years. Ley said, "President Loosevelt he good man. He no like Chinese law. Next yea he make us flee. Then I come back."[49]

10

Oswego County Jail— Oswego, New York

The British first developed the area of Oswego, New York, when they built a fort there in the 1720s. After the War of 1812, the area became more settled and the first county jail was placed in the basement of the Oswego County courthouse in 1822. The city also had a jail in the basement of the city hall and it was called the "Black Hole."[1]

The first talk of building a separate county jail in Oswego came in January 1835 when a petition was made to erect a jail in Oswego.[2] It was not until 1848 that a bill providing for a county jail was passed.[3] Then proposals were made to build the county jail in June of 1849.[4] The jail was built in 1849 in East Park and the jail in the courthouse was discontinued.[5]

The jail in East Park lasted until a new stone jail was constructed on the southeast corner of East Second and Schuyler Streets in Oswego in 1853. The stone jail was forty-five by seventy-five feet and two stories tall. Later that year, a huge fire broke out in the town and a cinder blew into the window of the jail setting some straw on fire. The prisoners were liberated and saved the building from destruction. The jail lasted until 1882 when it was discontinued.[6]

A new rotary jail was built on the same site as the old jail in 1887 by the Pauly Jail Building Company at a cost $30,000 to build. The rotary jail was made of iron and steel and had two floors with ten cells on each floor. The rotary was surrounded by a fireproof brick structure. With each revolution, the toilets were flushed with water collected in a circular tank around the top of the structure.[7]

This rotary jail was electrically operated. When the sheriff or guard wished to gain access to a particular cell, he touched a button and the table turned until the cell he wished to enter swung opposite the door of the sheriff's office. It stopped there until the sheriff entered and transacted his business. After lodging his prisoner in the cell, if that was his purpose, he would move the turntable until the next cell he wished to access came up opposite the landing door. Also, this is how prisoners were fed. There were times when the mechanism would "strike" and fail to function. These times were difficult for both the sheriff and prisoners. The incarcerated men would go hungry as there was no way of getting food into their cells until the problem was located and repaired.[8]

The state prison commission directed the construction of a suitable department for juveniles and women as an annex to the Oswego County Jail in January 1902.[9] Plans for an annex to the jail for juveniles and women were presented for approval on April 2, 1902.[10]

The New York State Commission inspector determined that no part of the Oswego County Jail was fireproof in September 1905. He said "the prisoners are constantly exposed to the peril of being roasted alive."[11]

A riot occurred at the Oswego County Jail on January 23, 1907, and a plot for an escape was uncovered afterwards. During the riot, a long file was found in an inmate's cell. Two railroad robbers with a long term staring them in the face were thought to be plotting to make an escape from the jail. District Attorney W.B. Baker caught wind of a plot to break out of the jail by two men named Storm and Webb. There was also considerable talk of a new jail based on the theory that the present structure was not secure enough. A great deal of money had been spent in recent years to repair the county jail.[12]

In May 1908, after years of criticism, the State Prison Commission served notice on the county commissioners that they should close the rotary jail and build a new one. An inspector from the commission determined that the Oswego County Jail was in direct violation of the law in its imprisonment of juveniles in the facility. Secretary George McLaughlin recommended that a separate place away from adult prisoners be created for the children. The commission threatened to condemn the jail if the commissioners did nothing.[13]

The turntable did not always work as it should and as a result of such incidents and state recommendations, the county commissioners finally decided that the county would have to build a new jail after twenty-one years. So in 1908 a new jail was planned for $85,000—about **$2.2 million in today's money**[14]—on the East River Road between Fulton and Oswego.[15]

The Board of Supervisors decided on July 18, 1909, to use inmates at the Oswego County Jail to help in the grading for the new jail site. About a dozen prisoners would do the work.[16]

When completed the three-floor jail contained ninety-six cells. Each cell was equipped with a toilet and wash bowl with large steel cots suspended from the side. Each floor was divided into two sections of cellblocks. The new jail was completed in early December and was the most modern of its kind in the state. The sheriff's residence and office was connected to the jail. Sheriff John Dennis was the last sheriff in charge of the old rotary jail. The old rotary jail was closed at the beginning of 1910 and sold by the county to the Ames Iron Works for $10,000 in 1910.[17]

The 1910 jail lasted until the Public Safety Center was built in 1994 across from the old jail. Sheriff Reuel A. Todd is now in charge of the Oswego County Correctional Facility, which can handle up to 48 inmates.[18]

Murderers

A thirteen-year-old girl was locked up in the Oswego County Jail on the charge of murder on November 13, 1896. Fanny Scofield was jailed after Coroner Vowinkle determined she was responsible for poisoning the two-year-old daughter of Mr. and Mrs. Albert Field, who lived on a farm in the village of Mexico. The parents were out in the field working when their daughter awoke and asked for something to eat. Scofield gave the child some milk. Dr. W. Manlius Smith of Syracuse made an analysis of the contents of the child's stomach and found it to contain arsenic. The doctor believed that Scofield put "Rough on Rats" into the milk. Officials then believed that Scofield may have done the same to the Fields other child, who died in July. The body would be exhumed to make an examination. The teen-agers trip to jail was her first experience in a car and she had many questions to ask. The newspaper called her an attractive girl.[19]

A twenty-five-year-old man was arrested for murdering a twelve-year-old girl on May 25, 1905, and interred in the Oswego County Jail. Henry Manser, a farm hand, was found in the vicinity with blood on his clothes, which led to his arrest. Cora Sweet was murdered after she left her house and was on her way to Sunday school at the Baptist Church. She had suffered a fractured skull after being hit with a stone. Manser had been in the woods to gather ginseng when Sweet cut through the woods on a shortcut to church.[20] Manser later confessed to the crime. He assaulted the girl and then pounded her head into a shapeless mass with a stone. He was sentenced to death and sent to the state penitentiary to be electrocuted in the state penitentiary on September 12 for murdering the little girl.[21]

The last murderer to be held in the rotary jail was George A. Eddy, who was confined in the Oswego establishment for the murder of John A. Reid in Pulaski on December 1, 1909. Eddy's little daughter Ida came to see him at the jail on December 27 for the first time since he had been imprisoned there. Between tears of joy and sorrow, the father said to his daughter, "This is the best and biggest Christmas present I have received, but it hurts darling, to have you find me here." They enjoyed three hours together that day.[22] After his wife, Mae, was going to testify against him, Eddy pleaded guilty to manslaughter in the first degree and received a ten-year sentence in the Auburn Prison on May 20, 1910. A crowd flocked to the courthouse to see him plead guilty.[23]

Escapes

Six prisoners escaped from the Oswego County Jail on August 22, 1888. They escaped by digging a hole through the brick wall and crawling out. The inmates were awaiting trial and had been charged with felonies.[24]

A man somehow escaped from the Oswego County Jail on November 12, 1889, and an attempt to recapture him was foiled by a boat captain. Bert Snyder, who was serving time for grand larceny, escaped the jail and Sheriff Van Buren traced him to Fulton, where he found him on a canal boat. Snyder asked boat captain Bradner Montague where Snyder was. The boat captain answered by rushing at the sheriff with a revolver that went off and grazed the sheriff in the right cheek. Montague was taken into custody, but Snyder escaped capture as he had left the boat a few minutes before the sheriff had arrived.[25]

Two men escaped the Oswego County Jail while they were doing chores in the jail yard on August 28, 1901. Harvey Halstead was recaptured at Fulton after an exciting chase. Joseph Murray remained still at large.[26]

Five prisoners escaped from the Oswego County Jail via a cellar door on December 7, 1906. One of the "trusties" employed in the kitchen broke a lock on the door using an axe. The men who escaped were John Case, who was charged with assault in the first degree; Arthur Lessing and James

Sereno, who were held on burglary and larceny charges; Charles Raney, who was charged with arson; and Edward Fitzgerald, who was being held on a simple charge. They were all awaiting transfer to the State Prison.[27]

A trustee of the jail escaped during an uproar in the Oswego County Jail on February 20, 1907. Three prisoners caused the uproar in the jail and had to be chained to their cells, so Oscar Smith seized the opportunity to escape the jail; however, his freedom was short lived and lasted only a day until he was recaptured. Smith had been given the liberty of entire basement of the jail and was only serving a short term in the jail, but then faced additional jail braking charges in March when the grand jury returned.[28]

Three inmates escaped from the Oswego County Jail after securing a key to the storeroom on May 15, 1907. The trouble at the jail began at midnight when an outsider scaled the high fence surrounding the jail and smuggled in bottles of whisky to several prisoners. They were discovered the next morning and allowed to sleep it off until noon. There was a key at the jail that was used to gain access to a room on the top floor where the blankets were stored. Two of the inmate trustees, William James and Vernie Taylor, who were allowed the liberty of the corridor of the rotary jail and must have gotten hold of the key. When "Spot" Murray complained of an aching tooth and asked for a dentist, Turnkey Huntley let him out of his rotary cell and allowed him to walk about the corridor until the dentist arrived. The three then made their escape by accessing the roof, sliding to the ground on the fire escape and bolting over the high fence. Mrs. Huntley was looking out of her window and saw the escape, so she ran to her husband, the sheriff, who was in his office writing a letter. Although the sheriff followed the inmates into a freight and lumberyard, he couldn't find them. He expressed his disgust with the jail and called it nothing more than a "rat trap." Taylor was captured the next night and returned to the jail.[29] James was recaptured on May 26 in Oswego by Officers Roach and Mowatt. He told officers that he had took a trip to Canada on one of his schooners. Murray was still at large.[30]

Suicides

After being indicted for bigamy by an Oswego County grand jury, William J. O'Neill was arrested and placed in the rotary jail. He then succeeded in committing suicide by eating too much opium in his cell. The sheriff summoned two doctors who found O'Neill dead. Before his death, he turned on several gas burners and declared, "Let us turn on the gas in the cells, fill up the room with gas, then strike a match and blow up the jail." The twenty-six-year-old man was co-owner of a saloon with his brother.[31]

A prisoner was discovered in the process of gouging himself with a darning needle in a holding cell in the Oswego County Jail while awaiting the action of the Grand Jury on a charge of grand larceny in the second degree and burglary. Thomas Martin stabbed himself in the side, so the jail physician came to treat him and he was placed in the rotary for better security. The prisoner was addicted to morphine and he became extremely unsettled for lack of the drug during imprisonment. He was accused of robbing the room of a Scranton millionaire in the Redstone Hotel. His pal, George Page, escaped to Syracuse, but was arrested there and returned to Oswego. The two were wanted in several cities.[32]

Other Criminals

Three Union sailors were found guilty of assault in the second degree on July 20, 1889, and spent some time in the Oswego County Jail. Andrew Hageny, William Putman, and Michael Donovan had dragged Jesse Josephs, a mate on the schooner John Schulte, a mile into the suburbs, beat him and threw him into the cellar of a burned house. Josephs was able to crawl out of the house and turn them into the sheriff. The trio was then arrested and jailed.[33]

The state of New York had liquor laws dating back to the early 1900s and some people found themselves in jail for violating those laws. State Commissioner of Excise Culliman sentenced many men to fines and jail terms on September 12, 1901. This included the jailing of Charles Clute and Frank Cavanaugh of Fulton to the Oswego County Jail for sixty days and required them to pay a fine of $200.[34]

A man was jailed after he nearly killed a woman at her home in Seward. James Melling was charged with first-degree assault after gashing Mrs. Harriet M. Burton in the neck and leaving her in critical condition at the City Hospital. Judge Spencer placed him in the Oswego County Jail on April 10, 1907, to await the action of the grand jury in Pulaski in May.[35]

11

Grayson County Jail— Sherman, Texas

Grayson County was founded on March 17, 1846. Then in 1850 Sherman became an incorporated town within the county. It was named after General Sidney Sherman, a hero of the Texas Revolution. During and after the Civil War, north Texas outlaw bands led by Jesse James and William Quantrill were seen in Sherman. By the 1870s, Sherman's population had increased to around 6,000.[1]

A county jail was built in Sherman and located on the northeast corner of the South Travis and Jones Street intersection, but by the 1880s it was deemed inadequate to serve the county. In 1886 the Commissioner's Court declared the building of a new jail a "public necessity." A lot located in the 400 block between West Houston and West Lamar streets was purchased. The county leaders who brought the new jail in 1887 included County Judge E.P. Gregg and the county commissioners: W.A. Wells, W.A. Tibbs, and W.W. Crane.[2]

The new Grayson County Jail with a two-story rotary feature was built in 1887 by the Pauly Jail Building Company. The new jail was built at a cost of $100,000 and with a capacity of a hundred prisoners. The rotating cell section was escape proof, but it wasn't long before prisoners learned to block the rotary from turning. There was a dungeon cell in the cellar designed to contain difficult prisoners or terrible dangerous ones.[3]

After having too much trouble with the rotating cell section, it was torn out in 1912 and stationary cells with key openings were put in.[4]

The remainder of the jail was used throughout the first quarter century. In 1931 the kitchen located in the basement was reported in the newspaper as unsanitary, because coal dust and trash blew through the windows behind the stove. Also, the dungeon, which had only one steel door and no windows, opened into storage rooms near the kitchen.[5]

The Gothic tower of the jail was used for executions by hanging. A room in one of the towers had a trap door built in. Eight men were executed in the jail. The first hanging occurred on July 8, 1892, and the last one transpired on April 11, 1915. However, this massive stone tower structure with its great weight caused the masonry beneath it to crack in later years.[6]

County jails were sometimes used to temporarily house insane prisoners before they could be committed to a better facility. Such was the case with Nannie Woods, an African American, in the Sherman Jail in November 1900. She was judged insane by the county court and placed in the county jail. She raved from morning to night in the jail. Her principal hallucination was that a man was elected and defrauded the office.[7]

In 1928 the Grand Jury recommended to the 15th District Court the necessity of building a new jail facility due to the crumbling of the masonry, the unsanitary conditions, and the lack of facilities to house the insane. The members of the grand jury were: W.K. Taylor, foreman; T.E. Willett, J.A. Hardaway, J.S. Eubank, D.R. Vaughan, H.E. Boher, W.C. Shearer, W.J. Hogan, R.L. Radford, W.J. Rich, and J.D. Holley.[8]

In 1934 the jail was declared as "rapidly approaching the danger point" by architect John Tulloch and former city engineer A.A. McMillian. Two days after the report was issued, the Commissioners' Court ordered the entrance to the jail to be fenced off to prevent the possibility of visitors being injured. The jail was razed in January 1937. Part of the rotary jail remains today as part of the metal arch over Loy Park in Denison.[9]

Hangings

Hanging was the universal method of execution in America up to the 1890s.[10] 1892 was the worst year for hangings in America with one hundred and sixty-one blacks and sixty-nine whites hanged in one year, including the first one in the Grayson County Jail.[11] George Smith was hanged on July 8, 1892. It had been over thirteen years since a man suffered the death penalty in the county. Smith shot and killed City Marshal Isbell of Bells while trying to hold up a store in January 1891. He was housed in the rotary jail section until his conviction in May and then until the hanging.[12]

Two men who murdered a blacksmith in Denison, Texas, on May 28, 1892, were strung up in the gallows of the Grayson County Jail on May

12, 1893. John Carlisle and Charles Luttrell killed W.T. Sharman and were found guilty of the crime. They were arrested and placed in the Grayson County Jail until they were hanged for their crime. On the day of the hanging, several hundred people came to witness the hanging, including Mrs. Sharman and her son. As they walked to their deaths, each man carried a small bouquet of flowers and had flower boutonnieres. When they arrived at the platform, Sheriff Hughes asked Luttrell if he had any last words. Luttrell replied, "I don't know that I have much that I care to say, but I do desire now to state there has been no ill treatment on the part of Sheriff Hughes, and his guards, who have treated us kindly. They have been humane in every particular. I feel that some of the evidence against me has been manufactured, but I have no malice in my heart. I forgive everyone as I feel I have myself been forgiven. I feel that my loss on earth will be my gain in heaven." Then Sheriff Hughes turned to Carlisle and he said, "I haven't much I care to say except to thank the sheriff and the officers for their many kindnesses. We have been treated nicely. I have nothing more to say." At 2:18 p.m., Sheriff Hughes jerked the trigger and the bodies shot down, a fall of nearly seven feet. They were dead in minutes. The bodies were cut down at 2:30 p.m. and the prison physician declared them dead.[13]

Sidney Spears, a negro, was convicted in the April term of the Grayson County Court and sentenced to be hanged on June 4, 1900, but the Texas governor gave him a respite for a fortnight to consider a strong petition to commute his sentence from death to life imprisonment; however, the governor decided against changing the sentence and Spears was hanged for murder on June 18, 1900, in the Grayson County Jail.[14] Hundreds of people witnessed the hanging. His last words were, "May God save my enemies." Sheriff A.D. Shrewsbury sprung the trap that sent Spears to his death.[15]

Two men were hanged in the Grayson County Jail on August 9, 1912. One was Sellars Vines, who was convicted of shooting and killing Deputy Constable Fred Mounger on September 27, 1911. The shooting took place in the Houston & Texas Central Railroad yards in Wichita Falls. Vines was a fugitive from justice and was hiding in a box car near the freight depot. Mounger was the night watchman on duty that evening. He was making his rounds when he flashed a light in the railroad car containing Vines. The officer was not prepared to shoot and Vines shot him in the back, killing him instantly. Officers looked for the black man all that night and found him the next day about six miles outside of Sherman. He was lodged in the Grayson County Jail. A week before his trial, he escaped from the jail. As he was fleeing, Jailer Jeff Steele shot at him as he was jumping over a fence. The bullet struck the black man in the side of the face and passed through his mouth, tearing away a portion of his jaw and cutting his tongue in two. The other African American who was hanged was Wood Maxey. On the night of October 16, 1910, Maxey had been baptized in the Methodist church. On his way home, he stopped at the Crystal Café. Owner Manager Ernest Johnson asked him to take off his hat in the white man's place. Maxey refused and attempted to hit Johnson over the head with a ketchup bottle. Johnson grabbed a pistol and struck Maxey over the head. Then he tossed Maxey out the door. So Maxey went to the police station where he asked patrolman Buck Blaylock to arrest Johnson. Blaylock said he would have the man in city court the next day. Maxey grew mad at the officer and left the police station. He then went a friend's home and borrowed a single-barrel shotgun. Maxey returned to the restaurant and fired a shot at the manager from behind a telephone pole where he had hidden. The shot struck Johnson in the side of the neck, killing him instantly. Maxey ran and hid in an outhouse in the vicinity of his home where he was later discovered by Sheriff Lee McAfee. Maxey was tried in December 1910, but the trial resulted in a hung jury. He was retried in April 1911 and the jury found him guilty of first-degree murder and gave him the death sentence.[16]

Murderers

A man who shot and killed another man in Lark was placed in the Grayson County Jail on September 1, 1893. Lee Green was accused of killing E.A. Price. The murder occurred after Price insisted that Green apologize for whistling and making indecent remarks when he saw his wife and mother lift up their dresses while fording the Red River on foot. The two men met at Lark and Price slapped Green over the incident. Green drew his six-shooter and shot Price twice. Price died within five minutes. Green was arrested at Pottsboro and put in the rotary jail.[17]

An African American who murdered Deputy Marshal John Carlton of Hackett, Arkansas, in Denison, Texas, was placed in the Sherman Jail. A lynch mob had attempted to hang John Hogan. Hogan was not frightened of the mob and commented, "If they would give me a chance, I would kill several more."[18]

A prisoner killed another prisoner in the Sherman Jail in June 1896. W.W. Northcutt fatally stabbed Anderson Stinnett, a black man, who had been put in the same cell with him. Stinnett had been arrested for drunkenness.[19]

Albert Whitly was arrested in January 1904 in Helen on the charge of murdering Robert C. Francis and taken to the Sherman Jail.[20]

A woman came to the Grayson County Jail on September 19, 1908, and identified an inmate there as the man wanted in six murders in San Jose, California. Mary Zimmerman positively identified Bill Hatfield, a.k.a. James C. Dunham, the murderer. At the time of the murders, Zimmerman was living a mile from where the wholesale slaughter took place. The theory of the officers at the time was that the murders were committed for money, as Colonel McClincy had received a large payment late Saturday night, too late to put it in the bank, and the money, which amounted to several thousand dollars, was never found. At the time a hired man, who had escaped the carnage, was arrested and held. By some it was thought he did the killing and that he had also killed Dunham and buried his body, and there was a great deal of searching for it. This man was finally released.[21]

Dr. John W. Sherman was placed in the Sherman Jail without bond for the killing of his brother-in-law, Thomas D. Norman. While there, he secured a marriage license to wed Miss Cleo D. Lucas. However, the sheriff refused her admission to the jail and the ceremony was not held.[22]

The killing of a police officer caused a great stir among the Sherman people in September 1911. Officer Fred Munger was killed by an African American youth, who made his escape but was soon captured. He was placed in the Sherman Jail. A mob was formed to make a raid on the jail, so they were moved to McKinney. Two of the blacks had been charged with murder and a third charged with knifing the officer. After the mob quieted down, the trio was brought back to the Sherman Jail.[23]

Escapes

The federal prisoners in the Grayson County Jail, which numbered about sixty, revolted in October 1892. A total of eleven prisoners escaped in three attempts during one week. One of the escapees was Tom Moore, a condemned murderer, but he was captured several miles out of the city. By making the jailbreak, he forfeited his appeal and would hang for his conviction.[24]

A prisoner, who escaped the Sherman Jail in 1891 while awaiting trial in the federal court, was captured in Brooklyn, New York, in April 1896. J.W. DeArmond had been arrested in 1890 on the charge of murdering Ed Howell in the Chickasaw nation that year. DeArmond and four others escaped the Sherman Jail in 1891.[25]

On May 23, 1930, two prisoners escaped by carving a hole in one of the weakened walls by simply using a pair of scissors and a piece of metal from a plumbing fixture to gouge mortar from between bricks.[26]

The jailer was knocked senseless by four prisoners who escaped from the Sherman Jail in January 1908. Three of the men were recaptured, but Henry Cato remained at large. Cato was in the jail on the charge of murdering Alvin Frizzell, a young man whose dead body was found in a creek. Cato was jailed in the Sherman Jail without bond.[27]

Other Criminals

An old man was placed in a rotary cell in the Grayson County Jail on July 1, 1891, for embezzlement. James B. Smith, a bookkeeper, was charged with embezzlement after taking money from his employer, Eubank & Company. Sheriff McAfee arrested Smith when he crossed over from Arkansas into Texas. He told a reporter: "For the sake of my friends I ask you to not deal with me more harshly than you find it absolutely necessary in reporting the case. I cannot tell you how it came about. I only know that I was suffering from a stomach complaint and had taken some brandy for it. The result was that I became intoxicated, and for days before I left I was crazed. I don't know when I left the city. I woke up in a hospital in Galveston. Since then I have been sick and broken down."[28]

Safekeeping

Since the rotary portion of the jail was inescapable, the Sherman facility was sometimes used by other counties to keep their prisoners in a more secure jail than they had. For example, Cass County took John A. Williams to Sherman for safekeeping after he was convicted of murder on two counts, train wrecking and robbery in March 1891.[29]

Some prisoners were even moved from Sherman not because of the jail, but because of rumors that ill harm would come to them if they stayed there. Such was the case of William Duncan, who was charged with criminal assault on his little seven-year-old stepdaughter. Sheriff Shrewsbury decided to move Duncan to another county jail until his trial date arrived.[30]

Chittenden County Jail— Burlington, Vermont

Located on the banks of Lake Champlain, the town of Burlington, Vermont, was first settled in 1775, but it wasn't until after the Revolutionary War that it was organized in 1785. It soon became the most populous city in the state and the shire town (county seat) for Chittenden County.[1]

When the first Chittenden County Jail was built is unknown. However, a new county jail was built in Burlington in 1843. The work was supervised by Judge Van Sicklin. The material for the jail was blue stone from Isle La Mott.[2]

A rotary jail was considered in 1886 when a new jail facility was needed. A building committee of the Chittenden County Jail was selected and consisted of Senator Stevens, Representative Proctor and L.B. Howe, Esq. of Jericho in November.[3] The following year county officials discussed where to locate the new jail. Some wanted to build it to the northern part of the city away from heavily inhabited areas, while the others preferred a more central location.[4]

The jail commissioners visited the rotary jail in Crawfordsville, Indiana, and were most favorably impressed with the jail. The proposed jail would contain eight or ten cells housing two prisoners in each cell. In addition, the jail would have three cells for women and three for the criminally insane above the sheriff's office. It was expected to cost $18,000.[5]

The Chittenden County commissioners accepted plans for the new jail in April 1887. Plans for the rotary jail showed a two-story brick building thirty-eight feet by seventy feet for the jailer's residence. The building would include some terra cotta ornamentation and would be built by the Pauly Jail Building Company.[6]

Work on the new jail was suspended in November when the funds provided by the legislature—$19,000—ran out and the assistant county judges would not advance the money realized from the old jail property and from the special tax.[7]

After the short delay, the Chittenden County Jail was completed in January 1888 and put to use immediately. The county sheriff at the time was Joseph Barton. The commissioners paid the city of Burlington $1,000 for the lot. The building cost $8,800, the boiler and heating apparatus cost $700, and the steel and iron for the rotary jail and cells cost $11,000. The two-story structure was made of brick with a Mansard roof that practically encompassed another floor. The front part, which was square with irregular outlines and a wing extending to the rear, contained twelve rooms. The front entrances and hall were nearly midway on the frontage on Main Street, while to the left sat the dining room. Behind the dining room was the kitchen. A china closet sat between the two rooms. East of the kitchen was the sheriff's office, which had double entrances from the kitchen and outdoors. A pantry stood to the rear of the kitchen and it had a small door opening into the corridor of the jail through which food could be passed to the prisoners. Three large sleeping rooms and a bathroom were on the second floor, while three bedrooms were located on the third floor. The lower floor was finished in natural color hardwood and the upper floors were finished in pine painted in two light colors. All of the windows on the front had sliding blinds. The walls were plastered and hard finished with the exception of those in the parlor, hall and dining room, which were handsomely papered in buff and gold. The basement was divided into six apartments for various purposes, one being laundry. The exterior part of the jail was octagonal with grated and barred windows in each front. The revolving cage contained ten core-shaped cells, which were nine-feet high by nine-feet long. The cells were eight-feet wide at the outer end and four-feet wide at the inner end. The walls, ceiling, and floor of the cells were composed of three-fourths of an inch thick iron and all of the connected parts were strongly riveted.[8]

The cage worked on the same principle of a turntable, except it revolved on an immense hub at the center, resting at the top on sixteen small wheels. At the bottom were four arms projecting the outer rim with wheels on each to steady the cage as it revolved. A heavy iron door opened from the sheriff's office into the grated passage leading to the entrance of the cage. In the middle of this passage was a grated door dividing it into nearly square enclosures. Just beyond this grated door were two others opening to the right and left into the corridor, while opposite to it still another door opened into the cage. The last was a sliding door, which was operated by means of a lever outside of the middle door so that the prisoner would have no opportunity to assault the jailer when the door was opened for him to exit. The cage was revolved by means of a crank in a sort of closet which opens off from the sheriff's office just to the right of the entrance. This closet was secured by a combination lock. When a prisoner was to be placed in a certain cell, the cage was revolved until the cell stopped opposite the entrance to the cage; then a turn of the crank and the inmate was swung around to where the solid grating along confronted him, rendering escape impossible, were every door in the jail left open by chance. The cage could be revolved only by the crank, but there was an additional safeguard in the shape of a lever, which operated a bolt that had to be removed before the cage could be rotated. Escape was impossible.[9]

The cells for the female prisoners were located directly over the sheriff's office, opening off from the hall which was reached from below via an iron staircase. The bars were solid iron as well as the grated doors at the entrances of the cells, and the windows were heavily barred. Each cell was provided with two cots of iron lattice work hung by chains, and each had a water faucet and closet (toilet). There were five of these cells so that ten women could be confined, making the accommodations for thirty prisoners in the entire jail. The jail and sheriff's office were fireproof. The ceilings were of corrugated iron covered with brick over which was a layer of Portland cement. The entire structure was heated by steam from a boiler located in the basement.[10]

In July 1900, there were twenty-eight inmates in the Crittenden County Jail, including two suspected murders, named Farmer and Pooler, eight Chinamen, and two women.[11]

The last year of prohibition in Vermont was 1902. Edward Horton became the county sheriff that year as well.[12] By the following year, the people arrested for drunkenness had increased significantly. The Chittenden County Jail suffered from overcrowding in September 1903 and prisoners were forced to sleep in the corridors. There were over thirty inmates and the number was increasing. Most were in for drunkenness.[13]

Overcrowding occurred again in December 1904. A total of forty-one inmates were crowded into the jail. The rotary jail was called "the merry-go-round" and it was filled. Another nine prisoners slept on the floor in the corridor. Judges wanted a new jail, but they were unable to persuade the county commissioners.[14]

A couple was married in the Chittenden County Jail in March 1904.

John Latulippe and Miss Louise Lapan were married in the jail and the ceremony was witnessed by the jailers. Latulippe had been in the jail since February 12, but was released soon after his marriage.[15]

Overcrowding continued and hit a new record in March 1905. Two raids made late on a Saturday night resulted in the jail being jammed with forty-three inmates, the largest number that ever slept there. Twenty slept in the cells upstairs, twelve in the cells in the cage, and eleven in the corridor. In one cell, four girls were confined.[16]

In September 1905, the Chittenden County grand jury found the jail in shameful condition. Ten cells in the men's area were occupied by twenty-four inmates and the sheriff reported that there had been as many as thirty-six men in the cells. Also, there were twenty beds in cells occupied by twenty-four men. In the women's section, the five cells were occupied by two women and three men. No accommodations were allowed the sick or the young to be confined separately from the hardened criminals. They compared it to a Russian gulag.[17]

Work on a new jail structure began in August 1907 by the Pauly Jail Building Company, the same company who built the rotary jail. The building would be built on the same site. The prisoners in the merry-go-round portion would not be disturbed until the new walls were completed. The new structure would take about four months to complete.[18]

In 1968 the Vermont legislature decided to end its antiquated county jail system. Instead of county jails, the state turned to regional centers. Four of the county jails, including the Chittenden County Jail, became regional correctional centers in April 1969. Two of the fourteen county jails immediately closed their doors as a result, while the others continued for one more year as local lockups. The new regional correctional system was designed to provide rehabilitation programs for offenders as well as improved health, educational and psychological services rather than relying on strict incarceration.[19]

Nowadays, there is no longer a county jail for men. Instead, the Chittenden Regional Correctional Facility is located in South Burlington and it's only for women.

Murderers

Charles Corry was arrested for murder on September 24, 1904. He was charged with the crime for murdering his neighbor, Charles McLane.[20]

Benjamin Williams only spent a short time in the rotary jail in 1905, because he was found guilty of first-degree murder and sentenced to life imprisonment at the state prison in Windsor. Williams murdered Policeman James McGrath on May 12, 1904. He refused to see anyone and didn't seem to care where he went.[21]

Other Criminals

Frank Colligole was transferred to the Chittenden County Jail in February 1901 by Gov. William W. Stickney so that he could be properly and safely jailed until his trial date in Ludlow. The rotary jail was apparently more secure than the jail in Grand Isle County.[22]

Bookkeeper Bert Agan was arrested for embezzling $3,000 from the Elias Lyman Coal Company on January 24, 1903, and placed in the Chittenden County Jail.[23]

Two men who robbed the Crystal Pharmacy of money, cigars and cigarettes were caught by police and put in the rotary jail in March 1903. Louis Ouimette and Edmund Pratt both confessed their crime to police. At first both denied the crime, but then police interviewed Ouimette after Pratt left the station. He finally admitted the crime to police. Then Pratt followed with his own confession.[24]

John J. Fairchild was in the Chittenden County Jail in April 1907 awaiting trial on the murder of Noah Phelps of Milton. He was placed in quarantine after he was found suffering from diphtheria.[25]

With Vermont being so close to Canada, there were some criminals who crossed the border to escape justice. Three Russian Finns who were employed by a Canadian company to work in Vermont were arrested and placed in the Chittenden County Jail until they could be returned to Canada. Victor Seymour, Ami Caski and John Caski, were arrested for breaking immigration laws.[26]

Another who was arrested for breaking immigration laws was Alphonse Van Bever in December 1906. He brought in Celina Bonheur and her daughter from Canada, but claimed they were his wife and child. He was placed in the Chittenden County Jail until he could post bond. He later pleaded guilty and paid a fine before he was deported back to Canada.[27]

The Chittenden County Jail was to be the scene for the second act of a play by a prominent playwright. The play would be taken from the book, "A Wrecked Institution," by J. W. Ketchum, who was serving a seven-year sentence for the wrecking of the Farmers National Bank in Vergennes. The first act of the play would be in the interior of the defunct bank; the second act in the jail; and the third act in playwright D.H. Lewis' apartment in Vergennes. The play was performed in one-night stands throughout New England.[28] Ketchum was released from the rotary jail in March 1905 after spending thirty-four months there. He was transferred to the Addison County Jail to serve out the rest of his term. He applied for the transfer due to his ill health. The request was granted by the Attorney General of the United States. For the last few weeks of his stay in the Chittenden County Jail, the writer was confined to quarters on the second floor. During his stay in the rotary jail, he twice prevented jailbreaks by other prisoners.[29] Ketchum was released from the Addison County Jail in June 1907 after serving five years and two months of his seven-year sentence. The remainder of his sentence was forgiven because of his good behavior. He announced his plans to tour New England to present a play based on his book and his jail time experience. The tour would last twenty weeks. He was the principal in the drama. Thus, he hoped to rehabilitate himself in public esteem.[30]

A man tried twice to commit suicide in the Crittenden County Jail in July 1906. Sol Peppin, 40, slit his throat and opened a vein in his arm with a knife. He was then moved to the hospital for the insane in Waterbury.[31]

Mr. Graton of Burlington introduced a bill to provide a new jail in Crittenden County. The rotary jail had been condemned by two prior grand juries.[32]

In 1905, a total of eight hundred and forty-one persons were incarcerated in the Chittenden County Jail. That number went up to eight hundred and ninety-one the following year. In 1906, intoxication was the number one reason for imprisonment with six hundred and twenty-six incarcerated. Other reasons included breach of the peace (forty-eight), tramps (twenty-five), larceny (twenty-six), open and gross lewdness (fourteen), loitering (twelve), insane (ten), selling liquor (eight), grand larceny (eight), petit larceny (five), adultery (five), stealing beer (three), non-support (three), keeping a house of ill fame (two), horse stealing (two), rape (two), escaped from Vergennes (one), and other miscellaneous charges.[33]

Escapes

Daniel Butler tried to escape from the rotary jail in December 1903. As a result of the attempt to escape, he received an additional two years on his sentence of three years for burglary. He was sent to the state prison to serve out his term.[34]

Three inmates attempted an escape from the Chittenden County Jail in January 1894. Bissette, Jerome and Lessor, who were sentenced to be moved to the state prison, tried to escape from the jail using a knife that had been turned into a saw. They attempted to saw through the bars on a window. A chisel was also discovered in their cell.[35]

Drunkenness

Intoxication was the number one crime during the early 1900s and Volney Newell probably held the record for drinking. He claimed to have consumed two gallons of whiskey in a twenty-four hour period in late April 1902. He was arrested by Sheriff Reeves and Judge Hawkins threw him in the Chittenden County Jail to sober up.[36]

Vermont changed from prohibition to license in 1903 and saloons re-opened, resulting in more arrests for intoxication; therefore, resulting in more overcrowding of prisoners in the Chittenden County Jail. During prohibition, one hundred and twenty-eight drunks were arrested in 1902, while the number ballooned to four hundred nine the following year. The increase continued as four hundred and eighty-nine were jailed for drunkenness in 1904.[37]

Salt Lake County Jail—
Salt Lake City, Utah

A rotary jail existed in Salt Lake City, Utah, for twenty-two years before officials decided they had seen enough problems with the jail. The experience all began in 1887. Salt Lake County officials decided a new jail was needed after repeated escape attempts at their existing facility. By this time, the population of Salt Lake City was more than 40,000 and a larger facility was needed. Most of the population was Mormon, but some elements were not religious and crime was on the rise.

To investigate the types of jails available, Salt Lake City Mayor Francis Armstrong and Probate Judge Elias A. Smith traveled east to view the newest jails built. They stopped in Council Bluffs, Iowa; Omaha, Nebraska; and St. Louis, Missouri. At Council Bluffs, they visited the rotary jail that had recently been built there. The other two jails were more traditional establishments for criminals.[1]

Upon return, Mayor Armstrong said he favored the traditional square-caged jails, while Judge Smith liked the rotary jail. The final decision was to go with both types of jail into one structure. Besides the two-story rotary jail with 10 cells on each level, which could house 20 prisoners, the jail had twenty conventional cells and a dungeon—two dark cells—in the basement for inmates who violated the rules. The V-shaped rotary cells had hammocks for sleeping, while the regular cells had cots. Each had a stationary washbasin and a lavatory. Each cell had its own independent opening for entrance and exit. A hand lever was used to bring the rotary to a point where an inmate could be let in or out. The jail had the appearance of a Victorian-style house and was situated next to the County Courthouse, making it convenient for law enforcement officials to transfer prisoners to and from court.[2]

The local newspapers described the rotary jail as "a whirligig in a squirrel cage," a device that "looks for all the world like a huge rat trap," and as a "circular cell structure ... turning upon conical steel rollers, like a railway turntable, with which we all are familiar."

By July 4, 1888, the new rotary jail was ready and seven prisoners from the existing jail were transferred to the new facility. The jail was symmetrical and a central steeple gave it the appearance of a church.[3]

An unidentified inmate, who had been a newspaper reporter, wrote a lengthy description of the county jail in 1900: The front part of the jail is occupied by the sheriff and his family. It was spacious with modern conveniences. The two-story jail was built with bricks and the windows were heavily barred and covered with stout steel screens. The office has an entrance on the west side and is accessible from the residence. Here the inmate is made to unload all articles in his possession, which are then packaged, labeled and put away until his release. A heavy iron door and barred gateway leads to another room from which the prisoner enters a rotary cell on the first or second level. The mechanical apparatus for opening the barred gateway is ingenious. The rotary, which is placed nearly in the center of the room, is encased in an iron cage made of inch and a half bars. The rotary is a ponderous cylindrical drum, double deck, built of one-quarter inch steel iron firmly riveted together, having twenty cells, ten on each floor. The cells are conical in shape being eight feet at the entrance and two-and-a-half feet at the end. They are eight feet tall and ten feet long. Each cell is equipped with a water faucet and a lavatory. A couple of hammocks are swung on one side and each prisoner is allowed three heavy double blankets. The immense drum with its load of human freight is so nicely adjusted and balanced that a heavy lad of fifteen can turn it with ease. The dimensions of this revolving prison are eighty feet in circumference and eighteen feet in height. It makes about eight complete circuits each day, which is about forty-five miles a year. The position of the cells is changed daily, so that it would be difficult for any prisoner to make a successful attempt at escape. As there are eleven windows to the room, every cell is well lit during the day. Electric lights are used to illuminate at night. There is twelve-by-fourteen foot room for exercise and a similar room for meals with two long tables and benches.[4]

Bells are sounded to summon the prisoners. Four bells summons the prisoners to rise, make their beds, sweep out their cells, and wash. Three bells warns them the rotary will turn and get them out for exercise. As the prisoners emerge from their cells, a gate is slid to one side. The jailer sits behind another enclosure. Prisoners don't come near or within reach of the jailer, which precludes the possibility of an attack. Two bells is a signal to march single file through a gateway to their meals. Speaking is not allowed. The meal is over when one bell is sounded. Then they march back to the recreation cell for fifteen minutes of exercise, where conversation is allowed. Prisoners are fed three times a day, except for Sunday when they are fed twice. Breakfast consists of porridge and milk, stewed beef, bread, molasses, and coffee. Dinner consists of soup, bread, and water. Supper consists of roast beef, potatoes, bread, and tea. With the meat there is a plentiful supply of gravy. On Sundays there are extras, including a dish of bread pudding. Cleanliness is a must. Prisoners are given a bath weekly. The entire building is heated by steam.[5]

The worst prisoners were kept in the rotary where the bars were made with hardened steel and much more difficult to cut with a saw. The bars on the rectangular side cells were made of a softer metal. Plus, with the rotary, only one cell was opened at a time.

A couple of grand juries paid a visit to the rotary jail soon after it was completed. They found it in excellent condition and found the ventilation, heating, lighting, and food to be satisfactory. One grand jury reported: "We have visited the new County Jail and found that institution everything that could be desired." The grand jury also found "the attendants courteous and kind."[6]

A 1893 grand jury suggested that the dungeon was cruel and that inmates there sometimes created a nuisance with their outcries.[7]

New Jail Decided

The Salt Lake County Commission decided to build a new jail on April 12, 1909, at the urging of Sheriff Joseph E. Sharp. The new facility took more than a year to complete and was ready by July 7, 1910, spelling the end of the rotary jail there. The jail remained for a few years to come and the sheriff's residence was turned into a private residence for a while before it was turned into an apartment building. It came down as well in August 1927.[8]

Escape Attempts

The only successful escape from the rotary jail came on February 1, 1907. Mysteriously, when guards rotated the cellblock to get inmate

Charles Riis out for a court appearance, they round the cell was empty. During the night, Riis had sawed through the bars of his cell and escaped through the window. He used two blankets tied together to lower himself to the ground.[9]

On June 3, 1889, seven inmates escaped from the jail, but it was not the result of poor design of the rotary jail. The sheriff's theory was that inmate Ledford, who was in the corridor sweeping up, picked the lock on the door of the rotary and let the others out of their cells. Then they all assembled in a vacant cell and lay in wait for the jailer. Jailer Joe Burt opened the door, which connects the sheriff's office to the main hall of the jail, and was about to lock himself in when two prisoners sprang out of their cell at the side of the door and jumped him. Then the other five prisoners came out of the cell and joined in the tussle. They overcame the jailer and rushed out into the street. However, Burt pursued the prisoners and told one to halt. The prisoner stopped, threw up his hands and gave up. The police were called and Officers Cummock and Bateman ran down one of the prisoners, Frank Hilbert. The others got away.[10]

In December 1892, inmates tried to escape by springing the brake that held the rotary from turning. A guard by the name of Joe Burt was scheduled to go home at 5:30 p.m. and his replacement would come an hour later, leaving the jail unmanned. Burt delayed his departure and as he left, he heard the rotary turning, so he stopped the attempt before it could happen. The cells were inspected and the tools were found.[11]

Another escape attempt was tired in 1898 when a prisoner carved a pistol from wood and soap. He covered it "with tinfoil so as to appear first sight to be made of steel." The scheme was foiled when another inmate informed authorities.[12]

Joe Sullivan almost escaped from the rotary jail in January 1908. He had almost sawed his way out of the rotary into the corridor when he was discovered by Deputy Sheriff Corliss. His cell was searched and a steel hack saw was found as well as a deadly improvised slingshot. It was thought that he was given the steel saw by inmate Richard Deming. Sullivan was taken to the state prison for safe keeping. He had been charged with the murder of Salt Lake City policeman Charles S. Ford.[13]

Six months later, Deming was charged with destroying jail property and attempting to break out of the County Rotary Jail on June 15, 1908. Deming did not deny that he sawed a bar in cell number five in the rotary, but he boldly declared he did it at the suggestion of Sheriff Emery and

Deputy Sharp. He swore he entered into a conspiracy with them. The convicted murderer and life prisoner got caught after sawing about a quarter inch of a steel bar.[14]

Probably the last attempted escape from the rotary jail came in 1910, a year before the jail was closed forever. The attempted break was one of the boldest in the history of Utah prisons, and but for the watchfulness of the guards at the county bastille Jailer Carson might now be at the morgue and the county prison practically devoid of inmates. Lucian Driskell had planned the escape by having his brother, Tracey, smuggle saws and a revolver into his cell. However, the saws and later the revolver were recovered and the jailbreak was averted.[15]

A Hanging

Only one execution was ever held at the Salt Lake County Jail and it took place on August 7, 1896. Charles Thiede was convicted of murdering his wife by cutting her throat. The judge offered his a choice of execution: firing squad or hanging. When Thiede didn't make the decision, the judge made it for him and chose hanging. A new method of hanging a man was provided. A four hundred and thirty-pound weight connected to a rope wound through pulleys was designed to jerk Thiede upward instead of gravity doing the job. Thiede's arms were secured at his sides and his legs bound. He looked to the blue heavens for the last time before the lever was pulled. At 10:39 a.m., Sheriff Hardy drew a handkerchief from his pocket and waved it to signal the man behind the canvas screen to pull the lever. Thiede's body was jerked into the air. It took an agonizing fifteen minutes before Thiede died. His neck never broke as expected. Instead, he was strangled to death. This new method of hanging was never used again.[16]

Other Murderers

The Salt Lake County Jail housed other killers as well, but the jail was merely a holding area until a man was convicted and sent to the "Big House," a.k.a. prison. Such was the case with Peter Mortensen after the turn of the century. Mortensen was arrested for the murder of reputable

Salt Lake City businessman James R. Hay. When witness James Sharp took the witness stand at the preliminary hearing, he said that Mortensen had killed Hay because, "God (had) revealed it to me." The revelation resulted in longest jury selection process in Utah's history as more than eleven hundred people had to be screened before twelve good men were found. In the end, Mortensen was found guilty and was transferred from the county jail to Sugarhouse Prison for execution on November 20, 1903.[17]

In 1902, the jail held two murderers at the same time. Both were put in the rotary jail section as it provided better security than traditional cells. Roy Kaighn was being held for stabbing a traveling man to death. Williard Haynes killed a man was he was "half drunk and drug crazed."[18]

The miner, Matt Rosenquist, was accused of stabbing John Anderson to death in Bingham. "In the Scandinavian saloon, just about time to close up, he accused me of calling him a bum, which I did not do," said Rosenquist. "Then he struck me twice with his fist half doubled. I had no scuffle with him at all and did not use a knife. After I had gone to sleep the officer came and arrested me. I came from Johannesburg, where I worked in the mines. I have no relatives in this country."[19]

Deputy Sheriff Heaston of Bingham overhead the interview and said, "Part of that is true, but most of it, according to witnesses who testified at the hearing, is not true. The bartender and others testified that after Anderson struck or rather slapped him and told him to go home, Rosenquist walked toward the door and stopped in the doorway. Anderson walked toward him and here they were not noticed particularly. In a short time Anderson staggered back against the billiard table and soon fell to the floor. Nobody knew he was hurt and when the time came to close up they started to drag him out, when they saw blood and then discovered that he was wounded and dying. Bloodstains were on the door and billiard table. A man who was sitting outside the door testified that he saw Rosenquist running away from the place. When I went to Smith's to arrest him, I found that he had gone upstairs and gotten into another man's bed."[20]

Another murderer who spent some time in the rotary jail was Don Herbert, a sheepherder. He shot and killed Theodore Friese during a card game. Friese bet high on a poker hand and when Herbert could not cover the bet, Friese said the money was his. Herbert disputed this and Friese drew a gun on him. The sheepherder left the room and in a few minutes people heard shots. Herbert later turned himself in and said the shot was in self-defense.[21]

Injuries from the Rotary

The rotary jail had its problems with inmates sometimes getting in the way when it was rotated. Al Shavers was badly bruised when he got caught in the rotary jail as it was turned on February 25, 1898. Shavers was caught between the two walls when did not move quickly enough when the rotary was being rotated. However, the rotary was stopped in time to save him from being crushed to death. The black man was in jail for killing John W. Dent on Thanksgiving night. He was awaiting trial.[22]

Charles Falkenbing nearly got crushed by the rotary jail on June 1, 1904. He was in his cell when it was opened for him and his cellmate to get out and go to eat. However, the inmate delayed leaving the cell until the rotary started up again. The jailer saw the danger and yelled for the operation to stop. Fortunately, the operator was able to stop the rotary before it crushed Falkenbing. "These here roundhouses may be all right to live in, but I would rather have my room out on the square so I can go out when I get ready without takin' chances of havin' my daylights squeezed out," the prisoner said. After the incident, Falkenbing lost his appetite for supper. He was serving a thirty-day sentence in the rotary jail for vagrancy.[23]

Elmer A. Lane claimed he "got tangled up with the rotary at the county jail and almost broke his arm." He tried to plead guilty to interfering with a police officer, Judge Lewis did the unusual thing of not accepting the plea. The judge didn't accept the plea because Lane lied to him, according to District Attorney Fred C. Loofbourow. Lane stood trial and was found guilty by a jury. He was given six months in the rotary jail.[24]

Many Criminals Held

The rotary section was usually reserved for hardened criminals. A newspaper article listed some of the inmates in 1902. One was a man wanted on two continents for forgery. Another was an embezzler who sent his employer into bankruptcy. Another was a man who was serving three months for refusing to support his children. A 72-year-old ex–Union soldier was in for stealing, while another man was in for fraud. A black man, who was charged with vagrancy, filled "the jail with old plantation melodies to the music of guitar and mandolin, which chases away the blues of prison life." There was also a young Chinese burglar and robber who stole a horse. When a young African was told by the jailer that he might put him in a cell with the Mongolian, the black man responded, "I will be the best little black boy in Utah if you don't do dat again." The jail also had two women who were charged with robbing an Oregon tenderfoot of $1,100. And there was even a twelve-year-old boy who wanted to go to reform school, so back then juveniles were sometimes incarcerated in the rotary jail until they were found a place elsewhere.[25]

One of the more unusual criminals who ended up in the county rotary jail was James J. McDonnell. He attempted to murder two people using dynamite in a parcel.[26]

When James Riley was to go to trial in November 1904, other inmates in the jail came to his rescue to provide him with good-looking clothes for the trail as he needed new clothes. The inmates kicked in and gave him a double breasted blue sack coat, a spring block felt hat, a pair of trousers, a tie and a pair of shoes. Riley was being charged with blowing a safe.[27]

Otto Schermenich found himself in the rotary jail after being accused of assaulting Mrs. Gustave Schwan in 1904. The sheriff arrested him because he fit the description and had scratches on his face and hands. Otto declared that he received the scratches while working "while dumping slag at the smelter."[28]

James T. Monk spent some time in the rotary jail before being sentenced to two years hard time in prison for forgery. However, he declared that he wouldn't attend religious services in the penitentiary. Monk said, "I'll not go to church. You can depend on that. I'll see them in h—l first. Furthermore, I'm not going to associate with those d----d hoboes up there. You can see the president of that Free-Thinkers' church and tell them to interest themselves in my behalf."[29]

14

Sedgwick County Jail— Wichita, Kansas

Wichita developed as a trading post on the Chisholm Trail in the 1860s. The trail was used to drive cattle overland from ranches in Texas to Kansas railheads, thus earning the name "Cowtown." The city was first incorporated in 1870 and added a police force the following year. By the late 1880s, the population of Wichita and Sedgwick County had grown so much that a new jail was needed to house criminals.[1]

A contract for building a new Sedgwick County jail was let to the Pauly Jail Building and Manufacturing Company of St. Louis at a total cost of $47,250 on April 30, 1888. The company filed a bond for $50,000. The company obligated themselves to complete the building by the first day of September with a forfeiture of $25 for every day beyond that time. The building would cover a space of seventy-four feet and four inches by ninety-two feet and eight inches with a height of two stories, a basement, and an attic.[2] The jail included a rotary section of twelve cells on each floor, so it could house forty-eight inmates. When completed, the rotary section would weigh about fifty-six tons or one hundred and two thousand pounds.[3]

While the new rotary jail was being built in Wichita, the old jail there had a reputation of being unfit for habitation. Notorious cases included Judge Foster putting Thomas Gunter, eighteen, in the Wichita County Jail in early May 1888 as a hostage to force the return of his father, who was accused of killing a man in Indian territory.[4]

The new jail was completed in October 1888 and forty-two prisoners from the old county jail were transferred into their new quarters on the 14th at 6 a.m. without incident. The new jail could hold about sixty prisoners. This included cells for the sick and for women prisoners. The rotary section was equipped with a separate cage as the inmate came out of his cage, so that at no time would a prisoner come in contact with the jailer. The rotary jail alleged to be escape proof and fire proof as well. Also, the jail was equipped so executions—two of which were planned for November 1888—would be held inside the jail. The new jail would also house prisoners sentenced by the U.S. District Court in Wichita as there was no federal facility located in the area. The quarters for the sheriff were not yet completed.[5]

The following year, Mr. Rausch, the superintendent of the Pauly company, visited the city and installed a steel roller in place of the iron one that was used in the new rotary jail, because the iron roller would wear away from the friction of the constant turning of the rotary jail. He also made sure all the other parts of the jail were functioning correctly.[6]

In 1890, the District Court ordered that all criminals arrested in the Indian Territory of Oklahoma would be housed in the Sedgwick County Jail. In May, the jail contained seventy prisoners, eighteen of whom were there for murder, seventeen for horse stealing, six highwaymen, and the balance were being held for minor crimes. Most of the criminals were Indians and half-breeds, although most all nationalities were represented.[7]

By September 1890, the county jail had twice as many occupants— fifty-six—as opposed to other county jails in Kansas. Only ten of the prisoners were chargeable to Sedgwick County.[8]

In 1895 Wichita was having a problem with tramps. The tramps somehow got the idea that they could commit petty offenses and when jailed the county commissioners would not turn them out. These petty offenders often boasted when sentenced to the Sedgwick County Jail that they would stay as long as the commissioners desired to feed them. The county solved that problem by feeding them breakfast and then releasing them. Judge Hatton confirmed the city was solving the tramp problem, but what bothered him is what were the farmers going to do if all these men are driven into the country. He believed tramps from throughout the country were coming to Kansas.[9]

In January 1904, Judge D.M. Dale and County Attorney O.C. Eckstein inspected the Sedgwick County Jail and found it to be very unsanitary. They recommended several remedies, including plumbing repairs, new bed clothing and mattresses, painting cells, and the use of electric lights in bathrooms. They also recommended that inmates be required to clean their cells daily.[10]

In 1905, a reporter visited the Sedgwick County Jail and wrote an article about it. He noted that prisoners were given good food and were allowed to take a bath once a week. The inmates could amuse themselves by playing cards and checkers. He said no prisoner was allowed to use profane or vulgar language. If they broke the rules, they were confined to the dungeon and given only bread and water. He said the dungeon was calculated to break the strongest spirit in a few hours. It was built underground and was only a few yards square with no light.[11]

A prisoner at the Sedgwick County Jail wrote a letter that was smuggled out to Governor Edward W. Hoch about the conditions of the jail. He said the conditions at the jail were wretched and that prisoners only got two adequate meals a day. If a prisoner asked for more food, they were thrown into the dungeon or dark room. The newspaper speculated that the governor might launch an investigation of the jail.[12]

A fire occurred in the jail on March 8, 1915, and "smoked up" eight prisoners who were confined in the structure. Some of the prisoners got excited and broke window panes to get fresh air. A.G. Walden, fire marshal, said that had if the fire had gotten ten minutes more of a start some of the prisoners in the rotary cell would have perished. The only victim of the fire was the apple jack liquor that had been seized in a raid on bootleg joints in Colwich.[13]

In 1916, the county commissioners voted to spend $100,000 to build a new jail. Bids were accepted and W.W. Rose's plan was accepted. However, those plans to build the jail were later scrapped after the foundation had been dug, so a road crew had to cover up the hole created.[14]

In 1917 the rotary jail in Sedgwick County began having mechanical problems as it became stuck several times. The first time occurred in July when it froze up for 24 hours, resulting in one inmate not being released when his jail time was over. Sheriff Sarver said it was working "like a sawmill. And we never can tell whether it will work the next time or not." No coaxing or any other methods known to the sheriff's office would force it to move, so the next morning mechanics were called in. They raised the rotary section a foot on eight jacks, while the turning mechanisms at the top and bottom were overhauled in an attempt to make it work. In the event of a fire, it would take a minimum of ten minutes just to lower it to its base. Inmates would be killed. Five successive panels of jurors made official visits to the jail and condemned it. And while the jail had a capacity for fifty-four inmates, it has holding up to sixty-three inmates at one time.[15]

Then on August 24, 1917, the rotary was stuck again. This time it was stuck for nearly a week. Judge Pierpont had to close his court as a result of the rotary jail not working. Several inmates were trapped in it and couldn't get out to have their cases heard.[16] Eleven cases were held up as a result of the rotary not working.[17]

Officials feared a lawsuit as a result of the problem. They knew a fire inside the jail could have killed the inmates with smoke from a flaming mattress. As it was, if the rotary jail was working properly, it would take about forty-five minutes to get all prisoners out of the jail. A new jail was planned, but the bonds were declared illegal and the county had to fill up the excavation.[18]

After being stuck for a week, Judge Richard E. Bird ordered, "The rotary must be fixed. We will have to get those men out of there in some manner at once." Although a man had been working on it for a few days, he had not got it to work. Prisoners were fed through the bars, but they were not able to leave their cells.[19]

In 1919 the county commissioners decided to remodel the county jail. The cost to remove the rotary and replace it with cells was $27,000. Judge Bird ordered the jail closed in February 1919. He declared that it was unsanitary and unsafe and the county commissioners agreed. He further ordered the removal of ten federal prisoners. The capacity of the jail was then reduced to twenty-eight prisoners.[20]

Hangings

The first person to be executed by hanging in the new rotary jail was Lee Mosier on November 17, 1887. Mosier was convicted of murdering Hugh B. Lawler in cold blood by shooting him in the back of the head on September 16, 1887. The jury took only minutes to convict Mosier. Mosier's father pleaded with President Grover Cleveland to commute the sentence, but the President declined writing, "I am very sorry that my conception of public duty will not permit me to interfere in your son's case, but am much moved by my sympathy for his worthy and suffering parents."[21]

A year later, two black men were hanged in the rotary jail in November 1888. Jake and Joe Tobler were hanged at 10:24 a.m. on November 21 for their murders of James Cass and John Goodykountz on August 16, 1885, in the Indian Territory. The brothers confessed to killing the men in cold blood while they slept. On the morning of the hanging, about eighty witnesses were allowed to enter to the jail to view the hanging. The last words uttered by Jake when a clergyman was praying for them was, "Let up on that."[22]

Mrs. Lon Hoding made an attempt to hang herself in the Sedgwick County Jail in July 1899. She had been confined pending a sanity examination. She tore her garments into strips and twisted them into a rope to suspend herself for the cell window. She also attempted to poison herself with a drug that nobody knew how she got a hold of.[23]

An African American inmate at the Sedgwick County Jail was returned to Arkansas to be hanged in 1909. Walter Horton was arrested in Kansas three months prior to the requisition from the governor of Arkansas for his execution for a murder in 1903. Horton had been an unruly prisoner and as a result he was put on a bread and water diet for several days to induce him to pay attention to the jail rules. Sheriff Cogdell was happy to get the request and said, "He has been one of the worst prisoners we have had to deal with in a long time."[24]

Murderers

Two out of three murderers who were convicted in the Wichita Court on April 2, 1891, received the death sentence. The first murderer to be tried was Jake Pecora, who took the life of a man in Oklahoma. Pecora claimed the shooting was accidental and regretted it, so Judge Dundy sentenced him to ten years in the state penitentiary. He could be released in eight years for good behavior. A young man by the name of Ed Belden was sentenced to be hanged on June 26 in the Sedgwick County Jail by Judge Ryner. He had murdered Charlie Grant. Then a man going by the name of Adams was found guilty and sentenced to hang on the same date by Judge Dundy.[25] Belden, however, was not hanged on June 26 and on July 18, he received word that President Benjamin Harrison had commuted his sentence to life imprisonment.[26] Belden was sent to Leavenworth Penitentiary on October 10.

Also taken to Leavenworth to hang on January 14 was Clyde Mattox. He had been convicted of murdering John Mullen in 1889 in Oklahoma City.[27] However, a new trial was granted for Mattox by the Supreme Court and it resulted in a hung jury. A new trial was scheduled. In the meantime, the accused escaped from the county jail on February 7, 1894, and he was recaptured shortly after that. He was again tried in June 1894 and found guilty. The case was reviewed by the Supreme Court, who leveled a suspension of the sentence by Judge Williams, who had sustained the verdict. Then on June 27, 1895, Federal Judge John A. Williams sentenced Mattox to be hanged on October 11, 1895.[28] Mattox's hanging never occurred as it was commuted by President Harrison, thanks to the pleading of his mother, Mrs. Hatch. She also was able to get another sentence commuted, but this time by President Cleveland, so Mattox was released from prison.[29]

A full-blooded Chickasaw Indian who was married to a white woman was convicted of murder and sentenced to be hanged on June 2, 1893, in the Sedgwick County Jail. Ed Pickens, 32, was tried in the federal court and found guilty of murdering Jap Greet on October 20, 1886. Several years passed as he was not arrested until the summer of 1892. He was jailed in one of the revolving cells to wait until his sentence was carried out. President Cleveland was asked to commute the death sentence to a life sentence.[30] The President commuted Pickens death sentence on May 26 and gave him life imprisonment on the grounds that he was of very low order of intelligence.[31]

Mrs. Irene Leonard was given a 30-year sentence for murdering her husband, H.H. Leonard, in one of the most sensational trials in Wichita history in June 1896. She was taken to the Sedgwick County Jail and her lawyer was able to get Judge Dale to leave her there until his appeal of the case was heard. She was supposed to go to the state penitentiary and be confined at hard labor.[32]

Clyde Moore spent some time in the rotary jail before he was found guilty of murdering C.L. Wiltberger, a farmer, on December 7, 1901. Judge McBride sentenced the boy to twenty years in the penitentiary at hard labor on January 3, 1902. Moore's attorney made a strong plea to get the sentence changed to a reform school, but the judge held that Moore to be old enough to have known what he was doing.[33]

Escapes

Two murderers made a delivery (as an escape was called back then) from the Sedgwick County Jail on July 5, 1892. John Bly and Peter Snyder cut through a bar with acids in their cell in the basement. Bly was charged with killing an officer in Oklahoma City and was awaiting a second trial for the offense. Snyder murdered a soldier near El Reno and was awaiting transportation to Columbus, Ohio, to serve a seven-year sentence.[34]

Another inmate escaped from the Sedgwick County Jail the night of February 26, 1895. F.E. Harris, a United States prisoner, escaped from his cell by removing some bricks adjacent to the window. Harris had been quite ill, so Jailer Horner had removed him from his rotary cell and put him in a more comfortable cell due to his illness. Harris was arrested on December 11 by Post Office Inspector W.E. Cochran on the charge of fraudulently using the United States mails. He had been given a bond of $1,000, but he failed to pay for it so he was confined in the county jail. Sheriff Royse offered a $50 reward for his return.[35]

An attempted escape from the Sedgwick County Jail by federal prisoners was prevented when a delivery of saws, files, keys and nippers was discovered in the cells of Henry Lorangle, Thomas Ferguson and Alvin Ballard. They had partially sawed through the bars of their cells.[36]

Eight prisoners did manage the almost impossible escape from the rotary section of the Sedgwick County Jail on February 2, 1899. Soon after jailer Douglas Simmons retired for the night after checking the rotary jail, inmate Harry Tackett initiated his plan of escape. He poured acid on the large iron bars, locks and bolts and began sawing his way to liberty. He first sawed into the rivet holding the large lever that is used to operate the rotary, thus freeing the rotary. Then he sawed the lock on his cell and then a bolt at the bottom of the cage to loosen the brace to the sliding door of his cell. He could have escaped then, but he wanted to do more damage, so he sawed a large lock off of the rotary brake. This allowed the big revolving case to be moved at will. The inmates of the cell began to turn it cog by cog. Tackett walked around the rotary and told the inmates to get ready to escape. He then cranked the rotary allowing seven others to escape. Then they sawed the bars off of the west window to make their escape from the jail. All the prisoners made their way out safely, but C.H. Howard only wanted to go see his wife and family before returning to the jail as he only had a few days remaining on his sentence. The others who fled were Bill Rhodes, Harry Alley, James Robinson, Albert Adams, James Murphy and Ed Stewart.[37] Sheriff C.W. Simmons offered various rewards on February 4 for information or capture of five men who remained at large. The five included Fitzsimmons, an African American hotel waiter; Bill Rhodes, a horse trader; Harry Alley, a barber; Jim Murphy and Bill

Tackett.[38] Murphy was caught on February 9 in Trinidad, Colorado.[39] Tackett was later captured in Oklahoma and imprisoned there for yet another crime. Sheriff Simmons visited him at the Lansing Penitentiary in October to speak to him about the escape.[40] Robinson was captured at Newton. Adams was apprehended in Eldorado. Howard gave himself up to authorities. Rhodes, Fitzsimmons, and Murphy had yet to be found as of October 23, 1902.[41]

Two boys being held at the Sedgwick County Jail used spoons in an attempt to break jail, but were caught before they succeeded on October 23, 1902. The boys had been confined in the second floor boys' department of the jail. They used the handles of spoons to dig away at the mortar between the bricks and got out about twenty bricks before being discovered. Both boys were headed to reform school in Topeka.

A group of five men made a futile attempt at a wholesale jail delivery on May 15, 1910, but prompt action by the sheriff's wife and daughter prevented them from getting away. When the inmates started a commotion that night, Mrs. Cogdell and Miss Cora Cogdell, the sheriff's wife and daughter, got suspicious and called Undersheriff Boston and Turnkey Pulliam. When the two men arrived, they found that the inmates had torn loose the iron braces from their beds and pried loose several bars of the cell door leading from their cell to the corridor. When Sheriff Cogdell returned he added charges against the group for attempting escape.[42]

An inmate did make a successful escape on December 21, 1910, and was recaptured at his home before Christmas. Carl Elliott's Christmas present was an additional thirty days in jail for escaping. Strangely enough, he was within five days of his release.[43]

Other Criminals

As quickly as the new rotary jail was completed, it began housing inmates arrested by local and federal authorities for selling liquor to the Indians in Kansas and Oklahoma in some cases. For example, Judge Foster of the United States District Court sentenced four men—James Voss, A.J. Rodgers, Jack Sheehan, and Greenup Jones—in the Sedgwick County Jail for thirty days for selling liquor in the Indian Territory in Oklahoma.[44]

An unnamed inmate who had been confined in the Sedgwick County Jail for eleven years was declared insane by the probate court in August

1889 and sent to an asylum. He had been passed down from sheriff to sheriff as a regular attachment to the institution and no one appeared to know or care about the reason for his incarceration.[45]

Gus G. Nordmark was turned over to Sheriff Royse by Mexican police officers on December 23, 1895, for stealing $400.02 from the Postal Service. Nordmark had fled to Mexico to escape justice and was in the country for about sixty days before he was arrested. "Mexico is a great country," Nordmark said, "but I would rather live in the Sedgwick county jail six months than to live in the state of Sonora in Old Mexico for ten years." Nordmark had written the sheriff while in Mexico saying he had intended to pay back what he owed.[46]

Safekeeping

Because the rotary jail was considered more secure, some other counties asked the Sedgwick County Jail to house their prisoners if there was room. For example, Judge Reed, murderer of Isaac Hopper in 1892, was taken to Wichita because it was considered safer than the Cowley County Jail.[47]

A man convicted of murder in Sumner County was put in the Sedgwick County Jail for safekeeping after the Kansas Supreme Court sustained the decision in his conviction on April 6, 1895. Anderson Gray was convicted of planning the murder of Thomas Patton on May 5, 1984, while Thomas McDonald, the man who committed the actual murder, was acquitted.[48]

A young murderer was secretly brought to the Sedgwick County Jail because of the threat of mob violence. This volatile situation occurred because Judge Gillett allowed Johnnie Kornstett to withdraw his plea of guilty and put the county to the expense of a costly trial.[49]

Frank Clark, who was criminally charged with assaulting his fifteen-year-old sister, was brought to the Sedgwick County Jail for safe keeping as there were indications of a lynching party being formed in Wellington.[50]

A man accused of murder was brought to the Sedgwick County Jail for safe keeping on June 20, 1903. Ed Christy, who was charged with shooting D.L. Pierce of Peck, was brought to the jail after there were rumors of plots to hang the prisoner, who was in the Sumner County Jail in Wellington.[51]

To avoid a possible lynching, three African Americans were hastily removed from the Wichita police station and hurried to the Sedgwick County Jail on May 23, 1906. They were arrested in connection with the beating and robbing William Sutton, a grocer.[52]

While many prisoners were sent to the Sedgwick County Jail for safe-keeping, some were transferred to other jails for the same reason. John C. Moore, who killed his wife in Arkansas City, was transferred to the Cowley County Jail in Winfield from the Sedgwick County Jail in Wichita on October 24, 1906, for safekeeping as there was a great deal of excitement over the killing.[53]

Ellis County Jail—
Waxahachie, Texas

Waxahachie was founded in August 1850 as the seat of the newly established Ellis County. The community was incorporated on April 28, 1871.[1]

Sheriff Ryburn visited Fort Worth in December 1887 to see if he could make a deal with Tarrant County to take Ellis County prisoners until the new jail was completed the next year.[2] The rotary jail in Waxahachie was built in 1888 by the Pauly Jail Building Company. The jail had two tiers with ten cells on each tier.[3]

Ellis County also had a farm jail in the early 1900s; however, escape was easier from it than the rotary jail. One time nine men escaped from the jail in April 1915. The county farm jail was located two miles southeast of Waxahachie.[4]

The Ellis County commissioners gave the white prisoners a settee to enjoy in April 1911. It was placed in the runaround corridor by Jailer Maggart.[5]

The cage was dismantled in the 1920s and the building served as the home of the Relief Work Commission during the depression beginning in 1929. An addition was later added to the south side of the building and it continued to house a variety of commercial businesses, including law offices. The building still stands today and is listed with the Texas Historical Commission.[6]

Lynchings

In October 1905, the Ellis County grand jury indicted Albert Johnson, an African American, for the murder of J.H. Taylor. Taylor was found in an unconscious condition sitting in his buggy near Waxahachie. He had two severe fractures of the skull, which resulted in his death. He had been robbed of $75.[7] Johnson was convicted of the Taylor murder and sentenced to hang after a November trial. His attorney appealed. Two months later on January 12, he broke out of the county jail along with Monk Johnson, Dennis Borders, and Calhoun Williams. The black men dug a large hole in the brick wall after the men had been released from their cells in the morning for breakfast and exercise in the corridor. The men were recaptured. As a result of the jailbreak, Johnson's appeal was dismissed.[8] Johnson was hanged on March 30, 1906.[9]

An African American man was rushed to the Ellis County Jail for safekeeping after a lynch mob formed near India, Texas, on November 8, 1908. Ed Sharp had allegedly attacked and criminally assaulted a thirty-year-old white woman while she was milking a cow at the home of H. Didwell. Sharp allegedly used a large knife to threaten her life. A guard was put on the prisoner as farmers were rumored to be forming a lynch mob to string up the fellow.[10]

After having been tried for the same murder seven times, sentenced to death six times and having spent eight years in prison, Burrell Oates was to be hanged in Waxahachie on the night of November 29, 1912. It marked the end of the most remarkable case in criminal court history in Texas. Oates was originally charged with a murder along with another man after his gang held up a grocery store and killed its owner, Sol Anonoff on November 29, 1904. One member of the gang was found guilty and hanged. Another of the trio turned state's evidence. Oates, an African American, was found guilty, but appealed his case. He won the appeal based on an irregularity in drawing the names of jurors. At his new trial, he was convicted and sentenced to death again, but the Court of Criminal Appeals granted him a new trial on May 9, 1906, because the judge had failed to instruct the jury in his instructions that if the grocer's wife shot the husband by mistake, the prisoner was not guilty of murder. Oates was again tried and convicted, but on May 15, 1907, the case was reversed by the Court of Criminal Appeals on the grounds that the trial judge did not properly define murder as he directed the jury. After another trial, the case again came before the Court of Criminal Appeals on June 23, 1909, and a question as to the legality of the appointment of the trial judge was the ground for setting aside the verdict and again remanding the case for a new trial. Oates' fifth trial resulted in no verdict as to penalty with one juror standing for life imprisonment while the others demanded the death penalty. When Oates came up for his sixth trial, the judge transferred the case to Ellis County. Oates was again found guilty in the sixth trial; however, the jury did not specify the degree of murder of which Oates had been found guilty, so he was given another appeal. The seventh and final trial was held in Waxahachie on November 4, 1911. He was found guilty of murder in the first degree. His motion for appeal was denied.[11] Oates was hanged in Waxahachie on November 29, 1912. His last words were: "Goodbye. God bless you. I am ready to die. It's a drop here and a rise over there."[12]

Murderers

On March 5, 1888, a white man shot and killed an African American man over an old grudge in Fagan. Jefferson Stewart was arrested by three Graham County law enforcement officers and brought to the Ellis County Jail for murdering William Kelly. The grudge began the spring before when Stewart slapped another black man, John Hawkins, for sitting down at the same table with him that day. Kelly caused a disturbance at three or four places in Millbrook before facing Stewart in the billiard hall. Kelly threw a billiard ball at Stewart, who retaliated by shooting him. Stewart was scheduled to be tried at the next term of the Graham County District Court, but results of that trail are unknown.[13]

An African American, who shot and killed another black in 1916, was arrested and subsequently escaped from the county jail in Athens, was apprehended and put in the Ellis County Jail in December 1920. Deputy Sheriff H.G. McWhirter arrested J.B. Harmon in Italy (Texas) just as he was about to leave town. Harmon was charged with murdering "Buck" Lacy. Results of the trial are unknown.[14]

Stacey Powers was in the Ellis County Jail for twenty months on two charges of murder before he was released in February 1917 on a $5,000 bond for each murder. He had been charged with the murder of Travis and J.M. McCarty in the Sardis community of Ellis County. Results of the trial are unknown.[15]

After spending three years in the Ellis County Jail for murder, Lou Sapp was released from jail on bond by the criminal court of appeals on June 13, 1919. Sapp was arrested with his brother after the bodies of Dick

Watts and another man were discovered in the Big Thicket community of Hardin County. Sapp was sentenced to twenty years in prison, but appealed his case and won, so he was freed.[16]

Escapes

An inmate in the Ellis County Jail made an escape from the rotary jail on November 8, 1891. Albert Huntley carved a wooden key out of a broom handle to unlock the door. Then he used a rope to lower him from a third floor window. Huntley was in jail for forgery.[17]

Tom Varnell escaped from the Ellis County Jail, but he was recaptured and put back in jail in May 1893. When the prisoners were sent from the run-around to the rotary cages, Varnell made a dummy and placed it in his cell and stepped back into the run-around. Another prisoner called for a light and when Sheriff Merideth stepped into the side room to get it, Varnell made his break. Later, Varnell was found in Eden's building, which was more than a hundred yards from the jail. He was in jail for murdering old man Zand ten years before.[18]

Three men escaped from the Ellis County Jail sometime between midnight and daybreak on December 21, 1896. The men manufactured a key from a broom handle and unlocked the sliding door to the revolving cages. After springing this door at the bottom, the men crawled out into what is known as a "run-around." Then they cut through thick brick walls using an old knife and jumped down from the second floor. They then scaled a fence to gain their freedom. The men were identified as Walter Moreland, Joe Munkus, and Frank Chambers. There were some fifty prisoners incarcerated in the rotary jail at the time. The other prisoners couldn't escape because the steel bar held the revolving cages in position. The jail was set up so that only one cell at a time could be in a position of entrance or exit. Up until this time, the jail was thought to be perfectly safe.[19]

An inmate escaped from the Ellis County Jail on April 23, 1915, but he was recaptured less than a week later. H.I. Williams was captured by plainclothes officer Craven and Bandon on April 26 and charged with swindling. He had signed stolen checks in his possession at the time of the arrest. He was returned to Waxahachie.[20]

In most all cases, inmates are the ones who try to escape from jail, but occasionally someone tries to break into a jail. Such was the case when Garland Anderson was arrested for trying to saw through bars on the ground floor of the Ellis County Jail to gain entrance into the main runaround of the jail. He hoped to deliver steel saws to Lester Paulk, another Corsicana youth, who had been convicted of rape in of a young woman near Corsicana on August 7, 1925. Paulk had been given a ninety-nine-year sentence in district court during a trial that gained much attention. The case was transferred to Ellis County. Anderson was arrested in the act of sawing the bars and found himself placed in a cell in the rotary. Anderson had eighteen saws in his possession at the time of the arrest and he had driven to Waxahachie in a stolen car.[21]

Safekeeping

Because the rotary jail in Ellis County was deemed inescapable, it was often used by other counties to hold some for safekeeping. Issac Bruce, an African American, was convicted of raping a white woman and placed in the Ellis County Jail for safekeeping until his sentence of death was carried out. He was convicted by the district court in Hill County in the fall term of 1892. In April 1893, he sent a letter to the governor asking for clemency. Governor J.S. Hogg changed the sentence on May 18 to life in prison instead and ordered that he serve his term out in the Ellis County Jail.[22]

A young, ignorant African American was brought to the Ellis County Jail on June 11, 1899. Warren Bartlett had been charged with criminally assaulting the six-year-old daughter of Mr. Therford at Rice, Navarro County.[23] Bartlett was found guilty and given a life sentence, but the case was appealed on June 22.[24] Bartlett's sentence was changed to ninety-nine years in the penitentiary. His trial was rapidly rushed along, although his lawyers took exception to the speedy trial. Bartlett confessed to the crime when he was en route to the Hillsboro Jail and that confession was held against him in the case.[25]

Sheriff Bell of Hill County lodged Fred James in the Ellis County Jail for the murder of George Watts, a black barber at Hillsboro.[26]

Another killer was brought to the Ellis County Jail while repairs were being completed on the Dallas jail in September 1910. Frank McCue, who was charged with the murder of Earl Mabry in 1907, was brought to Waxahachie on September 14 for safekeeping.[27]

Other Criminals

A grand jury empaneled in February 1908 wrote that if they had interviewed reliable witnesses, the Ellis County Jail would be full of people who have violated local liquor laws. They were sure two places were selling liquor illegally; however, no indictments were issued.[28]

A Suicide

Jack White was found dead in his cell at the Ellis County Jail in November 1906. He had been charged with the murder of P.H. Pond. The prisoner drank prussic acid poisoning to commit suicide.[29]

Kanawha County Jail—
Charleston, West Virginia

Kanawha County was created on November 14, 1788, with the county seat at Charleston. At that time it was part of Virginia. When the first Kanawha County Jail was built is unknown; however, a teenage boy was confined in the county jail in Charleston, Virginia, on suspicion of having murdered his father in 1835. (The state of West Virginia was not formed until 1863.)[1]

On March 2, 1870, a band of Ku-Klux members released the prisoners from the Kanawha County Jail. The governor was going to call in troops to preserve the peace. At that time, the Ku Klux Klan was said to be extensive and civil authorities were often powerless against them.[2]

By the 1880s, Charleston had become the state capitol and its population had grown to more than six thousand and the county had more than forty thousand.[3]

In April 1887, all six prisoners of the Kanawha County Jail escaped by means of a tunnel, so the Kanawha County Jail was without any prisoners. The escape was made by means of a tunnel from the corridor of the jail into the jail yard, which was surrounded by a high board fence. They scaled the fence and escaped. The men were Samuel Finnigan, Jabez Burdette, Dick Fields (black), M.J. Lasker, Emanuel Williams and Asa Carr.[4]

The escape in 1887 may have spelled the end of that jail. A rotary jail was constructed the following year behind the Kanawha County Courthouse by the Pauly Jail Building Company. The one-story structure had eight cells and could house sixteen prisoners in the rotary section of the jail.

Due to the slow movement of the rotary jail, two men were burned in their steel cell in the Kanawha County Jail on August 23, 1909, before

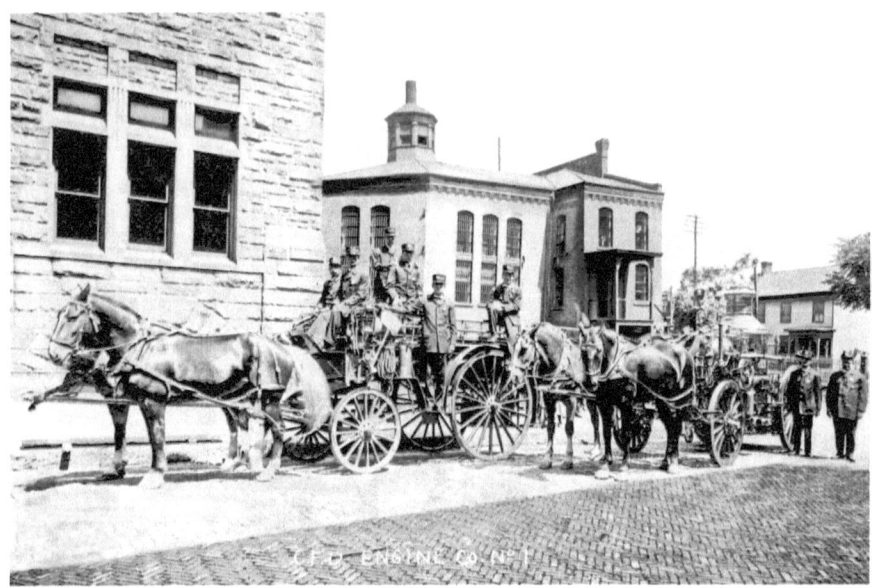

The Charleston Fire Department Engine Company No. 1 posed in front of the Kanawha County Jail for this photograph in the early 1900s.

jail could be rotated to the opening or the fire extinguished. The fire was probably started initially from a lighted cigarette. John R. Johnson, 18, and Charles Smurlow, 35, were burned practically from head to foot and presented a terrible sight with their skin falling off their bodies when they were released. Both were taken to Charleston General Hospital, but little hope was given. They both later died from their burns.[5]

The county government decided to investigate the assault of female prisoners by male inmates in 1909. An investigating committee took in evidence in December. Two teenage girls, aged fifteen and seventeen, who had spent some time in the Kanawha County Jail testified before the committee on December 22. They said they were visited by male prisoners at will and subjected to gross indignities. They also said a lot of gambling and drinking was done among prisoners and several jail officials. The girls had been released and were sent to a Salvation Army Rescue Home near Pittsburgh.[6]

One witness in the case—a painter named Nelson—testified that he saw a female federal prisoner, who was seventeen or eighteen, being assaulted by prisoners and that prisoners frequently unlocked her cell door and entered, remaining there for hours at a time. Some people testified that prisoners visited their houses and that on one occasion a jailer accompanied one of the prisoners. Evidence was also introduced that on one occasion a male prisoner held a female prisoner while another assaulted the girl. Some evidence was so horrible that it couldn't be printed in the newspaper.[7]

The Kanawha County Jail investigating committee made its report to Judge Burdette of the circuit court on January 8, 1910. It found the lack manner in which the jail was being run, the freedom allowed to prisoners, and the practices permitted were not conductive to proper management as would be expected by the public and required under the laws of the state. Many of the unsanitary conditions discovered were due to the neglect of the jailer. The committee found the food to be good, but that if the jailer had done his duty there should have been no beer or whisky carried into the jail only to be consumed by the prisoners. Six instances where prisoners were found to have had illicit cohabitation were singled out, but the committee declared these instances were a matter for a grand jury and the courts to handle. The conduct of the jail was found to be inexcusable and severely censured.[8]

The Kanawha County Jail was considered full in December 1914 and Judge Black had only begun to sentence some bootleggers found guilty of violating the Yost prohibition law. The jail had fifty-five prisoners and it was only built to hold a capacity of thirty-five inmates.[9]

In May 1917, a grand jury inspected the Kanawha County Jail and found conditions appalling. As a result, criminals convicted in the United States District Court were not required to serve any time in the local jail. The grand jury found the ventilation was poor and almost entirely lacking in the basement. They found dirty mattresses, unkempt, and unsanitary. The cells were unclean. They found iron bars were in some cases gummed with tobacco juices and bathing facilities inadequate and unsanitary. They discovered dirt in numerous places. They said the odor in the basement that was caused by the flushing of human excrements in the cells was very offensive and the toilet facilities very unsanitary. The provisions for confining insane persons were found to be totally inadequate. They found the stairway leading to the basement to be dark, dirty, and unsafe. Finally, they also found the jail to be overcrowded. As many as ninety-three prisoners had been housed there when the capacity was limited to forty.[10]

Being a night jailer is not the easiest position in the world, so John

Morgan declined his re-appointment to the position when Sheriff S.B. Jarrett offered it to him in April 1918. The vacancy occurred when Jarrett resigned the position, but agreed to stay until a replacement could be found.[11]

Twenty-one inmates at the Kanawha County Jail sent a letter to the newspaper calling attention to the conditions at the facility. They wrote that the city health inspector and pronounced the jail the worst in the state. They said the mattresses were so filthy and black that they were injurious to health. They said the jail is so crowded that three or four men were in cells built for one or two men. They said the commodes are sometimes only flushed once a day. They said the food was insufficient and not cooked in palatable condition. And last, they wrote that the pans the food is served in are unsanitary.[12]

A committee appointed to inspect the Kanawha County Jail in March 1919 found the jail not fit for use any longer. The jail was too small in size and obsolete in construction.[13]

Nationwide prohibition began in January 1920 when the Eighteenth Amendment to the U.S. Constitution went into effect. A reporter for the *Charleston Daily Mail* visited the jail on April 5, 1922, and wrote that conditions at the Kanawha County Jail to be awful. Prisoners were crowded in like sardines as one hundred and eighty-five inmates filled the jail built for thirty-five. Eleven of the inmates were women and African American women were put together with white women in one cell. The white men and African American men were segregated with the blacks being in a large room on another floor. The jail had only one bathtub for all the prisoners. In regard to some complaints about the jail, Sheriff Henry A. Walker said, "Of course, we cannot give each prisoner an individual room and all the comforts of home. If some of these women are so concerned about the way the prisoners are treated in the jail, why don't they take them into their homes and furnish them feather beds, upholstered furniture and everything?" The new jail on which work was being done would be ready in December.[14]

The rotary jail was torn down in 1924 to make room for an addition to the courthouse.

Nowadays, the Kanawha County Jail is only a memory as it has been replaced by the South Central Regional Jail, part of the state of West Virginia correctional system. Built in 1993, the jail holds about 500 inmates. The facility is located in Charleston and serves Kanawha and Jackson counties.[15]

Murderers

A mother was put in the Charleston Jail after killing her five-year-old daughter. Virginia Robinson became aggravated and beat her daughter to death with a hoe.[16]

Isham Mullins, who was charged with killing Henry Moore at Christmas 1887, delivered himself to authorities on February 13, 1888, and was committed to the Kanawha County Jail to await trial. He had previously escaped officers.[17]

An intoxicated man who killed another man was put in the Charleston jail in September 1892. John Clendenin had been drinking before he approached Joe Ulman's residence and started throwing stones at his home. Ulman came outside and Clendenin shot him dead with a pistol.[18]

Two men were charged with murder of a railroad detective and placed in the Kanawha County Jail in July 1911. Aaron Collins and John Dodson allegedly murdered Jack Horton at South Ruffner. A chase of the men lasted five days through Kanawha, Fayette, Nicholas, Raleigh, Boone, and into Lincoln County.[19]

Mert Cook was placed in the Kanawha County Jail in April 1918 after he was charged with the murder of Fred Jarrett, who had been killed two years previously. Deputy Sheriff E.E. Bragg arrested Cook at his home in Paint Creek. Just before Jarrett died he said, "Mert can tell who stabbed me." The two had worked together in the mines and may have gotten into a fight. Jarrett succumbed to his stab wounds.[20]

An African American woman fatally wounded her husband and admitted to the crime on August 12, 1918, in the Kanawha County Jail. Ida Bynum killed Tom because of his mistreatment of her. He died in the Charleston General Hospital early the next morning. She said that he had beaten her several times since they married in 1916. About a month before the incident, she said he beat her and her eleven-year-old son. The shooting occurred when Ida was putting her son to bed. Bynum jumped out of the bed and rushed at her with a razor declaring that he was going to kill her. She grabbed a revolver and shot him. She had applied for a peace bond for her husband (a restraining order these days) and kept the revolver handy in the house because she was afraid of him. She alleged that he had made threats following his arrest.[21]

Several inmates during these times were temporarily placed in the Kanawha County Jail until the county lunacy commission could decide whether they were insane or not and put in the asylum. For instance, Fred Bailey killed his wife at their home near Guthrie by beating her to death in September 1918. The commission visited Bailey in his cell in the jail and examined and interrogated him there. He was talking wildly and had been raving in his cell all night. He promptly admitted the killing. "It took me two hours to kill her," Bailey said after showing them his knuckles. During the interview, Bailey went into an incoherent ramble about the Kaiser, the Huns, spies, money, and his father-in-law.[22]

James Tomes, an African American, was being held in the Kanawha County Jail without bond after being accused of murdering another black man, Water Powell. Eddie Oliver, an eyewitness, said Powell drew something shiny from his pocket and fired a gun into Powell's shoulder. Powell died a few hours later in the hospital.[23]

A colored man pleaded guilty to second-degree murder of another colored man on February 8, 1919, and was given a sentence of twelve years in the state prison in Moundsville. Sam Davis had been held in the Kanawha County Jail since June of 1918 awaiting trial. Davis shot Albert Herring to death in Gallagher on June 21, 1918. Herring had assaulted and beaten a younger brother of Davis and when trouble arose between the two, Davis shot him with a revolver.[24]

Beatrice Matheny was convicted of killing her husband along the Dunbar car line below Charleston in March 1921. She was sent to Moundsville Penitentiary from the Kanawha County Jail in June 1922 to serve a year. Her sentence was lessened due to her ill health.[25]

Escapes

A prisoner who escaped the Fayette County Jail was captured in Charleston and put in the Kanawha County Jail until he could be returned for hanging. After Albert Voiers escaped jail, he fled to the woods in Kanawha County to hide out. There he was given food and shelter by relatives. Detective Tom Brannigan and Mayor Dunbar tracked Voiers to his brother's home and secured a search warrant. When they went to initiate the warrant, the armed Voiers resisted and shooting a hole through Brannigan's hat rim, but he was unhurt. A total of six shots were exchanged, yet nobody was injured.[26]

C.E. Adams sawed his way out of the Kanawha County Jail on May 8, 1907. He was captured in Santa Fe, New Mexico, in September. Adams was awaiting his sentence after being found guilty of arson from the burning of the depot in Kayford when he escaped. Judge Black sentenced Adams to nine years in the state penitentiary. He would begin serving the sentence when he returned from New Mexico.[27]

Six prisoners cut their way through the thin roof of the Kanawha County Jail and made their escape in late April 1908. The escape occurred in the afternoon, but their freedom was short lived as in less than two hours they were all captured before they could get beyond the city's limits.[28]

After an inmate escaped from the jail in Logan, Ohio, his brother-in-law dropped dead when he was told the news in April 1914. John Truslow, a.k.a. "Slippery John," sawed his way to liberty from the Kanawha County Jail in March 1914. He went to Ohio where he was arrested at Logan and put in the county jail. He also escaped from there and that is when Herbert L. Wagner died of a heart attack upon hearing the news. Papers were again being prepared for his extradition to West Virginia and the news proved to shocking for his brother-in-law.[29]

Three criminals fled from the Kanawha County Jail on July 4, 1918. C.C. Cook, a notorious crook, escaped from the jail for the second time in a month. The first time he escape was on June 8, but he was recaptured and returned. The other escapees were C. Kearns and Archie Crawford, an African American and felony prisoner being held for the grand jury. The three escaped during church services, which were held in a section of the jail known as the "bull pen." The perpetrators removed the window weight from the window sash and wrapped a weight with a blanket. Swinging the weight, they smashed the heavy cast-iron lock on the cell door. They then removed eight bricks from the wall that adjoins the Kanawha County Courthouse. A fireman saw the escape and sounded an alarm, but the escapees couldn't be found.[30]

Two unidentified colored prisoners escaped from the Kanawha County Jail in August 1918. They tore away a portion of the brick wall of the jail adjoining the county courthouse.[31]

A total escape of fifty inmates from the Kanawha County Jail was barely averted on February 2, 1919, but three inmates were successful in getting away. The escapees were named Kelly, Howard, and McTheny. They initially attempted to get out by sawing the cell lock, but were caught and confined to the dungeon. The three then dug their way through the brick wall and escaped through the cupola in the roof.[32]

Safekeeping

Perry Drake was brought to the Kanawha County Jail for safe keeping after he was implicated as an accomplice in the shooting of the Rev. Thomas P. Ryan on October 13, 1887, at his home in Roane County. Two other men who had been implicated in the murder were killed by a lynch mob called the "Consolidated Band." They hanged one man and slit the throat of the other man involved in the murder. Drake was not being held for the murder. He was arrested for illicit distilling. Drake was later released by Judge Guthrie because he couldn't be held in one county jail for a crime in another county.[33]

Mike Lee, the accused murderer of Jerry Hatfield, one of the noted members of the Hatfield-McCoy feud, was brought to the Kanawha County Jail for safe keeping in May 1890. He was due for trial in July at the Circuit Court in Logan County.[34]

An African American whom a mob sought to lynch in Williamson on July 15, 1899, was brought to the rotary jail in Charleston for safekeeping until he could be transferred to the state penitentiary. The mob followed Sheriff N.J. Keadle, two guards and the prisoner, Jim Dudley, all the way to Charleston, a trip of 150 miles. Dudley was duly convicted of shooting railroad conductor, A.J. Parlor, of the Norfolk and Western Railroad and given a fourteen-year sentence.[35]

An African American from St. Albans was taken to the Charleston Rotary Jail on July 12, 1892, to avoid a lynch mob that had formed after he stabbed a man in the chest with a large knife killing him. Charley Doome, a telegraph operator, had taken most of the black man's money in a craps game and he wanted to win his money back. Doome refused to play again and the two got into an argument. Then the unidentified man stabbed Doome.[36]

An African American wanted for murder in Jackson County, Ohio, was held in the Kanawha County Jail until officials could come and get him in December 1914. Isaiah Washington was arrested by Constable Rome Mitchell in Pratt and transported to Charleston on December 29. Washington allegedly murdered Eva Perkins, a black woman on September 30, 1913, by slashing her across the throat with a knife.[37]

Another African American was brought to the Kanawha County Jail for safekeeping after he allegedly killed a man in October 1915. Earl L.

Holmes Jr., was on his way home with a party of companions when they became involved in a fight with a number of African Americans. Stones were thrown and when one of the stones hit George Rhodes home, he came out and shot Holmes, who died an hour later in a hospital. Rhodes was brought to Charleston after the incident by Sheriff W.W. Hamilton of Mercer County.[38]

Alcohol Charges

The illegal making of liquor—moonshining—was a common occurrence in the mountains of West Virginia over the years. A large number of moonshiners were put in jail in late November 1890. A gang of twenty-two men were put in the jail for illegally making liquor.[39]

One of the first female moonshiners to be confined to the new rotary jail in Kanawha County was Lucy McClure. The handsome twenty-four-year-old woman was jailed on October 5, 1891, for being a moonshiner. More than a year before the arrest, federal authorities discovered that she was selling liquor along the Norfolk and Western Railroad. The feds tried to capture her, but she evaded them and they were frustrated in their efforts. Like the famed Annie Oakley, she was a fine shot with a rifle or revolver and owned a beautiful sorrel horse that helped her flee from authorities. She reputedly made hundreds of gallons of white lightening, but a decline of business resulted in her leaving for Lincoln County where marshals finally captured her.[40]

A hundred moonshiners, including twenty women, were taken to the Charleston Jail in April 1895. Marshal Doc Smith and a squad of deputies attempted to capture Lee Ward and others when Ward opened fire on them. The marshal returned fire and put four bullets in Ward, killing him. The rest of the moonshiners quickly surrendered.[41]

Other Criminals

An African American named William Jefferson was jailed in Charleston after Eureka detectives of Charleston were notified that he had fled to West Virginia from Montgomery County, Virginia, where he was charged with rape. Jefferson was captured in Huntington by Detective Mitchell, who turned him over to Capt. G.W. Baldwin in Charleston for requisition.[42]

Twenty-five African Americans were jailed on false charges on October 15, 1896, to prevent them from voting in the election. The United States deputy marshals charged them falsely for selling liquor. The newspaper called it was an outrage and initiated by Democrats that should be stopped.[43]

Sam Pierson, who was charged with the murder of Alex Dawson near Yankee Dam in Clay County, was taken to the Kanawha County Jail for safe keeping in September 1900.[44]

Thirty-seven of the forty-five striking coal miners, mostly Greeks, were arrested in September 1912 for intimidation of workmen. Lieutenant Adam Gaul and eight members of the state militia arrested the men who were attempting to prevent miners from returning from work at Dorothy, West Virginia. The miners were sentenced to sixty days in the Kanawha County Jail. A small band of men had been firing on the soldiers at various locations, so bloodhounds were sent out to track them down.[45] By March 1913, twenty-four of the miners received suspended sentences and were released. The other ten were given short jail terms. About five thousand miners were on strike at one time.[46]

An army deserter was held in the Kanawha County Jail in July 1918 until military authorities came and retrieve him. Harry Mooney, a confessed deserter from Camp Shelby, Hattiesburg, Mississippi, was arrested near his home on Davis Creek, five miles from Charleston by federal officers on July 19, 1918. Mooney tried to escape after his home was surrounded by officers, but he was brought to a halt when several shots were fired over his head. He claimed he had been granted a sick furlough on March 5.[47]

West Virginia Governor John J. Cornwell pardoned Basil Talbot of Charleston. He had been sentenced to ninety days in jail in the Kanawha County Jail for stealing a skirt; however, Talbot had already served ninety days before the trial.[48]

Strafford County Jail— Dover, New Hampshire

Dover is the oldest permanent settlement in New Hampshire, being settled in 1623. In 1633, Cochecho Plantation was purchased by a group of English Puritans who planned to settle in New England. They renamed the settlement Bristol and built a meetinghouse surrounded by an entrenchment with a jail nearby. The town was renamed Dover in 1637 by the new governor. Strafford County was one of the original five counties organized in New Hampshire in 1769.[1]

The first jail built in Dover was a small, wooden edifice in 1774, two

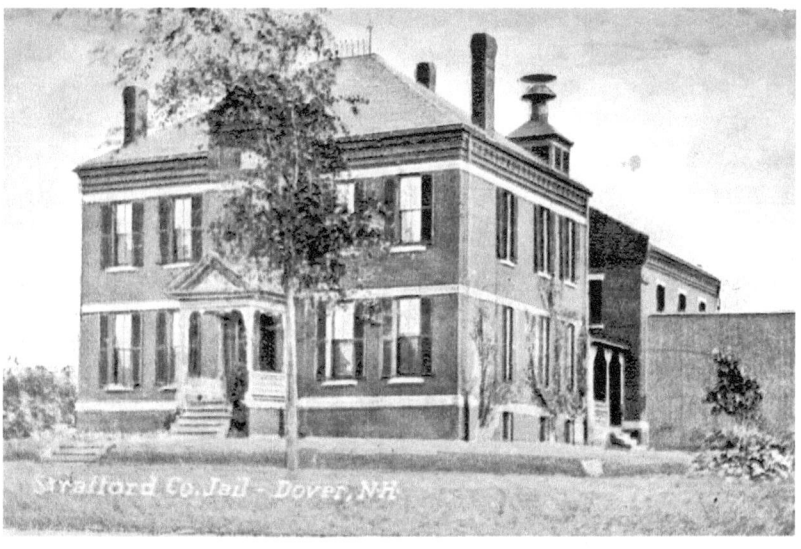

The Strafford County Jail was located in the rear of the facility and was torn down in 1918 for scrap for the war effort. This image comes for a postcard made at the time of its existence.

years before the Revolutionary War. Dover and Strafford County continued to grow over the next century and by 1888 a newer, larger jail was needed to house prisoners. The Pauly Jail Building Company was hired to construct a rotary jail with a jailer's house on the top of a hill across the Cochecho River from Washington Square.[2]

The two-level rotary jail contained 16 cells in all, eight on each level. A hand crank was used to turned the jail, so that no two cells lined up with the single door at any time. People called it the "Revolving Jail." Along with a couple of separate cells for women and others, the jail had a total capacity of fifty-six prisoners.[3]

The Strafford County rotary jail was in use until 1908 when a new jail was constructed. The jail was then torn down in 1918 in order to obtain scrap for the war effort. The jailer's quarters were left intact and turned into a private home. Today, the home is occupied by the McCoole family.[4]

The Longest Inmate

Rather than paying a judgment rendered against him for $1,500, Alfred W. Jones served nine years in the Strafford County Jail until the rotary jail closed in 1908. Jones had grown a beard for that length of time and claimed he would die in jail. The man had refused to take the poor debtor's oath, even if he were allowed to do so, because he said that would be tantamount to an acknowledgment of his debt. Suit was originally brought against him for the alleged abuse of Arthur A. Cripp, an orphan whom he raised Jones had become known as the "lion of the Teneriffe." He was 59 years old and a giant in stature.[5]

A Riot

Six prisoners who were confined in the revolving section of the Strafford County Jail began a riot in April 1895. They broke up chairs and other pieces of flammable furniture and set them ablaze. Mrs. Scates, the jailer's wife, was ill and powerless to stop them, so she had to send for assistance. On arrival of police officers, the jail was filled with smoke and the prisoners were nearly suffocated. Everything was removed from the cells and the rioters were left two to a cell and their right arms shackled and nothing but the bare floor to sit on. Mrs. Scates then refused to feed the inmates while she remained in charge of the jail.[6]

Murderers

An enormous crowd was present at the railroad station when Joseph E. Kelley arrived in Dover to be jailed in the Strafford County Jail on April 22, 1897. He had been charged with murder of a cashier of the Great Falls National Bank in Somersworth.[7] Three days later at the arraignment in Somersworth, he pleaded guilty to the murder of Joseph A. Stickney. Kelley had hit Stickney in the head and cut his throat with a razor. After the hearing, Kelley was returned to the Strafford County Jail for safe keeping until September when his sentence hearing would be conducted by the supreme judicial court. In October, he changed his plea to not guilty and was remanded for trial.[8] At the trial it came out that Kelley had stolen $6,000 in silver after killing Stickney. He then escaped to Canada where he was discovered three days later in a whorehouse dressed as a woman. After the jury was empaneled and the trial went three days, the defendant pleaded guilty and accepted the sentence of death.[9]

Alfred W. Jones was arrested and incarcerated in the Strafford County Jail in February 1898 for the murder of his mother, Sally W. Jones, who was poisoned to death on December 3, 1896.[10] Jones had been a model prisoner since coming to the jail and gained some weight on jail food. He was continually praying and advising other inmates to turn from evil and follow the teachings of the Bible. At the trial in April, the jury couldn't decide on a verdict after being out for nineteen-and-a-half hours, so Judge Carpenter discharged the jury and the case was continued. Jones was given a bail of $2,000.[11] The case against Jones was dropped September 21, 1898.[12]

Mrs. Lizzie Provinchia spent about eight months in the Strafford County Jail before the court sentenced her to twenty-five years in the state penitentiary on October 4, 1899. She was found guilty of killing her housekeeper, Annie Cox of Rochester on January 21, 1899. A large crowd gathered at the railroad station to see her off. She was accompanied by Sheriff James E. Hayes.[13]

Five men were incarcerated in the Strafford County Jail in July 1900 for the murder of Thomas Dobbins and John McNally and serious wounding of Joseph Gagnon. The bank robbing gang included John Farrell, Frank

Gold, William Scott, John Brown and John Williams. However, Farrell and Williams were discharged from the crime at a hearing only to be arrested immediately on suspicion of taking part in a robbery of the Cold Spring Brewery in Lawrence, Massachusetts. Guards were doubled at the jail when an attempt to break the prisoners out was feared.[14] Then a party of police officers from Massachusetts came to the Strafford County Jail and identified two of the men, John Williams and John Brown, as the men who shot at them during the robbing of a liquor store in Lynn. During this crime, Patrolman Joyce of the Lynn police force was wounded in the arm.[15]

A fifteen-year-old boy was charged with murder and confined in the Strafford County Jail on February 24, 1901. Frank Ballard was accused of killing Josephine E. Jenkins at Lee Hook. At first the Coroner John R. Ham determined the shooting was accidental. However, County Solicitor Scott and Deputy Sheriff W.W. Cushman reviewed the case and determined otherwise. Ballard still alleged it was an accident. He said,

> I did not understand the use of firearms and had never handled a gun. I had been told by Mr. Jenkins never to touch the gun, but had a strong desire to learn how to shoot it. After Mr. Jenkins left the house on that Monday morning, Mrs. Jenkins went to the yard to hang out her washing. I thought it would be a good time to try the gun. I got five cartridges and the gun and went to the woodshed. The kitchen door was open. The door between the kitchen and dining room was also open and the muzzle of the gun was pointed in through the kitchen door. I put two cartridges in the gun, then snapped it back in position for shooting. I went to raise the hammer of the gun, when my thumb slipped and the hammer flew back. There was a loud report. I heard a scream and when the smoke cleared away, I saw the form of Mrs. Jenkins lying on the floor. I did not see her before the gun was discharged.[16]

Martin Albert Glass was arrested for the murder of his brother, George W. Glass, in June 1902. A Boston insanity expert examined him as to his mental condition as his attorney based his defense on insanity. County Solicitor Scott didn't think Glass was insane when he killed his brother.[17]

Two men were indicted by the Strafford County grand jury for the murder of Miss Katherine Ryan and were jailed in the rotary section of the Strafford County Jail. Dr. Harry H. Stackpole was charged with murdering the woman, while Elmer E. Ryan was indicted as accessory before the fact in her death.[18] The case against Dr. Stackpole was dropped by the state on February 20, 1908.[19]

Escapes

There were a few escapes made from the jail during its existence, but they may not have been made from the rotary part of the jail. They were likely from other areas of the jail.

One of the escapes was a mystery. No one has solved the mysterious escape of a man named McArthur, a horse thief. He was an inmate in the rotary section of the jail until he began to complain of leg troubles. Then he was placed in the women's quarters, a more pleasant part of the jail outside the rotary section. During this time, his meals were carried to him by Jailer Frank Libbey. One day Libbey received a call and had to go out of town, so his youngest daughter was to take McArthur meals to him. When she carried his meal in, the room was vacant. Presumably he left though the window. When he could not be found, many people claimed he must have had outside help because his leg was bandaged and not in good condition. McArthur couldn't have safely jumped from the window, nor could he have walked very far by himself. The mystery was never solved.[20]

Julius Arthur Simpson escaped from the Strafford County Jail on July 17, 1891. He was implicated in a murder. He was a former Baptist minister turned burglar, horse thief, forger and bigamist.[21]

An escape attempt was foiled in June 1895 when Jailer Hayes accidently discovered two window bars nearly sawed off and other evidence of a plot for a wholesale jail escape. Suspicion pointed to Fred Davis and Silva Tatro, two notorious criminals. Davis was allowed some freedom in the corridor and the pastime of sweeping the jail floor by the kindhearted jailer. Both were closely confined after the discovery.[22]

A prisoner escaped officers while he was being returned to the Strafford County Jail. R.W. Burley slipped his handcuffs and escaped from Deputies Cushman and Seavey. The deputies couldn't chase after Burley as they had to watch the other twenty-two inmates they were transporting. Burley jumped from the barge in which they were being moved and cut across a vacant lot. He was later captured by the Dover Police in Durham when he went to see a mother and her child. He had been arraigned in the Supreme Court on the charge of breaking and entering.[23]

Three prisoners sawed their way to freedom from the Strafford County Jail on January 21, 1906. They used a plank to scale the high walls and get out of jail. The three men were confined in the walk and not the revolving rotary jail. Thirty-two other inmates in the walk decided not to follow the trio. The inmates had been given the liberty of the walk near dark. The men who escaped were being held on breaking-and-entering charges. They were William Hanna of Lynn, Massachusetts, and John Rogers and Cleophas Vallie of Portsmouth. The three men had difficulty in sawing three of the bars, so they bent them outward in order to squeeze through and drop to the ground, some ten feet below. They then found a plank, placed it against the wall and then climbed to liberty. Rogers and Vallie were recaptured on January 22.[24] A couple of days after the escape, two others were charged with aiding Rogers' escape. Elmore Grenier was charged with concealing and hiding Rogers, while his sister, Rosie Grenier, was charged with furnishing him a steel saw to make the escape.[25]

An escaped convict was recaptured by Sheriff George W. Parker and returned to the Dover Jail in early July 1906. Michael Cummings had escaped from the jail on June 17. He was recaptured at the Cochecho city railroad station. Cummings had but a week to serve on his sentence for breaking and entering a house in Rochester.[26]

Other Criminals

On March 10, 1900, a mother was charged with assault with intent to kill her baby and was placed in the Strafford County Jail when she could not post bail. Mrs. Mary S. Fredette was accused of the crime after her baby was found buried in a snow bank behind a billboard that screened a vacant lot. The child was barely alive when the discovery was made, but recovered and likely survived. The woman, who is only eighteen, abandoned the child because her husband refused to life with her unless she disposed of the child.[27]

An assistant cashier of the Cochecho National Bank was convicted of embezzlement and was given a five-year sentence. Harry Hough would serve the first year in the Strafford County Jail and the remaining four years in the jail at Manchester. He was convicted of stealing $10,000 from the bank.[28] Hough's attorney had requested that he serve out the rest of his five-year sentence in the Strafford County Jail in October 1900. He had been incarcerated in the jail for a year and was supposed to be transferred to the state penitentiary.[29]

A man who was released from state prison in Massachusetts in May 1907 was arrested again by Dover authorities on the expiration of his term and put in the Strafford County Jail to face charges of stealing a horse from Hon. J. Frank Seavey of Dover in 1901. Thomas Coleman had served a term for stealing a horse in Massachusetts. He also served a term in prison in Maine.[30]

Arthur Marcoux was arrested and interred in the Strafford County Jail without bail on June 16, 1907, after he nearly killed his nineteen-year-old sweetheart, Miss Annie Drapeau. He attacked her in the woods and left her for dead.[31]

Suicides

A prisoner committed suicide in the Strafford County Jail on May 29, 1895. Augustus Buckman cut his throat with a razor, which he borrowed from a prisoner in the cell next to him. Buckman was about sixty years old and was sent to the jail from Rochester five weeks before awaiting the action of a grand jury on the charge of improper conduct.[32]

An inmate tried to commit suicide while in the Dover Jail in February 1906. Frank S. Brewer tried to cut his throat with a jack knife while in jail for trying to sell stolen chickens. Brewer had been caught just before Christmas at the Boston and Main railroad station. He was indicted by the Strafford County grand jury.[33]

The Jail Today

The present day Strafford County Jail was built in 2003 and can hold more than four hundred prisoners, according to Captain Weisgarber.

Daviess County Jail—
Gallatin, Missouri

Gallatin was first settled in 1837 and named after Albert Gallatin, the only Secretary of the Treasury to serve under two presidents—Thomas Jefferson and James Madison. Daviess County had been established the year before and Gallatin became the county seat.[1]

The first Daviess County Jail was constructed in Gallatin in 1841. The two-story structure was made of logs and served the county until 1858. It was called the "pit" jail. The second county jail was built of stone and was located in the northwest corner of the public square in the county seat of Gallatin. Plans were laid for this jail in 1856 and the building was put to use on November 15, 1858, at a cost of $3,300.[2]

By the 1860s, lawlessness had reached new heights with criminal gangs including the James Brothers. Frank James killed Captain Sheets, a cashier at the bank in Gallatin during a robbery on December 7, 1868. After the crime, Jesse James's horse ran away from him. A constable caught up with him and said, "You are my prisoner." Jesse put a revolver to the constable's head and the officer threw up his hands. Jesse then jumped on Frank's horse and they rode off. Later they met up with a farmer on a horse and stole the horse out from under him. Frank was brought to Gallatin for trial in 1882 for the murder of Captain Sheets as well as two other murders. He was accused of murdering Frank McMillian of Wilton, Iowa, and Conductor Westfall during a Winston, Missouri, robbery on July 15, 1881.[3] He spent nearly a year awaiting trial in the Gallatin jail until he was taken to St. Louis for trial on the murder of Westfall and Sheets in November 1883.[4] The following year all the cases against Frank James were dismissed. Interestingly, Jesse James once wrote a letter to the editor of the *Kansas City Times*, saying he'd turn himself in for trial to any place in Missouri, except Gallatin.[5]

Then in 1885, a grand jury condemned both the jail and the courthouse, so plans were made to build a new jail and courthouse. Plans for a third jail were discussed in April 1885 by a committee of three members: William M. Bosafoh, A.M. Irving and Thomas Yates. However, an election on October 6, 1885, failed to gain majority approval for the new construction of a jail.[6]

However, after the jail was consumed by fire the next year, county commissioners approved the planning for a new jail on March 23, 1886. Irving was appointed as a special commissioner to supervise the erection of a new jail and jailer's quarters. Irving proposed a rotary jail to be built by the Pauly Jail Building and Manufacturing Company of St. Louis, Missouri. The initial plan for the rotary stated that the jail would provide better protection for the sheriff in handling prisoners, better lighting, better ventilation, more security from fire, and better sanitation. He also wanted an additional system of cells to be used for the detention of prisoners for less than $1,000 each. The court accepted the report on March 1, 1887, and ordered the jail built on land donated by the City of Gallatin on part of the Richards Block along West Jackson Street.[7]

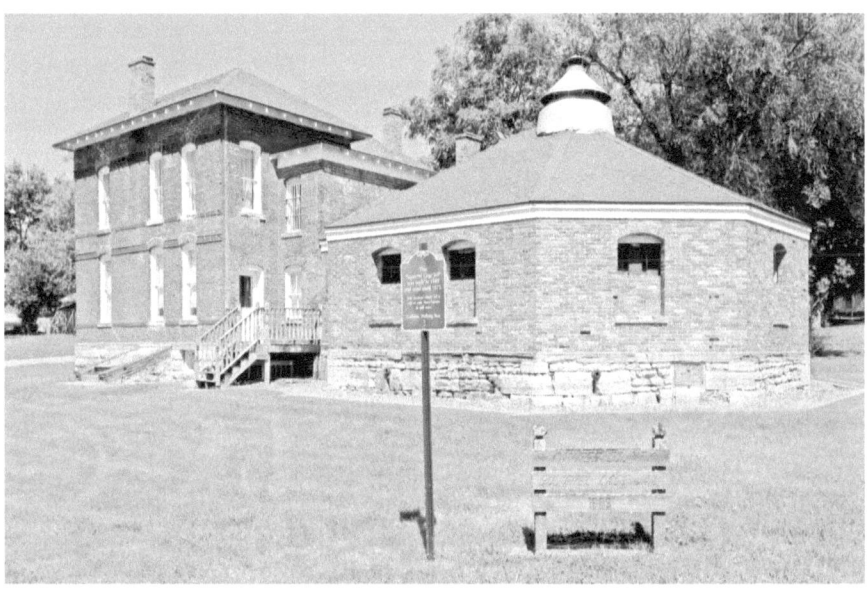

The old Daviess County Jail was placed on the National Register of Historic Places on February 23, 1990, in Gallatin (author photograph).

The design was the same as the other rotary jails built up to that time, but some minor changes were made to the locking device and the gear mechanism. It contained eight cells that were secured with steel bars. Each cell had two metal beds on the left side of the cell. Straw mattresses were used originally used for bedding. Cells were eight-feet tall and seven-and-a-half feet long with the toilet opening in the rear. The octagon shaped brick jail had small windows with iron grating for security and for lighting as the facility had no electricity. The top of the jail had a large air ventilation vane and smoke stack. The jail also featured wide fascia board.[8]

Connected to the rotary jail was the two-story sheriff's residence. It was separated by a steel door, so that no inmates could enter the residence even if they escaped from the rotary. The sheriff's residence also contained two cells for women or juveniles located on the second floor. The toilet in the cells was a round hole cut in the floor. The irregularly shaped sheriff's residence was made of brick in an Italianate motif design. The win-

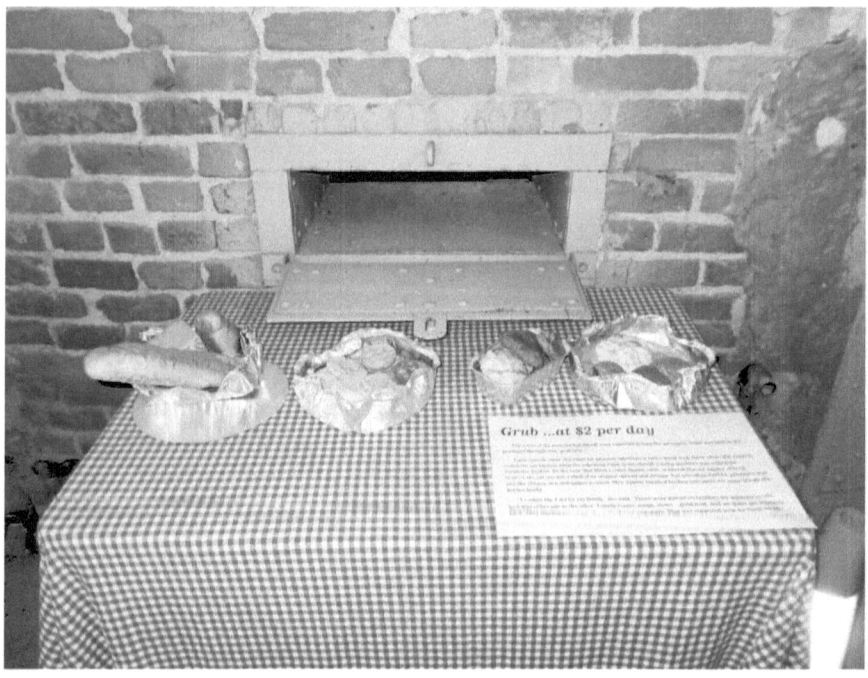

Meals for inmates were shoved into the rotary jail using this "grub hole"—a security measure for the sheriff's wife, who prepared the meals (author photograph).

dows had iron grating for security. The house was built with two brick chimneys at the roof's southern slope. The kitchen was located on the first floor. The sheriff's wife would make meals for the prisoners and pass the meals into the cells through a "grub hole" into the corridor of the rotary jail. From there it was passed into the individual cells. In this manner, the wife wasn't exposed to the inmates. Prisoners were fed once a day in the early days of the jail, according to Trudi Burton, curator Daviess County Historical Society. "I cooked like I did for the family," said Mary Louise Appley, wife of Sheriff Harold Appley, the last sheriff to reside in the house and cook for the prisoners in the jail.[9]

In its original state, the jail worked like a lazy Susan where pie-shaped cells sat on a turntable. The cells and turntable were surrounded by a stationary circular wall of iron bars. The jailer used a hand crank to turn the rotary and the cells were lined up to a single entrance door in the outer stationary cell, which was operated only by the jailer.[10]

Work on the rotary jail commenced in October 1887. When completed by the following year, the Daviess County Jail had room for nineteen inmates and cost $11,261.15 to build.[11]

The rotary worked well, but sometimes adjustments were needed. Balance adjustments were made manually using a wrench on four arms underneath the squirrel cage. Jailers usually balked at such maintenance due to the extremely tight crawl space in the area often raw with sewage.[12]

During the summer months, the structure would become extremely hot and inmates would wrap their hands around the steel bars to cool themselves. As a result, several inmates got their fingers and hands caught when the rotary moved, explained curator Burton. However, there are no recorded injuries. She also explained that inmates weren't provided any toilet paper in the early days. In 1920 Gallatin put in a new sewer service, and the jail's toilet facilities were updated accordingly.[13]

The jail had no bathing facilities, so a large tub of water was brought in occasionally for the inmates to bathe with their clothes left on thus washing their bodies and clothes at the same time. This was done especially before the circuit court judge visited the facility, so that the inmates wouldn't "smell so bad to the judge," explained the curator.[14]

By the 1950s, the rotary jail was still usable, but in need of some repairs. As the population of the county decreased at times the jail contained only one prisoner. The turntable continually caused the jailers no end of problems, as the heavy floor caused the gear system to break down.

After a time, the sheriff had to turn the jail like a top, literally putting his shoulder to the wheel to move it. By the early 1960s, the county had enough of the rotary contraption. A fierce debate raged in the county between those who thought the jail was unfit for human occupation and those who thought it should be kept intact because of its historic value. In the end, economics outweighed sentiment. The county just couldn't afford to build a new jail.[15]

At that time the county only had funds for the sheriff and a part-time deputy. So, the sheriff's wife kept the books, did the jail work, and took care of the dispatching. Most of the prisoners were local people. But that began to change when the interstate highway was completed. The jail bordered on being a place of cruel and unusual punishment. The pie-shaped cells were small. The cots had no sheets—blankets only were used. There was almost no ventilation, and the iron floor was cold enough to drain the body of heat. Bathing facilities were located in the outer circle. Prisoners ran the risk of amputation if their arms were hanging through the bars when the cells were rotated. And the single exit and need to rotate the cells made the jail a death trap should the place catch on fire. In 1964 the state condemned the jail as a fire hazard, so the inner circle of ironworks were removed and scrapped. The configuration of the rotary section of the jail was partitioned in half with male inmates housed on the east side and women on the west side. Beds were put in what used to be the corridors.[16]

The final straw came on November 1, 1974, when County Sheriff Appley condemned the rotary jail as being unfit to receive prisoners. Before this Circuit Judge Kenneth Lewis had refused to place prisoners in the Daviess County Jail for many months. In a letter to Presiding Judge Robert Owings, the sheriff stated: "Due to the present condition of the Daviess County Jail, which does not, in my opinion, meet any of the suggested minimum standards of county, state or federal jail committees as to health and sanitation, ventilation, lighting, prisoner safety, visiting facilities and the impossibility of a continual supervision of the prisoners, I feel it my duty, not only for my own personal liability but that of any prisoners, to condemn this jail as of November 1, 1975, until such time as reasonable quarters can be provided for incarceration of suspected, apprehended or convicted violators of the law."[17] A few days later, the sheriff and his wife were eating dinner when a snake fell out of the dining room ceiling.[18] The sheriff's residence was still used for local radio dispatching for several years to come.[19]

The Daviess County Commissioners offered to donate the rotary jail to the Daviess County Historical Society in May 1986. The historical society wanted to do a study on the costs involved in renovating the jail. The study showed that many repairs were needed and project to restore it would take community support as the costs exceeded the financial limits of the society. The repairs needed included a new roof and replacement of water-damaged rafters in the jail area of the building. The rock foundation would need repair in two areas. The basement steps would have to be replaced. The electric wiring would have to be replaced. Gas lines would have to be buried. The structure was officially deeded to the society later in 1986.[20] The historical society then made repairs to the rotary jail in the early 1990s. The squirrel cage was rebuilt by inmates at Western Missouri Correctional Center in Cameron. Afterwards, the cellblock could once again be rotated like is used when it was a functional jail. Now it is turned for special events like Halloween, when the jail is turned into a haunted house to raise money for its maintenance. The museum also has exhibits on the James brothers and other important historical characters in the area.[21]

A total of 17 Daviess County sheriffs used the rotary jail. They were:

1888: Gabe W. Cox	1930: Frank Sweany
1890: O.P. Walters	1934: W.T. Hutchison
1892: E.S. Lankford	1938: Frank Sweany
1896: William A. Johnson	1942: Harry Reeder
1900: R.D. McCray	1946: Frank Sweany
1904: William T. Hutchison	1954: A.F. Clements, Jr.
1908: J.A. Blair	1958: S.L. Houghton
1920: J. Frank Gildow	1970: Harold Appley
1926: B.B. Houghton	

The society decided to put the building on the National Register of Historic Places, so a lengthy application was completed. On February 23, 1990, the Daviess County Rotary Jail and Sheriff's Residence was listed in the National Register of Historic Places.[22]

Nowadays, the jail is open for tours by contacting the Daviess County Historical Society. Security cameras were recently added to protect the contents of the historical society in the jail.[23]

Murderers

A Mexican man was thrown in the Daviess County Jail after he killed a black man as the result of a card game in April 1890. John Moore attacked

James Trosper with a beer bottle. He then dragged him out in the alley and dumped him. The sheriff and another man took the black man to another place where he could be treated by doctors, but he died anyways. Moore was arrested and put in the Daviess County Jail.[24]

A twelve-year-old boy begged to be jailed after killing a fourteen-year-old butcher with a knife in February 1908. John Dougherty had been allowed to go home to wait trial in April because of his age. The boy was returned to the Daviess County Jail and asked to be locked up for the murder. "I just can't stay at home any longer," Dougherty begged the jailer. "Won't you please lock me up?" The jailer complied.[25]

A former Gallatin city clerk was convicted of second-degree murder on October 14, 1920. Hugh Y. Tarwater had murdered Wesley L. Robertson, the veteran publisher of the *Gallatin Democrat*, on December 23, 1919. The newspaper had printed stories alleging drunkenness on Tarwater's part. Tarwater went to publisher's office to talk him about a libel suit. Tarwater's defense was insanity and self-defense. He was put in the Gallatin County Jail in February and lost some eighty pounds by the time of the trial.[26]

A woman received the minimum sentence for stabbing her husband to death in March 1938. Bertha Leisure of Trenton was found guilty and had to pay a $100 fine but only had to serve three months in the Daviess County Jail.[27]

Orville "Ink" Ware's murder case was moved to Daviess Circuit Court in May 1953 as a result of change of venue. He was housed in the Gallatin rotary jail until he could be tried for the murder of Lawrence "Sonny" Lewis. The murder occurred on December 4, 1951, at the climax of a card game dispute. The first-degree murder charge resulted from a disagreement between the two, which ended when Lewis went home and returned with a .38 caliber revolver. Ware declared that Lewis fired at him five times and missed each time. Then Ware fired once with a .16-guage shotgun and killing Lewis.[28]

A Daviess Circuit Court found William "Bill" Hampton guilty of second-degree murder and set his punishment at ten years imprisonment. Hampton shot and fatally wounded Richard "Teeny" Black at Saale's Tavern in Chillicothe on May 4, 1959. Hampton had been in the Daviess County Jail since January when his case was moved from Livingston County on a change of venue.[29]

The last murderer housed in the Daviess County Jail was a man who was found guilty of second-degree murder on March 19, 1970. Cletus Edward "Bill" Whiteaker of Cameron was given a ten-year sentence in February 1971 and sent to the state penitentiary. He spent some time after the murder in the rotary jail before he was sent to the Livingston County Jail when his case was given a change of venue. Whiteaker was found guilty of murdering his wife, Berry Whiteaker, forty-three, after a quarrel outside the Submarine tavern in Gallatin. Mrs. Whiteaker had got into an argument with two other ladies in the tavern. They left the tavern and took the discussion to a car parked outside. Then Mr. Whiteaker arrived and shot out the front window of the car. He then dragged his wife from the car and shot her during a scuffle. She fell to the pavement as her husband bend down and fired a second shot at her head from close range. She died almost instantly. Curtis Kohler of Climax Springs, Missouri, heard the shots from inside the tavern and rushed outside to see Mrs. Whiteaker on the pavement. He approached and yelled at Mr. Whiteaker, who turned and fired his .38-calibre pistol at Kohler. The bullet whizzed past Kohler's head. Kohler then wrestled the gun away from Mr. Whiteaker and held him at gunpoint until Sheriff Harold Appley arrived. The trial revealed that Mr. Whiteaker had said before he killed his wife, "If I can't have you."[30]

Escapes

There were a couple of incidents in which prisoners silently managed to remove enough of the brick walls and gain access to other areas of the jail or the outside until they were caught.

Two men bored a hole through the brick wall to escape from the Daviess County Jail in February 1890. William Clark, a horse thief, and forger Jim Johnson used a case knife and a fire poker to break though the wall and escape.[31]

Two men sawed their way out of the Daviess County Jail in August 1898. They sawed the iron bolts in their cell and the outside windows of the jail to escape. Five other prisoners confined there decided not to escape.[32]

Two men serving a ninety-day sentence for carrying concealed weapons managed to escape from the Daviess County Jail in January 1899. Ed Conley and Adam Brown from Pattonsburg cut their way through like a rat through a cracker box and escaped. This jail escape prompted a grand jury investigation, and condemnation of the jail as "unsafe for the safe keeping of prisoners." The county court approved the condemnation, but provided no means for repair.[33]

On December 27, 1921, Stanley Benton and Leonard Hopper escaped from the Gallatin County Jail, according to original jail logs.

Jess Lipps escaped twice from the Daviess County Jail in April 1925. Each time he was recaptured.[34]

Two men tripped the lock on their cell door and climbed through a hole in the roof to make good their escape from the Daviess County Jail in September 1929. Rewards were offered for the apprehension of Roscoe Johnson and Clifford Kerns.[35]

Then on January 24, 1931, two men escaped from the Gallatin County Jail, but they were apprehended less than a week later near Parnell. Alfred Roach and Albert Letta were recaptured by Nodaway County deputies at a nearby farm. They had pried the sheet metal off the roof of their jail celling to flee. Roach was in jail on a charge of stealing geese along with his wife.[36]

Three men escaped from the Daviess County Jail on August 31, 1967. The jail was not being guarded at the time of the escape, because Sheriff Leland Houghton and his wife were visiting a hospitalized deputy in St. Joseph at the time of the break. The escapees used a steel rod to break through the outer wall of the cellblock. They then stole a car which had been impounded during the investigation of another case. However, they were recaptured by Missouri State troopers in Liberty within an hour of the break.[37]

The last escape occurred in September 1970 after the jail was reconfigured and the rotary no longer worked. Wilburn Earl McAfee, twenty-two, managed to pry his way through the roof of the jail about the time the beauty contest crowd came out of the auditorium across the street. He was seen briefly on the roof, but witnesses thought him to be a prankster and he made his escape out of town. Police officers searched for him all night and he was apprehended him while he was hitchhiking on Highway 13 near Jameson by Marshal Doug Roberts. Roberts was Gallatin's night marshal and just happened to be on his way home from duty. McAfee was in jail on a charge of disturbing the peace. A felony charge for jailbreak was added to his charges.[38]

A Suicide

One prisoner killed himself by taking poison in the Daviess County Jail on May 29, 1941. Glenn Reynolds, 22, of Pattonsburg, Missouri, was being held on a statutory charge. He was visited by his wife the day before and she had just given birth to a daughter.[39]

Other Criminals

A former police judge pled guilty to the fraudulent use of the mail and was given a three-month sentence in the Daviess County Jail on September 23, 1920. John W. Everman, a prominent Gallatin stockman, implored Judge Arba S. Van Valkenburg to fine him and not humiliate him with a jail sentence.[40]

A mob attacked and severely beat a banker in Jamesport, Missouri, before he was put in a car and rushed to the Daviess County Jail for safe keeping in February 1925. Former depositors of the closed bank thought that George B. Koch, the former president of the closed People's Exchange Bank, was trying to escape. A grand jury indicted him on grand larceny.[41]

During Prohibition (1920–33) many people were arrested and jailed for federal alcohol offenses, including the making of moonshine, transporting or possession of alcohol, and drunk and disorderly. For example, Bert Shellman was found guilty of illegal possession and was sentenced to eight months in the Gallatin Jail and fined $200 in May 1923. During the same month, John Campbell was given four months in jail and a fine of $300 for the manufacture of alcohol.[42]

Some of the last inmates in the Daviess County Jail were arrested after robbing the Tradin' Post on February 26, 1975. Two men had entered the store on Highway 6 and asked for a bottle of liquor. Owner Everette Linville reached to pick the bottle off the shelf and felt the barrel of a pistol on his neck. The men took the cash from the register and some cash from Linville's billfold. They also stole a .22 caliber rifle. Linville called the sheriff, who then put out a call to State Police. Trooper Richard Johnson and Sergeant Myron Garrett spotted the car and stopped it. There were four adults and a child in the car. The adults were taken to the Daviess County Jail. Judge Charles Brandom set the bond at $5,000 and the adults couldn't meet the bond, so they were put back into jail. The four were

Steven Lee Andrews, Richey Junior Tew, and Mrs. Donna Fay Hurst of Tulsa, Oklahoma, and Sandra Sue Smith of Weatherby.[43]

The Jail Today

Nowadays, Daviess and DeKalb counties have joined forces to open the Daviess/DeKalb County Regional Jail, which is located in Pattonsburg, Missouri. It has two buildings that have a capacity of more than two hundred inmates.[44]

Pueblo County Jail— Pueblo, Colorado

Pueblo's roots can be traced back to 1842 when the small Fort Pueblo was established. Then Pueblo County was organized in 1862. In the early days of Pueblo County, there was no jail and prisoners were detained in whatever makeshift quarters that were available at the moment. In 1868, a citizen by the name of R.N. Daniels built a stone structure in downtown Pueblo and rented to the county as a jail. Apparently it was poorly constructed, as escapes were frequent. After several months, the county commissioners erected a brick building on the courthouse square. The cells were made of planks that were spiked together and fitted with iron doors. The place was unfit for any human being to live in, the ventilation being defective so the odor was horrible, and in addition the bed bugs were numerous. In the early 1870s, Pueblo County built a two-story jail on the west portion of the courthouse block. This made it convenient for the sheriff to bring the inmates to court for trial. Then Colorado became a state on August 1, 1876.[1]

Meanwhile, the town of Pueblo built a one-story adobe jail located on North Santa Fe Avenue.[2] Several prisoners were confined in the Pueblo city jail in 1875 in conjunction with a missing man by the name of William Vance. A reward of $100 was offered for the recovery of Vance dead or alive.[3] Two years later silver was discovered and the Colorado Silver Boom began happening, bringing more people to the state and increasing unlawfulness.[4]

In 1886 or 1887 the county commissioners decided it was time for a new jail. They awarded a contract to the Pauly Jail Building Company of St. Louis to build a rotary jail. The commissioners accepted the plans for the new jail drawn up by E.P. Milhofer of the Pauly Company on July 30, 1888. The location would be at 1501 Martin in the northwest part of Pueblo on high ground, providing an excellent view of all parts of the city. The building would be three stories high, sixty-three feet wide and one hundred and eighteen feet in length. The exterior would be brick with stone trimmings. The roof would be wooden and covered by slate. The basement would be reserved for a dungeon for lunatics as well as the fuel and boiler rooms, a kitchen, a bakery, a storeroom, and a cellar. All windows would have iron window guards. A dumb waiter would carry food to all parts of the jail. The sheriff's and jailer's office would be located on the first floor in addition to the employees' dining and sleeping rooms. Entrances to these rooms would be through a large vestibule in the middle of the building. The second story would contain a solitary cell, a hospital cell for males, sixteen steel cells capable of holding four persons each, and the second story of the rotary jail. The third story would contain the hospital cell for women and sixteen cells like the ones on the second floor for juveniles and misdemeanor inmates. The new jail would contain thirty-seven steel cells. The cells would be made with steel plate with patent steel bar grates and escape was impossible. The rotary section would contain twenty pie-shaped cells on two levels. In the center of the ventilating space a stationary hollow cast iron shaft or stack would be placed. The ventilating space would contain a complete scientific system of water supply and sewer drainage. The rotating of the cells would be done by a system of shafts and gears, operated and controlled from the jailer's office. At the bottom of the cells projecting parts would be attached to the rear of the cells, extending toward the central shaft. These arms, rollers and rim keep the rotation true. The circular grating would have an opening at the front giving access from any cell to the prisoner's corridor when the opening of the cells was brought opposite. While admitting the prisoners to and from cells thru the vestibule, the jailer was protected by partition grating. The side doors of the prisoner's corridor, partition door and the sliding steel door were all controlled by the jailer's vestibule. Each cell was two-feet by six-inches wide at the rear to seven-feet-six-inches wide at the front, eight feet deep from front to rear and eight-feet high. The rear of the cells had a plate niche placed and secured into place with suitable holes in seats, fitting to hoppers. The niches were one-foot-nine-inches wide by three-feet high. Escape was impossible.[5]

Final contracts were awarded on September 6, 1888. The total price for the new jail was about $80,000. Work was completed exactly a year later and all fifty-nine prisoners from the old jail were marched to the new jail by Sheriff T.G. McCarthy. The prisoners ranged from men convicted of petty larceny all the way up to those convicted of murder. They were placed in cells on the second and third floors and not the rotary jail, which was not quite ready. A few weeks later, the rotary cellblock was completed and some of the inmates were interred there.[6]

The city continued to run a jail, but it was not very secure and escapes were common. Once two inmates were seized from the jail by a lynch mob and hanged. A mob of armed citizens came to the city jail and removed two Mexicans by force. Then they took them to the Fourth Street Bridge where they hanged both of them. The two unnamed prisoners had been charged with murder earlier in the day on September 13, 1919.[7]

In May 1927, Federal Attorney George Stephan asked the federal district court for an order transferring between twenty and thirty prisoners from the Pueblo County Jail to the Denver bastille, because two federal prisoners had escaped from the Pueblo jail within a week. One of the prisoners was James Tracey, a narcotic suspect being held for the grand jury. The other was Wilbur Haskett, who was serving a nine-month sentence for violating the prohibition law. Twenty-four prisoners were later moved to Denver.[8]

Also in 1927, a Pueblo Grand Jury condemned the use of the rotary jail, but finances to replace the jail were not available at that time. This decision spelled the end for the rotary section of the jail and the county commissioners started making plans to replace it. They eventually decided to remove the rotary jail section and replace it with cells. An article in the *Pueblo Chieftain* called the rotary jail an "archaic torture chamber used in the early days." The positive feature of the rotary jail was that no prisoner ever escaped from the rotary section during its use. The rotary section was removed by the Bernstein Brothers Metal Company in 1931.[9]

The jail continued to be used without the rotary section until the 1960s. A consulting architect once described the structure as "the only jail I know of that wore a girdle." He was referring to the steel beams and bars that had been installed on the outside of the building to keep the outside bricks from collapsing.[10]

In October 1968, the old Pueblo County Jail went up for sale to the public. Bids were accepted until November 7. Only two bids were received for the jail, so the county commissioners were looking for more bidders. The old jail was referred to as a "shocking monstrosity" by the Pueblo County Board of Visitors.[11] After another round of bidding, the old jail was sold to the Rabbi Nathanial Pollack in December for $2,400. Workmen began removing the steel bars and cells. The steel was sold as scrap with half of the salvage profits going to Pueblo County.[12]

In 2012 the Pueblo County Sheriff's Office Detention Center housed an average of five hundred and forty-five offenders on daily basis. The facilities hold individuals arrested on misdemeanor and felony charges and about one third of its population is sentenced to serve their time in the jail.

Murderers

Two men were shot to death by another man at a dance in Salt Creek the night of November 23, 1901. Antonia Tata was arrested for the murders and placed in the Pueblo County Jail since the crime was committed in Pueblo County. Tata was the master of ceremonies for the dance. After he was attacked by the two other men, he pulled out a gun and shot Farris Gonzales three times and Jose Martinez twice. Both were killed instantly.[13]

A duel between two men left one dead and the other interred in the Pueblo County Jail on October 20, 1902. Yard foreman W.S. Bailey killed his assistant, A.W. Wilson, in a duel with revolvers. The two men had an old grudge and decided to fight it out. Standing about fifteen feet apart, the two men exchanged bitter words before drawing their revolvers. Wilson was too slow and Bailey's revolver cracked with the bullet ripping into Wilson's side. Wilson turned and ran about a hundred feet before falling dead.[14]

A Dr. C.O. Rice shot and killed policeman Silas Martz and was put in the rotary jail, according to *The Coffeyville Daily Journal*, October 10, 1903.

A former county treasurer was killed in the Trinidad post office by a local politician on April 8, 1905. Joseph Johnson shot John H. Fox in the back of the head while he was reading a letter. Johnson immediately surrendered to Sheriff Davis and was put in the local jail under strong guard as a mob of about a thousand people formed with the avowed purpose of lynching the murderer. Johnson was put on a train to Pueblo to be housed in the county jail to avoid the hanging.[15]

The night jailer was nearly killed by a prisoner in the rotary jail on

April 16, 1908. Jeff Steel was found lying unconscious on the floor of the Pueblo County Jail suffering severe head wounds. The evidence pointed to Ed McDonald, an African American. McDonald was serving a short sentence for petit larceny. Deputy Sheriff Sam Fabrizio found a key and a piece of pipe behind a radiator close the rotary cell of McDonald. Close investigation showed that there was foot tracks from the door of the rotary cell to the radiator.[16]

A man eventually confessed to killing another man in a cold case and was incarcerated in the Pueblo County Jail on November 9, 1908. Cleveland "Smoky" Nunn had been under suspicion for a long time in the choking death of Thurman Walker. Walker's decomposed body was discovered in the Arkansas River on September 12 with a leather strap drawn tightly around his neck. Nunn claimed self-defense, but said he shot Walker to death, which conflicted with the evidence found. Robbery was thought to be the motive to the crime, since Nunn was originally arrested for forgery of a check belonging to Walker.[17] Nunn was sentenced to life imprisonment at hard labor in the state penitentiary. Judge Essex declared: "This case presents one of the most cold-blooded murders ever tried in the courts of Colorado."[18]

A man wanted for murder in California ended up in the Pueblo County Jail and was identified in 1909. C.C. Collins was using an alias, Charley Barr, when he was put in the jail. Detective Sergeant Joseph Redmond worked with San Francisco officials to uncover the identity of the man. Barr would likely be sent to California for killing Deputy Sheriff William Larkin there after serving a fourteen-year sentence in the Colorado penitentiary in Colorado for a holdup.[19]

A man was placed in the Pueblo County Jail for safekeeping after causing a train wreck, which killed the engineer and injured many passengers. Tom Gerbrick, thirty-eight, pleaded guilty before Judge J. Ed Rizer in district court to the crime of causing the wreck of the Santa Fe limited No. 6 at the Apishapa Bridge seven years before. Gerbrick used nitroglycerine to blow up the train. The judge gave him a sentence of thirty to forty years. "That's an awful jolt," muttered Gerbrick after the sentence was pronounced on September 15, 1910. He had expected a twenty-year sentence. After a short stay in Pueblo, he would be taken to the state penitentiary to serve out his sentence.[20]

The Colorado governor commuted sentences of two men in the Pueblo County Jail the day before they were scheduled to be hanged.

171

Governor Oliver Henry Nelson Shoupe decided to save the lives of Clifford Sprouls and Cruis Romero. Sprouls had been found guilty of killing W.W. Green. Romero was found guilty of participating in the murder of a Mexican rancher.[21]

A murder suspect was captured on August 8, 1919, in the Green Horn range foothills forty miles south of Pueblo. "Rufe" King was arrested for the disappearance of Reuben Gutshall at Maple Hill, Kansas. He was placed in the Pueblo County Jail until he could be extradited, although he said he would go to Kansas willingly without any extradition papers.[22]

Brothers tried to emulate bad men of bygone days. One brother ended up nearly dead and the other landed in jail looking at a twenty-to-thirty year sentence in August 1926. Leslie and Forrest Gonce held up Under Sheriff Daniels and Deputy Sheriff Fiscus when the sheriffs attempted to arrest the brothers. A posse was formed to search for the fleeing boys. The twenty-one-year-old Forrest was taken into custody without a fight after relatives tipped off police on the boy's whereabouts. However, his younger fourteen-year-old brother reached in his shirt for a revolver and was shot three times by the deputy sheriff.[23] Leslie survived the shooting and the bullets were left in his body.[24]

Escapes

In a strange scenario, a man playing the violin helped four men escape from the Pueblo County Jail. The jailer had let one inmate play the violin during the evening and while he performed four prisoners sawed off a portion of the window casing, worked a big stone out of place and were able to escape.[25]

Thirteen prisoners made their escape from the Pueblo County Jail by sawing a hole through the roof with a steel shoe shank the night of May 4, 1889. Only one of the men was recaptured.[26]

A woman who disguised herself as an African American nurse carrying a dummy baby attempted an escape from authorities. Mrs. Allie Garvin was arrested at the Santa Fe Depot by Deputy Sheriff John Scofield and Patrolman H.D. Harper and placed in the Pueblo County Jail. The woman was originally arrested November 9, 1906, on a charge of bigamy and put in jail to await trial. However, she was sent to St. Francis Hospital on November 16 for an illness thought to be an appendicitis. To escape authorities and conceal her identity, she blackened her face and made up materials to look like a baby in her arms. Garvin's sister also helped her in the escape. A hack driver alerted police to the attempted escape via train. Her sister was also charged with abetting a fugitive from justice. Both were put in the women's cell at the county lockup. Her husband is already in the county jail on a sixty-day sentence for nonsupport.[27]

A guard was credited with stopping a jailbreak from the Pueblo County Jail when he fired shots at the escapee on December 27, 1919. Inmate James R. Jewell, alias Sam Green, was seriously wounded by the shot. Turnkey Ed Coates was badly beaten by the prisoners before help arrived.[28]

Using a spoon, two men escaped from the Pueblo County Jail on August 17, 1921. Earl Dyer and Raymond Woods, who were awaiting trial on burglary and grand larceny charges, tunneled out of the jail using only a spoon to dig a hole through the solid brick wall and gain freedom. Two men answering their descriptions boarded a freight train to make good their escape.[29]

Two federal prisoners were able to escape from the Pueblo County Jail on May 12, 1927. One of those prisoners was James Tracey, a narcotic suspect. He was able to put on a coat and walk out of the jail when nobody was looking. Another of those prisoners was Wilbur Haskett, who was serving a nine-month sentence for violation of the prohibition law. He escaped by breaking the lock on his cell and when someone brought him a suit of clothing. The event triggered the U.S. district attorney to declare the jail unsafe.[30]

Suicides

While awaiting trial for petit larceny, L.M. Ball took matters into his own hands and hanged himself in his cell in the Pueblo County Jail on January 11, 1895. He used a dog chain to complete the job. He had been accused of stealing things from his own employer. He was going to get married in the near future.[31]

Mack B. Cart, a railway switchman, became despondent in the Pueblo County Jail and attempted suicide by drinking carbolic acid. Fortunately, he was saved by prompt medical aid on December 19, 1900. He was in jail for running away with another woman from his wife.[32]

Three women prisoners tried to commit suicide in the Pueblo County Jail on February 10, 1908. Ella Hosmer was the first to try to killer herself. The jail matron dropped a pair of scissors on her way out of the cell and Hosmer jabbed the sharp end into her wrist before the scissors were taken away from her. Then she seized a hat pin and tried to drive it into her heart. The pin broke. Hosmer was then carried to her steel cot and strapped down. Ollie Campbell and Annie Lee also attempted suicide by soaking the ends of parlor matches and drinking the solution. Both were saved. All had been arrested for shoplifting.[33]

Another woman tried to commit suicide in the Pueblo County Jail using bi-chloride of mercury tablets on August 2, 1913. Irene Demos was saved from death when jailers had her stomach pumped out. She and her former husband had allegedly stolen money and jewelry from her a Greek restaurant owner.[34]

Other Criminals

An entire gang was placed in the Pueblo County Jail after they were captured by Sheriff W.A. Moses. The notorious band of cattle thieves had operated for the twenty years in eastern Colorado and had stolen hundreds of cattle and horses. Bill Barren and Jim Lowe were the leaders of the gang.[35]

A former Baptist preacher was sentenced to four months in the Pueblo County Jail for unlawfully living with a woman on January 8, 1898. C.S. Rooks was living with Mary Johnson, formerly one of his flock in Nebraska. Rooks was also tarred and feathered in Kansas for similar acts.[36]

The postmistress of Pinkhampton was placed in the Pueblo County Jail for stealing money from registered letters on May 19, 1899. Mrs. Alpha T. Hendrickson was said to perfume her baths at the jail, making her the daintiest prisoner the institution has ever held.[37]

Disciplinarian J.E. Shields was murderously assaulted and the men responsible for the attack were put in the Pueblo County Jail on March 8, 1908. As the result of an outbreak of drunken Indians, the jail building was set on fire and two men narrowly escaped certain cremation.[38]

On November 8, 1927, rumors that striking miners in the southern Colorado coal field planned to free ten I.W.W. leaders from the Pueblo County Jail. When twenty-four automobile loads of strikers left Walsenburg, a report spread that they were to meet another hundred carloads of strikers to invade Pueblo and free their strike leaders. Sheriff H.C. Tiemnes immediately threw up a guard of a hundred deputies armed with shotguns, machine guns, rifles, side arms and fire hoses to remain on duty and stop the threat. However, after several hours and with nobody showing up, he sent home about half of the deputies.[39]

One of the I.W.W. strike leaders was released from Las Animas County Jail but he was rearrested and placed in the Pueblo County Jail, on November 29. Thousands of handbills had been distributed in other states calling for the miners to stop work.[40]

Newspapers usually write about criminals and their sentences, but once a Pueblo publisher was written about by many newspapers when he was convicted of income tax fraud on January 21, 1931. Frank S. Hoag received a sentence of five months in the Pueblo County Jail and a fine of $1,500. Hoag pleaded guilty to the charges and asked for probation.[41]

Safekeeping

Because the rotary jail was more secure than other jails, some men were brought there for safekeeping. Such was the case of Billy Davis, who was brought to the Pueblo County Jail after he narrowly escaped being lynched by twenty-five African Americans in January 1891. Before the mob could get hold of Davis, Sheriff Herad had the prisoner safely secured in the county bastille.[42]

Another criminal brought to the rotary jail was Benjamin Radcliffe, who was brought to the Pueblo County Jail on May 10, 1895, to insulate him from mob violence. Radcliffe had been accused of killing three school trustees for refusing to employ his daughter at the Michigan Creek schoolhouse in Park County.[43]

Two men were placed in the Pueblo County Jail for safekeeping after one of them confessed and implicated two others in the conspiracy to wreck the Florence & Cripple Creek suburban train on November 15 and 17, 1903. Charles McKinney confessed his part and said that Sherman Parker and W.B. Davis were responsible for the wrecking. Thomas Foster was also put in the county jail for his involvement. Parker and Davis, wanted felons, were also involved in the murder of two men in the Vindicator mine explosion.[44]

On October 9, 1905, a bank owner was brought to the Pueblo County rotary jail for safekeeping as depositors had made threats against his life in southern Colorado. Isaac Schiffer was placed under arrest for embezzlement and given a $100,000 bond as he awaited trial for his failed Bank of Alamosa.[45]

The United States government turned over a prisoner to the Pueblo County Jail for safekeeping until he pled guilty in district court in April 1907. A. Johnson was supposed to be housed in the Prowers County Jail, but he was moved to Pueblo due to its security and proximity to the U.S. Court in session in Pueblo. After Johnson pleaded guilty, he was sentenced to five years in the penitentiary in Leavenworth, Kansas. However, he was also wanted in Lamar for the killing of Marshal Frisbie.[46]

Then in 1909 Henry Starr, the Oklahoma-Colorado bandit, was moved to the rotary jail for safekeeping on June 10 because of a plot to liberate him from the Lamar jail. He was held on a $10,000 bond as he was charged with a bank holdup in Amity, Colorado. Sheriff Simpson had received word from pals of Starr that they would attempt to break him out of jail.[47]

Two prisoners were brought to the Pueblo County Jail due to unrest in Canon City State Prison in November 1929. Howard Royston and George Abshier, condemned members of a bank robbing gang who were scheduled for execution in February 1930, had turned to religion for comfort.[48] The pair was confined in the rotary jail until November 28 when they were whisked away to the state penitentiary to spend some time on death row until their scheduled hanging on February 15.[49]

Then the leader of the gang, Ralph Fleagle, was brought to the Pueblo County Jail on December 11, 1929, after his request for an appeal was denied. Fleagle was also scheduled to be hanged but not until March 29 for the slaying of A.N. Parish, president of the Lamar First National Bank during a holdup.[50]

Chapter Notes

Introduction

1. www.brainyquote.com/quotes/quotes/
r/richardwri392244.html.
2. "Talking of Prisons: Eminent Speakers at the Meeting in the Grand Opera House, Scenes in County Jails Are Graphically Portrayed by Secretary Hart, Gov. McGill Advocates the Suggestion for a Pardon Board, the Graded System of Convicts at St. Cloud Proves Successful," *The Saint Paul Globe*, October 22, 1888.
3. Nicholas Pevsner, A History of Building Types (Princeton: The Princeton University Press, 1976), 147.
4. *Ibid.*
5. *Ibid.*
6. Walter A. Lunden, "The Rotary Jail or Human Squirrel Cage," *Journal of the Society of Architectural Historians*. Vol. XVIII, No. 4 (December 1959: 149–150).
7. "Big Jail Delivery: 'Bill' Tackett Saws Through Iron and Steel, Eight Criminals Escape, Officers Hot on the Trail of the Fugitives," *Wichita Eagle*, February 3, 1899.
8. Chad Randl. *Revolving Architecture*, Princeton Architectural Press, New York, 2008.
9. *Ibid.*
10. *Ibid.*
11. "The New Jail," *Red Wing Daily Republican*, May 8, 1886.
12. *Ibid.*
13. *Ibid.*
14. www.brainyquote.com/quotes/quotes/
b/barbaradem325852.html.

Chapter 1

1. Application for United States Patent No. 244,358, July 12, 1881.

2. *Ibid.*
3. *Ibid.*
4. *Ibid.*
5. *Indianapolis News*, July 13, 1881.
6. Douglas K. Miller, "The Salt Lake County Rotary Jail," *Utah Historical Quarterly* 75.4, Fall 2007, 322–41.
7. Arthur Hopkins, *Prisons and Prison Buildings* (New York: Architectural Book Publishing, 1930), 46–47.
8. "No More Rotary Jails," *Wichita Beacon*, October 9, 1917.

Chapter 2

1. www.paducahky.gov/history-city-paducah.
2. "The Commonwealth," *The Courier-Journal*, October 25, 1881.
3. "The New Jail: It Is to Be Turned Over to Jailer Edwards Next Week, a Nice Batch of Prisoners Already on Hand," *The Paducah Daily News,* May 27, 1882.
4. "The New Jail," *The Paducah Daily News,* June 3, 1882.
5. "The New Jail Occupied," *The Paducah Daily News,* June 10, 1882.
6. "The Commonwealth," *The Courier-Journal*, June 29, 1882.
7. *Ibid.*
8. "Dungeon Is Being Built in County Jail Basement, Jailer Eaker Will Use It to Punish Unruly Prisoners—Brick Used in Construction," *The Paducah Evening Sun*, August 14, 1906.
9. "The Jail Report," *The Paducah Evening Sun*, September 22, 1906.
10. "Recommend New Jail for County, Physicians and Magistrates Find Old Building Unfit," *The Paducah Evening Sun*, February 23, 1910.

11. "Will Strengthen the Jail Walls, Ease with Which Prisoners Escape Shows Weakness Of Prison," *The Paducah Evening Sun*, May 25, 1910.

12. *Ibid.*

13. *Ibid.*

14. www.jailexchange.com.

15. "He Met His Doom, 'Devil' Winston Died Game in Expiation of the Horrible Murder of His Mistress, the Last Hours of the Wretch's Life, and the Tragic Details of His Untimely End," *The Paducah Evening Star*, November 19, 1897.

16. "Strung Up, Charles Hill, Who Brutally Assaulted a Young Girl, Is Taken from Jail in Paducah, Ky., and Hanged, an Armed Mob Forces the Jailer to Give Up His Keys—The Lynching Occurs in the Courthouse Yard—The Victim Makes an Appeal for His Life," *The Public Ledger*, June 10, 1892.

17. "He Met His Doom, "Devil" Winston Died Game In Expiation of the Horrible Murder of His Mistress, The Last Hours of the Wretch's Life, and the Tragic Details of His Untimely End," *The Paducah Evening Sun*, November 19, 1897.

18. "Freeman's Death in County Jail, Hiram Smedley Said Someone Took Box of Drugs from His Cell," *The Paducah Evening Sun*, November 1, 1909.

19. "Can Now Come Home, the Grand Jury Has Adjourned and the Sports May Be Happy—Criminal Term of Court Over, There Were About 16 Convictions—The Docket Disposed Of—Jail in Good Condition, Other Court News," *The Paducah Evening Sun*, September 24, 1898.

20. "Osburn's Slayer Must Serve His 2 Year Sentence, Lewis Futrell Loses Appeal from Verdict in Circuit Count," *The Paducah Evening Sun*, December 15, 1910.

21. "Tramp Moved as Victim Dies, Fulton Man's Alleged Slayer Taken to Jail at Princeton, Police Chief Lives," *The Courier-Journal*, February 6, 1930.

22. "Life Term in Prison Is Drawn by Roy Springer When Convicted of Having Slain Kentucky Merchant—Troops on Guard," *The Cincinnati Enquirer*, May 16, 1930.

23. "Man Killed, Wife Shot, Half-Brother of Woman Held in Paducah Jail," *The Courier-Journal*, May 16, 1932.

24. "Thirteen Prisoners Escape Jail, Jonas Smith, for Murder, Is Among Those Who Got Out," *The Paducah Evening Sun*, July 10, 1909.

25. "Jail Delivery, Tom Hollihan and Pete Griffin, Slick Prisoners, Get Away, Dug Through the Walls, They Had a Hammer and a Case Knife to Assist Them in Their Work, Thought They Were Helped," *The Paducah Evening Sun*, October 13, 1899.

26. "Yellow Boy Caught Up at Louisville," *The Paducah Evening Sun*, March 17, 1906.

27. "After Bolin, Detective Goes to Louisville for Prisoner, Stole Chief Collins' Dinner, Robbed Car and Broke Jail in Paducah," *The Paducah Evening Sun*, December 1, 1906.

28. "Second Escape for This Pair, Held at Madrid for Jailbreaking in Paducah and Get Away, the *Paducah Evening Sun*, January 28, 1910.

29. "Breaks Out of Padacuh Jail; Shot to Death, Daniel Blackwell Killed in Grantsburg, Illinois," *The Journal-Courier*, June 2, 1919.

30. "Fugitive Ends Life in River Near Paducah, Raymond Philley, 32, Breaks Officer's Grip, Leaps to Death, Accused of Slaying, Alleged Murderer Was Recaptured After Jail Break," *The Courier-Journal*, April 5, 1926.

31. "4 in McCracken Jail Use Spoon to Escape, Recaptured on Roof of Prison Kitchen by Jailer and Deputy," *The Courier-Journal*, April 2, 1933.

32. "6 Prisoners Lock Jailer in Cell and Flee in McCracken County, Deputy and Trusty Covered with Pistol When They Start to Lock Up for Night," *The Courier-Journal*, February 27, 1934.

33. "Six Prisoners Make Get-Away but Are Caught," *Kentucky Advocate*, February 27, 1934.

34. "The Commonwealth," *The Courier-Journal*, January 6, 1883.

35. "Hiram Smedley Sentenced to Five Years in State Penitentiary for Forging Name to County Warrant, Former County Court Clerk Convicted Second Time for Peculations During His Term of Office," *The Paducah Evening Sun*, April 30, 1910.

36. "Confederate Pardoned, Sent to Jail for Claiming Pension as Union Soldier," *The Courier-Journal*, July 25, 1913.

37. "Paducah Jail Is Filled by Raiders," *The Courier-Journal*, July 21, 1924.

38. "Officers Taken in Liquor Case, Illinois Sheriff Denied Custody of Bank Bandit Leader

Held in Paducah," *The Courier-Journal,* November 4, 1932.

39. "Willis Case, Will Come Up in the Cadiz Court Wednesday," *The Paducah Evening Sun,* May 12, 1905.

40. "In Paducah Jail for Safekeeping, Fulton Prisoner Is Removed from Mayfield, It Was Feared the Crowd, Incited by Hickman Men, Would Attempt to Lynch Him, Broke and Ran from Guard," *The Paducah Evening Sun,* August 1, 1906.

41. "Bridges Case Continued," *The Paducah Evening Sun,* August 9, 1910.

42. "Life Term, Homer Bridges' Sentence at Murray, Slayer of Ernest Lowery at Hazel, Is Found Guilty of Murder," *The Paducah Evening Sun,* November 23, 1910.

43. "Right Person Is Caught, Though Other Is Sought, Leonard Wilson Not Wanted for Killing Henry Cherry, but Harry Shaver, Confessed When Arrested on Other Charge, Said It Was Self-Defense," *The Paducah Evening Sun,* November 10, 1910.

44. "Life Term, Voted for Lee Carter by Jury at Clinton, Was Charged with Murder of Millionaire's Son, Farmer Mysteriously Shot Near Horse Cave, Science Hill Programme," *The Courier-Journal,* May 27, 1911.

45. "Two Men Killed, Negro Slays Two White Men in Fight Near This City, Sheriff Rushes Slayer to Paducah Jail," *The Hickman Courier,* January 4, 1912.

46. "Sheriff Slain by Deputy, Graves Countain Is Moved for Safekeeping After Killing Officer Over Salary," *The Courier-Journal,* March 7, 1922.

47. "Waives Examination, Mrs. Walters Held Without Bail and Sent to Paducah Jail," *the Courier-Journal,* October 24, 1923.

48. "Dowdy Placed in M'Cracken Jail, Marshall County Man Was Visited by Mob While at Benton," *The Courier-Journal,* March 14, 1925.

49. "Negroes Admit Fulton Slaying, Dee Plant Killed by Blow from Ax Near Hickman; 4 Say Robbery Motive," *The Courier-Journal,* October 31, 1928.

50. "Four Negroes Confess at Trial on Charge of Having Killed Kentuckian, 25," *The Cincinnati Enquirer,* May 14, 1929.

51. "Mob Flogs Prisoner in Smithland, Victim Taken for Ride, Beaten as 5 Masked Men Overpower Jailer," *The Courier-Journal,* October 18, 1933.

52. "Married Too Soon," *Hopkinsville Kentuckian,* April 13, 1915.

53. "Suspect in Paducah Blast Is Baptized," *The Courier-Journal,* July 27, 1923.

54. *The Courier-Journal,* June 12, 1924.

55. "Paducah Jail Empty Few Hours," *The Courier-Journal,* July 24, 1932.

Chapter 3

1. Pease, Theodore Calvin. *Collections of the Illinois State Historical Library,* The Laws of the Northwest Territory, 1788–1800 (1925).

2. Randl, Chad. *Revolving Architecture,* New York: Princeton Architectural Press, 2008.

3. *Ibid.*

4. *Corrections Now,* Vol. 12, Issue 2, October 2010, Kimberly D. Dodson, Ph.D., The Rotary Jail of Montgomery County, Indiana: An Early Experimental Penelogical Design.

5. *Ibid.*

6. *Ibid.*

7. "An Empty Jail," *Attica Daily Tribune,* May 6, 1915.

8. "Indiana Brevities," *Crawford County Democrat,* October 31, 1918.

9. *Hammond Lake County Times,* December 15, 1928.

10. www.rotaryjailmuseum.org/history.html.

11. "Suggests New County Jails by Federal Aid," *The Daily Reporter,* August 9, 1938.

12. Sign at the Rotary Jail Museum.

13. www.montgomeryco.net.

14. *Elkhart Weekly Review,* October 21, 1885.

15. "Henning Hanged for Murdering Mrs. Vollmer, He Talked Fifteen Minutes on the Scaffold—Sketch of His Life and of the Crime for Which He Died," *The Indianapolis News,* May 27, 1886.

16. "Murdered Her Child," *Logansport Pharos-Tribune,* May 19, 1895.

17. "Escaped Punishment," *Logansport Journal,* February 9, 1896.

18. "Life Sentence, Otto Walker Convicted of Murder in the First Degree," *The Jamestown Press,* March 6, 1908.

19. "Crawfordsville Man Held, Alleged Slayer Said to Be Wearing Victim's Trousers," *The Indianapolis Star,* October 16, 1916.

20. "First Degree Murder and Life Sen-

tence, Verdict of Jury Late Friday Afternoon in George Farlow Trial, Defendant Sentenced Today, Will Be Take to State Prison Monday," *Shelbyville Democrat*, April 26, 1917.

21. "Hoosier News Briefly Told," *The Wanatah Mirror*, December 27, 1917.

22. "Taken to Crawfordsville, Woman to Be Tried in Montgomery County on Murder Charge," *The Indianapolis News*, April 24, 1918.

23. "Murder Laid to Attack Attempt, Prosecutor Believes Young Man Slew Teacher Through Fear of Exposure, Discards Other Motives, Farm Laborer, However, Says He Killed Young Woman in Fit of Anger," *The Indianapolis News*, August 30, 1932.

24. "Farm Hand Sentenced to Life for Killing Teacher, Morris Greet, 22-Year-Old Indiana Youth, Had Feared Death Sentence," *Great Clipper*, January 23, 1933.

25. "State Intelligence," *The Ripley County Journal*, September 6, 1883.

26. "Indiana State News," *Winchester Journal*, April 3, 1885.

27. "Sensational Jail Delivery, Four Prisoners Gain Their Liberty from the Crawford County Jail in a Very Mysterious Manner," *The Republic*, May 18, 1892.

28. "Prisoner's Daring Jump for Liberty," *Knox Stark County Democrat*, May 31, 1900.

29. "Prisoners Escape Jail," *Hammond Lake County Times*, August 4, 1909.

30. "Arthur Gasaway Escapes Jail, Chief of Police Brown Receives Word from Crawfordsville, Is Not Located Here, Former Brazil Man Escapes from Montgomery County Jail Fearing Penitentiary Sentence," *Brazil Daily Times*, November 26, 1913.

31. "Two Local Men Among Quartet Making Escape, Had Just Been Sentenced for Auto Banditry—Cattle "Rustler" With Absentees," *The Indianapolis Star*, March 18, 1928.

32. "Escaped Youth Calls to Police, One of Four Men Who Broke Jail at Crawfordsville Surrenders Himself," *The Call-Leader*, March 19, 1928.

33. "Two Escape from Jail," Men Saw Way Out of Montgomery County Jail, Jump Twenty Feet to Ground and Escape," *Rushville Republican*, May 14, 1930.

34. *The Indianapolis Star*, January 29, 1932.

35. "Telegraphic," *Shelbyville Daily Democrat*, March 12, 1886.

36. "Firebug Charges His Mania Up to Whisky," *Indianapolis Star*, April 2, 1909.

37. "Preacher's Noise in Jail Stirs Prisoners' Wrath," *The Indianapolis Star*, March 18, 1914.

38. "Sentences are Given Members of 2d, Indiana," *The Huntington Press*, March 24, 1918.

39. "Negro Is Accused of Long Series of Thefts, Loss $5,000 to $6,000 for Crawfordsville Store, Grocher Also in the List, *Indianapolis News*, August 31, 1920.

40. "Gets Term in Prison, Crawfordsville Man Sentenced for Theft of Merchandise," *Attica Daily Tribune*, October 13, 1920.

41. "Girl Robbers Taken to Jail, Pair Robbed Store of Dresses and Coats Used in Style Show, Value $1,000, Mother Is Also Prisoner, the *Call-Leader*, September 15, 1927.

42. "Youths, 16, 19, Held as Liquor Runners," *The Indianapolis Star*, May 23, 1930.

Chapter 4

1. "Nodaway County Missouri, Volume 1," B.F. Bowen & Company, 1916.

2. *Ibid.*

3. *Ibid.*

4. "Maryville," *Maryville Daily Forum*, January 29, 1976.

5. "Horrible Accident, Charles W. Fry Has His Head Crushed and Dies in Twelve Hours," *Maryville Republican*, June 30, 1904.

6. *Ibid.*

7. "Nies Dies of Burns, Injuries in Jail Explosion Prove Fatal, Others Are Better," *Maryville Daily Democrat*, December 12, 1927.

8. "College Girl Is Fined $10 on Bad Check Charge," *Maryville Daily Forum*, May 28, 1949.

9. "Twelve Get Prison Terms in Nodaway Courts During '54," *Maryville Daily Forum*, December 31, 1954.

10. *Ibid.*

11. "County Jail: Local Facility Hasn't Rocked Since Rolling Cage Was Frozen," *Maryville Daily Forum*, March 12, 1977.

12. *Ibid.*

13. *Ibid.*

14. "Jail Registration Urged by Professor," *Maryville Daily Forum*, January 18, 1978.

15. Cronk, Susan, "Nodaway County Jail," Blog.

16. www.insideprison.com.

17. *Ibid.*

18. "To St. Joe for Safekeeping," *St. Louis Post-Dispatch*, October 8, 1896.

19. "Montgomery's Slayer, Trial of John Joyce for Murder Begun at Maryville," *The Sedalia Democrat*, April 12, 1898; "John Joyce Acquitted, the *Sedalia Democrat*, April 22, 1898.

20. "Causes Daughter's Death, Confession of a Dying Girl Implicates a Missouri Farmer in Her Murder," *Omaha Daily Bee*, January 5, 1899.

21. *The Holt County Sentinel*, March 30, 1900.

22. "Man Pleads Guilty to Murder of Son," *Jefferson City Post-Tribune*, October 15, 1935.

23. "Time at Jail," *Maryville Daily Forum*, May 28, 1949.

24. "Missouri, Condensed Reports of the Latest News from All Parts of the State," *Union Record*, December 15, 1887.

25. "Four Break Jail, Two of the Quartet Are Arrested at Burlington Jct., Escape Through Wall, the Two Thompson Boys Are Still at Large—Gibbs Notified Sheriff Dowden," *Maryville Daily Democrat Forum*, April 9, 1919.

26. *Ibid.*

27. "Jail Breaker Is Captured, Irwin Swearingen Arrested in K.C.—Sentenced from This County," *Maryville Daily Forum*, January 27, 1930.

28. "William Helpley Is Captured by Milwaukee Police, Man Who Broke Jail Here, Sept. 21 Identified by Fingerprints," *The Maryville Daily Forum*, November 18, 1931.

29. "Seek 2 Who Sawed Their Way Out of Jail," *Jefferson City Post-Tribune*, June 24, 1935.

30. "Breaks Jail When Sheriff Is Gone, L.R. Seals Chisels Hole in Ceiling and Gets Out of Second Story," *The Maryville Daily Forum*, June 28, 1937.

31. "Two Break from Bedford Jail by Sawing Bars," *The Maryville Daily Forum*, October 2, 1950.

32. "Nodaway Co. Jail Escapee Captured," *Macon Chronicle-Herald*, March 12, 1953.

33. "Jail Escapee Draws 2-Yr. Prison Term," *The Maryville Daily Forum*, June 20, 1959.

34. "Two Prisoners Cut Bars, Drop 14 Feet to Gain Freedom Today in Nodaway County Jail Break," *The Maryville Daily Forum*, April 18, 1960.

35. "Earl Emery, Jail Escapee, Turn Self In," *The Maryville Daily Forum*, July 29, 1964.

36. "County Jail Escapees Are Captured," *The Sedalia Democrat*, October 3, 1973.

37. "Negro Preacher Shot, Rev. Wm. Johnston of Maryville, Mo., Killed by an Officer," *The Norfolk Weekly News*, August 31, 1899.

38. "Proceedings of City Council," *The Palmyra Spectator*, November 12, 1891.

39. "May Release the Judges from Jail, Famous St. Clair County Case Reaches the Federal Court in St. Louis, Would Not Levy Certain Tax, Bonds for Railroad Which Was Never Built Repudiated by Taxpayers—Writ of Habeas Corpus," *The St. Louis Republic*, November 24, 1901.

40. "Judge Neville Released from Maryville Jail, Promised Judge Phillips That He Would Not Attempt to Sit on the Bench," *The St. Louis Republic*, December 23, 1902.

41. "Son Joins His Father in Local County Jail," *The Maryville Daily Forum*, August 9, 1938.

42. "First Night of Their Honeymoon Spent in Nodaway County Jail," *The Maryville Daily Forum*, February 10, 1940.

43. "A Giant Brute, a Desperate Character Arrested for Outrage at Bedford, Iowa," *Burlington Hawk Eye*, May 24, 1890.

44. "A $4,800 Liquor Fine, *Chillicothe Constitution*, February 28, 1907.

45. "Committed Suicide," *Maryville Republican*, May 19, 1904.

46. "Ex-Sheriff Kills Himself, After Drinking Heavily Was Arrested and Fined—He Went Home and Took Poison—Was a Wealthy Man," *Sedalia Weekly Sentinel*, January 16, 1904.

Chapter 5

1. "History of DeKalb County Sheriff's Office," *Office of Sheriff DeKalb County*.

2. *Ibid.*

3. *Ibid.*

4. Lunden, Walter A., "The Rotary Jail, or Human Squirrel Cage," *Journal of the Society of Architectural Historians*, Vol. 18, No. 4, December 1959.

5. "Court-House Struck by Lightning, Fire Started at 10:30 O'clock Sunday Night, Citizens Work Faithfully—Damage Estimated from $3,000 to $4,000," *The Republic*, June 22, 1905.

6. *St. Joseph Gazette*, October 8, 1938.

7. "Death Verdict for Girl Slayer, Martin

181

Paulsgrove, Who Killed Sweetheart, Convicted of Murder," *St. Louis Dispatch*, October 16, 1905.

8. "Is He Insane?" *The Chillicothion-Tribune*, March 22, 1907.

9. "Elze Meek Is Not Guilty of Murder Charge, Slayer of Overseer Culley Is Insane and Was Not Responsible, Accused, Who Was Taken into Court Bound in Straight Jacket, Will Be Sent to State Hospital," *Chillicothe Constitution*, October 17, 1925.

10. "Sheriff Smith of Maysville Shot While Looking for Still," *Chillicothe Constitution*, October 11, 1921.

11. "U.S. Agents Arrest DeKalb County Sheriff, Officer at Maysville Is Accused of Abetting a Bootlegger," *The Chillicothe Tribune*, February 9, 1923.

12. "Prisoner Is Given 2 Years for Sale of Whisky from Jail, Judge Reeves Compliments Jury for Verdict and Reprimands Sheriff for Permitting Prisoner Such Freedom," *Chillicothe Constitution,* October 1, 1923.

13. "Missouri Notes," *The Macon Republican*, August 15, 1889.

14. "Missouri State News, Wholesale Jail Delivery," *The Taney County Republican*, February 7, 1901.

15. "Chivalry Worked Both Ways, It Sends Earl Bell to Jail for Six Months, but Keeps Him Out for Six More," *Kansas City Journal*, May 5, 1897.

16. *The Holt County Sentinel*, January 11, 1901.

17. "Indicted for Election Fraud," *Chillicothe-Tribune,* Nov. 2, 1907.

18. "Held as Suspect in Two Robberies," *Jefferson City Post Tribune*, December 29, 1930.

19. www.ddcrj.com.

20. *Ibid.*

Chapter 6

1. www.pottcounty.com.

2. Roenfeld, Ryan and Warner, Dr. Richard, *Tales from the Squirrel Cage Jail, Volume 2*, 2013.

3. *The Nonpareil*, July 26, 1936.

4. Roenfeld, Ryan and Warner, Richard. "History of the 'Squirrel Cage' Jail" Undated.

5. *Ibid.*

6. *Ibid.*

7. *Ibid.*

8. "'Squirrel Cage Jail' Over 130 Years Old," *Historical Society of Pottawattami County Member Journal.*

9. *Ibid.*

10. *Laurens Advertiser*, Nov. 10, 1888.

11. *Ibid.*

12. www.hauntedhouses.com/states/ia/squirrel_cage_jail.htm.

13. *Ibid.*

14. *Ibid.*

15. "County Jail at Keokuk on List to Be Closed," *Fort Madison Evening Democrat*, February 1, 1969.

16. "Jail Closed at Council Bluffs," *Creston News Advertiser,* November 29, 1969.

17. www.pottcountysheriff.com/general-info/history.php.

18. www.thehistoricalsociety.org/museums/squirrel-cage-jail.html.

19. *Ibid.*

20. https://en.wikipedia.org/wiki/Jake_Bird.

21. "Newell Sent to Prison," *Rock Valley Bee*, January 19, 1906.

22. "Governor Refuses to Halt Execution, Brown Will Be Hanged, Pal Loses His Appeal," *Mason City Globe-Gazette*, July 23, 1962.

23. "Kelley," *Rock Valley Bee*, September 20, 1962.

24. "Didn't Need the Keys," Eleven Prisoners Walk Out the Unlocked Doors of the County Jail, Three of Them Recaptured—How They Effected Their Escape, *The Council Bluffs Nonpareil*, December 6, 1888.

25. "Council Bluffs Jail Breaker Surrenders," *The Mason City Globe-Gazette*, June 9, 1937.

26. "2 Men Saw Way Out of Council Bluffs Jail," *The Mason City Globe-Gazette*, September 18, 1942.

27. "Three Escape from Jail; One Captured on Downtown Street," *Iowa City Press-Citizen*, October 22, 1948.

28. "Hunt Escapees in 2 Robberies," *The Des Moines Register*, July 20, 1949.

29. "Four Break Out of Council Bluffs Jail," *Carrol Daily Times Herald*, December 9, 1958.

30. "Mob Crimes for Lives of Negroes, It Breaks Down the Doors of the County Jail at Council Bluffs, Eager for Vengeance, a Thousand Men Were Determined to Avenge Assault on Women, Eloquence Stays Mob, When Near Success the Earnest Pleas of Congress-

man Smith Stopped Attack," *The Des Moines Register*, December 29, 1903.

31. "Given 90 Days in County Jail," *Council Bluffs Nonpareil*, August 22, 1944.

32. "Pardon Frees Boy, 15, from Jail in Bluffs," *The Des Moines Register*, May 30, 1952.

33. "Reopen Murder Case at Clarinda, Return Huseman to Page County Jail," *The Council Bluffs Nonpareil*, July 10, 1949.

34. *Ibid.*
35. *Ibid.*
36. *Ibid.*
37. *Ibid.*
38. *Ibid.*
39. *Ibid.*
40. *Ibid.*

Chapter 7

1. "The Rotary Iron Jail," *The Interior Journal*, Nov. 17, 1885.

2. "Do Drop In' and Get Shot, the Details of the Nightly Row at McNulty's Saloon, Scenes in the Jail, a Missing Mute Turns Up All Right—Counterfeit Cigar Labels—Sunday Gleanings in the Bluffs, Behind the Bars," *Omaha Daily Bee*, December 27, 1886.

3. "Need of a Jail," *The Nebraska State Journal*, August 26, 1908.

4. "Scaffold and Noose, How the Douglas County Condemned Will Be Hanged," *Omaha Daily Bee*, December 4, 1885.

5. "News of Nebraska," *The McCook Tribune*, December 3, 1885.

6. "A Touch of Romance in the Closing Hours of Murderer Neal, Dog-Like Fidelity with Which a Fallen Woman of Omaha Has Clung to Him," *Lincoln Weekly Nebraska State Journal*, September 25, 1891.

7. "Foiled by Officers, the Omaha Mob Did Nothing for the Want of a Leader," *Lincoln Semi Weekly State Journal*, August 8, 1893.

8. "Higgins Is Lynched, Thurston County Murderer Swung from a Bridge, Sheriff Met by Masked Men, No Resistance by the Officer, and Prisoner Given but Little Time to Make a Statement," *The Columbus Journal*, September 4, 1907.

9. "Crowd gathers at Omaha Jail," reported *The Alliance Herald*, July 2, 1908.

10. "Convicts August Kastner, Accused Man Held to Be Responsible for Policeman's Death, Jury Finds Him Guilty of Murder, Re-

turns a Verdict of Murder in the Second Degree for Killing Officer Dan Tiedeman Last June," *Omaha Daily Bee*, February 27, 1898.

11. "Omaha Notes," *Lincoln Nebraska State Journal*, January 31, 1900.

12. "Riot at South Omaha," Angry Crowds Make Merciless Attack on Greeks, Torch is Applied to Several Buildings and Inmates Beaten and Shot by Vengeful Mob—Windows Smashed in Others," *The Alliance Herald*, February 25, 1909.

13. "Without a Goodbye," *Omaha Daily Bee*, April 5, 1893.

14. "Some Men Who Have Been Mayors," *The Courier*, December 7, 1901.

15. "In the Toils for Whisky Selling, George W. Baker Under Arrest—Another Haul Expected To-Day," *Lincoln Weekly Nebraska State Journal*, May 1, 1891.

16. "Federal Building Notes," *Omaha Bee*, August 10, 1898.

17. "Ed Hudderd's Great Luck, Pardon Extended by Governor Boyd, Hudderd Eloped with Mrs. Peterson of Sarpy County and Got Eleven Months in Jail," *Lincoln Semi Weekly Nebraska State Journal,* July 1, 1892.

18. "Given a Fere (Sic) Rein, Bank Wrecker Mosher a Prisoner at Omaha Only in Name," *Lincoln Semi Weekly State Journal*, October 27, 1893.

19. "Heavy Sentence for Bartley," *Barber County Index,* June 30, 1897.

20. "Joseph Bartley Is Liberated, Passes from Penitentiary on Pardon Brought from Gov. Savage," *The North Platte Weekly Tribune*, January 7, 1902.

21. "Millionaires Must Serve Time, Jail for Richard and Comstock in Thirty Days, Court of Appeals in Order, Men Convicted of Land Frauds in Nebraska Must Serve Sentence in Douglas County Jail and Pay Fines Mandate Is Received, the *Kearney Daily Hub*, November 8, 1910.

22. "Indian Smashes the Jug, Supposes That Destroys All Evidence Against Him as a Bootlegger," *Omaha Daily Bee*, August 21, 1907.

23. "Two Chinese Must Get Out, Judge Munger Orders the Deportation of a Pair of the Local Colony," *Omaha Daily Bee*, October 29, 1905.

24. *Lincoln Weekly Nebraska State Journal*, May 31, 1889.

25. "Keep in Confinement, a Story Which

If True Places Omaha Police Officials in a Bad Light," *Lincoln Weekly Nebraska State Journal*, June 13, 1890.

26. www.weitz.com/project/douglas-co-corrections/.

Chapter 8

1. https://en.wikipedia.org/wiki/Warren_County_Courthouse_(Indiana).

2. "Broke Jail," *Williamsport Warren Leader*, October 28, 1871.

3. *Ibid.*

4. "Specifications Rotary Jail and Cells," *Warren Republican*, July 1, 1886.

5. "Warren County's Penal and Benevolent Institutions," *Warren Republican*, January 1, 1891.

6. "Report of the State Board of Charities, Upon Our County Institutions," *Williamsport Warren Review*, October 15, 1891.

7. "About the Court House," *Williamsport Warren Review,* November 26, 1891.

8. "Reports of the Grand Jury," *Williamsport Warren Republican*, April 4, 1897.

9. "Grand Jury's Report, or the Condition of the Jail and the County Asylum, a New Jail Recommended," *The Warren Review,*" November 18, 1897.

10. "Report of the Grand Jury, March 16, 1898," *Williamsport Warren Republican*, March 24, 1898.

11. "Our County Jail," *Williamsport Warren Republican*, February 7, 1901.

12. *Williamsport Warren Republican*, November 21, 1901.

13. "Courthouse Gone, High Wind Prevented the Firemen from Saving It," *Jasper Herald,* January 25, 1907.

14. *Attica Fountain Warren Democrat*, February 9, 1907.

15. "The Proposed New Court House and Jail for Warren County," *The Warren Review*, April 18, 1907.

16. www.jailexchange.com.

17. "Welch Has Been Caught," *Covington Friend*, August 13, 1897.

18. *Ibid.*

19. "Attempt to Break Jail," *Lock Haven Express*, March 9, 1893.

20. "Broke Jail," *Williamsport Warren Republican*, November 11, 1893.

21. *Attica Fountain Warren Democrat*, December 21, 1893.

22. "Cronkhite Is Caught, Warren County's Ex-Treasurer Arrested at Los Angeles, Cal., Violet Ink Used by His Wife Leads to the Clew—A Sheriff's Clever Work," *The Indianapolis Journal*, March 25, 1894.

23. "Indiana State News," *Thorntown Argus*, June 9, 1894.

24. "Cronkhite Free," *Williamsport Warren Review*, December 10, 1896.

25. "He Played Detective, A.B. Britten, Class Leader and Sun-School Superintendent in Jail at Williamsport," *Attica Fountain Warren Democrat*, June 20, 1895.

26. *Williamsport Warren Republican*, April 21, 1898.

27. "Everybody Takes a Kick at a Rolling Stone," *Williamsport Warren Republican,* March 24, 1898.

Chapter 9

1. "Razing of County Jail Recalls Early History," *The Post-Crescent*, Aug. 9, 1940.

2. www.wikipedia.org.

3. "The New Jail Project Being Considered," *Janesville Daily Gazette,* March 24, 1885.

4. Ryan, Thomas Henry, *History of Outagamie County, Wisconsin.*

5. *Ibid.*

6. *Ibid.*

7. "The First Prisoner," *Appleton Post*, June 9, 1887.

8. "At Last," *Appleton Crescent*, June 4, 1887.

9. "State News," *Oshkosh Daily Northwestern*, August 25, 1891.

10. "State News," *Oshkosh Daily Northwestern*, September 22, 1898.

11. *Ibid.*

12. *Ibid.*

13. *Ibid.*

14. www.measuringworth.com.

15. "Local Firm Bought Jail, Iron & Metal Co. Bids for Old Outagamie Co. Structure," *Manitowoc Daily Herald*, April 11, 1906.

16. "Says Jail Is No Good, Manitowoc Man Causes Big Sensation at Appleton," *Manitowoc Daily Herald,* December 4, 1906.

17. www.outagamie.org.

18. "State News," *The Weekly Wisconsin*, April 20, 1889.

19. "Wisconsin Small Talk," *The Weekly Wisconsin*, October 17, 1891.

20. "Badger Brevities," *The Weekly Wisconsin*, January 30, 1892.

21. "Tried to Dig Out of Jail, a Short Term Prisoner at Appleton Prevents a Jail Delivery," *The Centralia Enterprise and Tribune*, December 29, 1894.

22. "State News," *Oshkosh Daily Northwestern*, March 19, 1898.

23. "Horse Thief Escapes," *Oshkosh Daily Northwestern*, November 5, 1901.

24. "The News Condensed," *The New North*, August 11, 1904.

25. "Break Jail at Appleton, Outagamie Structure Appears to Be Unsafe One," *Oshkosh Daily Northwestern*, September 1, 1904.

26. "Breaks Appleton Jail," *Oshkosh Daily Northwestern*, January 14, 1905.

27. "Neenah Woman's Luck," *Oshkosh Daily Northwestern*, April 25, 1905.

28. "State News," *Oshkosh Daily Northwestern*, March 6, 1906.

29. "News of the State," *Oshkosh Daily Northwestern*, Jan. 4, 1892.

30. "Caught in the Cage," *Oshkosh Daily Northwestern*, February 9, 1894.

31. "A State in Brief," *Oshkosh Daily Northwestern*, November 7, 1891.

32. "Indians Must Go to Jail, Those Who Have Been Found Guilty of Sale of Liquor," *Oshkosh Daily Northwestern*, June 13, 1900.

33. *Ibid.*

34. "Indians Pay Fines," *Oshkosh Daily Northwestern*, June 10, 1903.

35. "Schabo on the Stand," *The Centralia Enterprise and Tribune*, June 19, 1897.

36. "For Second Murder," *Oshkosh Daily Northwestern,* March 21, 1899.

37. "Peter Ross Found Not Guilty," *Green Bay Weekly Gazette*, May 3, 1899.

38. *Ibid.*

39. "Kaukauna Man Still Missing, Michael McCarthy of That City Is Missing, and His Body Is Not Found Yet, Weave Evidence About Prisoner, Story That He Offered to Produce Missing Man Alive for Two Thousand Dollars Is Denied, *Janesville Daily Gazette*, October 30, 1905.

40. "Short Notes," *Oshkosh Daily Northwestern*, November 27, 1905.

41. "Claims He's Not Insane," *Oshkosh Daily Northwestern*, January 9, 1897.

42. "Finally Run to Earth," *Oshkosh Daily Northwestern*, October 22, 1903.

43. "Killed Himself in Jail," *The Weekly Wisconsin*, June 23, 1894.

44. "Roby Sentenced to Jail," *Oshkosh Daily Northwestern*, May 1, 1890.

45. "Danger in Use of Stamps," *Oshkosh Daily Northwestern*, June 26, 1901.

46. "State Notes," *Janesville Daily Gazette*, August 11, 1902.

47. "Unlucky Horse Thief," *Oshkosh Daily Northwestern*, Feb. 9, 1906.

48. "Charge Is Serious, Alleged Assault by Youth Paroled from State Reformatory," *Oshkosh Daily Northwestern*, September 13, 1906.

49. "An Innocent Prisoner," *Oshkosh Daily Northwestern,* July 7, 1905.

Chapter 10

1. Slosek, Anthony. Oswego County historian, June 1982 paper.

2. *Oswego Palladium,* January 7, 1835.

3. *Oswego Palladium,* April 18, 1848.

4. *Oswego Palladium,* June 5, 1849.

5. *Ibid.*

6. *Oswego Daily Palladium,* February 2, 1882 .

7. "Work for Convicts, the Prison Association Endorses the Fasett Bill—A Revolving Prison," *The Sun,* April 16, 1889.

8. McDougall, Florence, *History of Oswego County Jail,* 2013.

9. "Report on the State Prisons, Slight Decrease in Numbers of Convicts, Houses of Detention," *Democrat and Chronicle,* January 20, 1902.

10. "Prison Commission, Reports of Inspections and Improvements—Committee Named," *Democrat and Chronicle,* April 3, 1902.

11. "Prisons Fire Traps," New State Commission Organizes and Receives Reports," *New York Tribune,* September 6, 1905.

12. "Signs of a Plot to Empty the Jail, District-Attorney Said to Be in Possession of Information Leading Him to Believe That Prisoners at Oswego Have Active Friends Outside," *The Post-Standard,* January 29, 1907.

13. "County Jail Is Condemned, State Prison Commission Speaks Plainly to Oswego, Supervisors Call Meeting, Whole Matter Will Be Canvassed Thursday—New Site Among Rec-

ommendations," *Syracuse Post Standard,* June 2, 1908.

14. *Ibid.*

15. "Oswego County's New Jail Will Be Completed Soon," *Syracuse Post Standard,* November 15, 1909.

16. "Prisoners to Aid in Building New Jail," *Syracuse Post Standard,* July 30, 1909.

17. *Ibid.*

18. www.oswegocounty.com/jail.shtml.

19. "Crime of a Little Girl, Accused of Having Murdered an Infant by Administering Arsenic in the Milk," *The San Francisco Call,* November 14, 1896.

20. "12-Year-Old Girl Murdered, Assaulted While on Her Way to Sunday School—A Farm Hand Arrested," *The Sun,* May 30, 1905.

21. "Brute Electrocuted, Henry Manser Executed in New York Prison for Murdering Little Girl," *Paducah Sun,* September 12, 1905.

22. "George Eddy Visited by His Daughter and His Father-In-Law," *The Post-Standard,* December 28, 1909.

23. "Ten Years for Eddy for Murder of Reid, Accused Slayer Changes Plea Because Wife Was to Go on Stand—To-Day He Will Be in Auburn Prison—Friends to Make Effort to Secure Pardon," *The Post-Standard,* May 21, 1910.

24. "Telegrams in Brief," *Democrat and Chronicle,* August 24, 1888.

25. "A Boatman Harbors an Escaped Prisoner," *The Sun,* November 15, 1889.

26. "Escaped from Prison," *Poughkeepsie Eagle-News,* August 29, 1901.

27. "Escapes from Three Jails, Oswego, Yates, and Franklin County Institutions Lose Prisoners," *New York Times,* December 8, 1906.

28. "Oscar Smith Is Found, Made His Escape from Oswego County Jail, Time Had Nearly Expired," *The Post-Standard,* February 25, 1907.

29. "Another Break from County Jail, Three Prisoners Escape in Oswego—One Subsequently Captured, but Two Are Still at Large—Two of the Prisoners Were 'Trustys,'" *The Post-Standard,* May 16, 1907.

30. "James Back in County Jail, Escaped Prisoner Apprehended by the Oswego Police," *The Post-Standard,* May 27, 1907.

31. "William J. O'Neill Committed Suicide, Was Under Indictment at Oswego for Bigamy, Evidently Despondent, the Young Man Was Well Known in Certain Circles in This City—

Ran a Saloon at No. 81 Hudson Avenue When Arrested," *Democrat and Chronicle,* April 28, 1901.

32. "Used Needle on Himself, Prisoner in Oswego County Jail Discovered in the Act," *Syracuse Post Standard,* August 17, 1908.

33. "Found Guilty of Assault," *The Kingston Daily Freeman,* July 20, 1889.

34. "Excise Violation Convictions," *Democrat and Chronicle,* September 13, 1901.

35. "Held for Grand Jury, James Melling Accused of Assaulting Mrs. Harriet M. Burton," *The Post-Standard,* April 11, 1907.

Chapter 11

1. https://en.wikipedia.org/wiki/Sherman,_Texas.

2. www.rootsweb.ancestry.com.

3. *Ibid.*

4. *Ibid.*

5. "County Jails Date to 1887," *Sherman Democrat,* July 4, 1976.

6. *Ibid.*

7. "Texasettes," *Alpine Avalanche,* November 23, 1900.

8. *Ibid.*

9. *Ibid.*

10. www.capitalpunishmentuk.org.

11. www.legendsofamerica.com.

12. "That Is Pretty Tight, Such Were George Smith's Words as the Trap Fell, Grayson County's First Legal Execution in Thirteen Years—He Killed a City Marshal," *The Galveston Daily News,* July 9, 1892.

13. "Double Hanging, Expiation of the Foul Taking Off of Sharman, the Widow and Children of Sharman, for Whose Assassination the Men Died, Witnessed the Execution," *McKinney Democrat,* May 18, 1893.

14. "Murderer Respited," *El Paso Herald,* June 6, 1900.

15. "Sidney Spears Swings, from a Sherman Scaffold for the Killing of His Wife," *Wise County Messenger,* June 22, 1900.

16. "The Hanging of Vines and Maxey, Execution of Two Negroes Witnessed by Large Crowd in Sherman, History of the Crimes, Vines Killed Constable at Sherman and Maxey Paid Penalty for Murder of White Man," *Wichita Daily Times,* August 11, 1912.

17. "Killing Near Denison, Killed for Resenting an Insult to His Wife—Talked Too

Much," *The Austin Weekly Statesman*, September 7, 1893.

18. "A Cool Criminal, a Negro Murderer Laughs in the Faces of a Crowd of Men Who Were Trying to Take Him Away from the Officers," *Galveston Daily News*, November 9, 1887.

19. "General News," *McKinney Democrat*, June 9, 1896.

20. "State News," *Advocate*, January 30, 1904.

21. "Woman Identified Suspect in the Sherman Jail," *The Abilene Reporter,* September 25, 1908.

22. "Was Near Marriage, Dr. Sherman, in Jail for Killing, Got License, but the Sheriff Refused to Permit the Ceremony," *Advocate*, March 9, 1911.

23. "Negroes Are in Jail Here, Were Brought to McKinney Thursday Night, Officers Feared Mob, Sherman People Stirred Up Over Killing of Fred Munger Wednesday Night," *McKinney Daily Courier Gazette*," September 29, 1911.

24. "Prisoners in Revolt, the Sherman Jail Is Broken Three Times and Ten Prisoners Escape," *Lemars Semi-Weekly Sentinel*," October 9, 1892.

25. "Texas News Notes," *Shriner Gazette*, April 16, 1896.

26. *Ibid.*

27. "Local and Personal," *Advocate*, January 18, 1908.

28. "An Old Man's Sad Story, Behind the Bars of the Sherman Jail, a Little Brandy for His Stomach's Sake Leads to His Downfall— His Spirit Broken," *The Galveston Daily News,* July 2, 1891.

29. "Williams Wants to Be Arraigned," *The Galveston Daily News*, March 5, 1891.

30. "Moved for Safe Keeping," *Bryan Morning Eagle*, September 19, 1909.

Chapter 12

1. www.wikipedia.org.

2. "The New Jail," *The Burlington Weekly Free Press*, June 23, 1843.

3. "City and Vicinity," *The Burlington Weekly Free Press*, Nov. 26, 1886.

4. "The New County Jail, What Shall It Be? And Where Located?" *The Burlington Weekly Free Press*, January 14, 1887.

5. "City and Vicinity," *The Burlington Weekly Free Press*, March 25, 1887.

6. "The New County Jail, Plans Adopted by the Commissioners for the Structure—The Site Undecided," *The Burlington Weekly Free Press*, April 29, 1887.

7. "Weekly News Summary," *The Vermont Watchman*, November 17, 1887.

8. "Chittenden County Jail, Where Our Criminals Will Rest in Revolving Cells," *The Burlington Weekly Free Press*, January 20, 1888.

9. *Ibid.*

10. *Ibid.*

11. "Happenings of a Week Among the Citizens of the Green Mountain State," *Middlebury Register*, July 27, 1900.

12. *Ibid.*

13. "Drunkenness Has Increased," *Boston Globe*, October 29, 1905.

14. "About the State," *The Barre Daily Times*, December 20, 1904.

15. "State News," *Middlebury Register*, April 1, 1904.

16. "Burlington's Criminality; County Jail Crowded as It Never Has Been Crowded Before," *The Barre Daily Times*, March 20, 1905.

17. "Like a Russian Prison, Is Chittenden County Jail, Says the Grand Jury," *The Barre Daily Times*, September 16, 1905.

18. "New Jail on Old Site, Work of Construction Begun Tuesday Morning," *The Burlington Free Press*, August 29, 1907.

19. "County Jail System Ends, Replaced by Regional Centers," *Bennington Banner*, April 1, 1969.

20. "Corry Now Behind Bars," *The Barre Daily Times*, September 24, 1904.

21. "Burlington," *Boston Globe*, October 15, 1905.

22. "Colligole at Burlington," *Barre Evening Telegram*, January 30, 1901.

23. "Trusted Clerk Arrested, Bert Agan, Employed by a Burlington Coal Company, Accused of Embezzling $3000," *Boston Globe*, January 25, 1903.

24. "Louis Ouimette and Edmund Pratt Own Up to Sunday Morning's Burglary," *The Burlington Weekly Free Press*, April 3, 1903.

25. "Prisoner Has Diptheria, John J. Fairchild Is Isolated in Chittenden County Jail," *The Barre Daily Times*, April 4, 1907.

26. "Taken Back to Montreal, Four Men Who Are Charged with Breaking Immigration Laws, the *Barre Daily Times*, June 1, 1905.

27. "Van Bever Paid Fine, Settled Case for Bringing Woman and Child into United States," *The Burlington Free Press*, January 29, 1907.

28. "A Wrecked Institution," *Middlebury Register*, May 6, 1904.

29. "Ketchum at Middlebury," *Middlebury Register*, March 3, 1905.

30. "Ketchum Will Tour Vermont with Dramatic Company," *Vermont Phoenix*, June 28, 1907.

31. *Vermont Phoenix*, July 13, 1906.

32. "Steady Inflow of Bills, Some Being Important Measures, *Vermont Phoenix*, October 19, 1906.

33. "891 Persons Jailed," *Burlington Weekly Free Press*, January 10, 1907.

34. "FOUND GUILTY OF BURGLARY," *The Barre Daily Times*, December 10, 1903.

35. "The Vermont News," *Vermont Phoenix*, January 26, 1894.

36. "Champion Whiskey Drinker," *The Burlington Free Press*, May 1, 1902.

37. "Fort Ethan Allen No Criterion," *The Barre Daily Times*, February 3, 1905.

Chapter 13

1. Douglas K. Miller, "The Salt Lake County Rotary Jail," *Utah Historical Quarterly* 75.4 (Fall 2007): 322–41.

2. *Ibid.*

3. *Ibid.*

4. "Chapter from an Old Man's Life," *Deseret Evening News*, Feb. 17, 1900.

5. *Ibid.*

6. Douglas K. Miller, "The Salt Lake County Rotary Jail," *Utah Historical Quarterly* 75.4 (Fall 2007): 322–41.

7. *Ibid.*

8. *Ibid.*

9. *Ibid.*

10. "Seven Prisoners Escape from the County Jail," *The Salt Lake Herald*, June 4, 1889.

11. *Ibid.*

12. *Ibid.*

13. "Sullivan Almost Escapes from Jail," *The Salt Lake Tribune*, Jan. 22, 1908.

14. "Deming Testifies About Odd Plan," *Deseret Evening News*, June 15, 1908.

15. "Accused Murderer Plans Jail Break," *The Salt Lake Tribune*, Feb. 16, 1910.

16. *Ibid.*

17. *Ibid.*

18. *Ibid.*

19. "Talk with Rosenquist," *The Salt Lake Tribune*, Nov. 4, 1897.

20. *Ibid.*

21. "Card Game Leads to Cold Murder," *Deseret Evening News*, Dec. 30, 1907.

22. "Shavers' Close Call," *The Salt Lake Herald*, Feb. 26, 1898.

23. "Narrow Escape from Death in the County Jail Rotary," *The Salt Lake Tribune*, June 1, 1904.

24. "Elmer A. Lane Has Peculiar Experience," *The Salt Lake Tribune*, March 5, 1909.

25. "Prison Life in the Big Rotary of the County Jail," *Deseret Evening News*, March 1, 1902.

26. "Captured Dynamiter Arraigned in Court," *The Salt Lake Herald*, Aug. 31, 1899.

27. "Was Arrayed in All His Glory," *The Salt Lake Tribune*, Nov. 22, 1904.

28. "Suspected of Schwan Assault," *The Salt Lake Tribune*, Nov. 17, 1904.

29. "Snow King Sentenced," *The Salt Lake Tribune*, March 27, 1898.

Chapter 14

1. https://en.wikipedia.org/wiki/Wichita.

2. "Editorial Notes," *Fort Scott Daily Monitor*, May 1, 1888.

3. "Men Trapped in Ancient Jail Rotary: If Fire Should Break Out 24 Men Would be Cremated—No Power On Earth Could Remove Them, Rotary Bucks Like Bull Elephant, Refuses to Work, Shutting Prisoners in—Entire Jail Branded a Disgrace to a Civilized Community," *The Wichita Daily Eagle*, July 20, 1917.

4. "Boy Held for Murder, to Be Released on His Own and His Mother's Bond, He Is Now Confined in the Wichita Jail Where His Health Is Endangered by Its Filthiness," *The Daily Commonwealth*, May 11, 1888.

5. *Ibid.*

6. "A Jail Improvement," *The Wichita Daily Eagle*, December 14, 1889.

7. "A Jail Improvement," *The Wichita Daily Eagle*, December 14, 1889.

8. *The Wichita Daily Eagle*, September 26, 1890.

9. "Tramp Must Work, He Has Invaded Wichita and Run Against a Big Snag, the *Wichita Daily Eagle*, March 3, 1895.

10. "Must Keep It Clean, Recommendations in Regard to Sedgwick County Jail," *The Wichita Beacon*, January 11, 1904.

11. "Jail Not So Bad: What the Interior of the Segwick County Jail Looks Like," *The Topeka Daily Capital*, April 16, 1905.

12. "Sedgwick Jail Bad Says Prisoner," *The Topeka Daily Capital*, September 16, 1908.

13. "Fire Threatens Prisoners, Smokes Eight Men in Rotary at County Jail and Destroys Some Liquor," *The Wichita Daily Eagle*, March 9, 1915.

14. "Rose's Plan Accepted, Twelve Architects in Competition for Sedgwick County Jail," *The Gazette Globe*, September 18, 1916.

15. "Jail Rotary Is Still Temperamental," *The Wichita Daily Eagle,* July 23, 1917.

16. "Men Trapped; Rotary Again Out of Order," *The Wichita Daily Eagle,* August 29, 1917.

17. "Rotary Still Out of Order," *The Wichita Daily Eagle*, August 30, 1917.

18. *Ibid.*

19. "Judge Bird's Talk Makes Rotary Work," *The Wichita Daily Eagle*, September 2, 1917.

20. "28 Prisoners Is Limited Judge Sets for County Jail, Any Number in Excess of This Must Be Sent to Other Places for Detention, Commissioners Agree," *The Wichita Daily Eagle*, February 15, 1919.

21. "Firm as a Rock, Dies with a Single Desire Expressed and That Is to Show Game, the Mandates of the Law Carried Out in Full, Officers Pale Before the Task—Mosier Seemingly the Least Concerned of Those Present," *The Wichita Daily Eagle*, November 18, 1887.

22. "Joe and Jake, the Crime for Which Joe and Jake Tobler Stood Under the Gallows, How Two Sleeping Cattlemen Were Murdered and Robbed in the Indian Territory, Callous Behavior of the Two Men on the Scaffold—Their Last Night on Earth," *The Walnut Valley Times*, November 22, 1888.

23. "She Hung Herself, Mrs. Lon Hoding Attempts to End Her Life," *The Wichita Daily Eagle*, June 20, 1899.

24. Unruly Prisoner to the Gallows, Sedgwick County Jail Doors Open on Horton, Sheriff Says He Has Been One of the Worst Prisoners He Has Had to Handle During Four Years," *The Wichita Beacon*, July 29, 1909.

25. "Sentenced to Be Hanged, the Last Act but One in Two Oklahoma Tragedies, Adams and Belden Condemned to Death—How the Death Sentences Were Pronounced and How the Condemned Took It—Speeches of the Prisoners and Scenes in the Court Room," *Wichita Eagle*, April 3, 1891.

26. "Belden Very Happy, the President Yesterday Commuted the Sentence to Life Imprisonment—How He Received the News," *The Wichita Daily Eagle*, July 24, 1891.

27. "Sent to Leavenworth, Belden and Mattox Sent to the Penitentiary Last Night," *The Wichita Daily Eagle*, October 11, 1891.

28. "After Three Trials, Clyde Mattox, the Oklahoma Murderer Must Hang October 11," *The McPherson Daily Republican*, June 27, 1895.

29. "Clyde Mattox One of Bad Men of Territory, Most Important Witness for Maust Twice Pardoned by Presidents, Sentenced to Hang in Wichita," *The Wichita Daily Eagle*, January 25, 1912.

30. "Will It Crack? Ed Pickens Will Have That Question Answered About His Neck on June 2, an Extra Effort to Be Made in His Case for Executive Clemency," *The Wichita Beacon*, April 22, 1893.

31. "Sentence Commuted," *Newton Daily Republican,* May 26, 1893.

32. "Thirty Long Years, in the Penitentiary at Lansing Was Mrs. Leonard Was Given, for the Murder of Her Husband, H.H. Leonard, Motion for a New Trial, Was Overruled and Judge Dale Passed the Sentence Yesterday, Her Attorney's Prayed an Appeal to the Supreme Court," *The Wichita Beacon*, June 27, 1896.

33. "A Boy Gets 20 Years, Clyde Moore Sentenced to Prison for Wiltberger Murder," *The Topeka Daily Capital*, January 4, 1902.

34. "Break Jail, Two Murderers at Wichita Make Good Their Escape," *The Atchison Daily Champion*, July 6, 1892.

35. "Makes His Escape, Sedgick County Jail Wouldn't Hold Mr. Harris," *The Wichita Daily Eagle*, February 28, 1895.

36. "Jail Delivery Prevented," *Fort Scott Daily Monitor*, December 2, 1896.

37. "Big Jail Delivery, "Bill" Tackett Saws Through Iron and Steel, Eight Criminals Escape, Officers Hot on the Trail of the Fugitives," *The Wichita Daily Eagle*, February 3, 1899.

189

38. "$300 Reward!" The *Wichita Beacon*, February 4, 1899.

39. "One More Caught, Jim Murphy the Jailbreaker Nabbed in Colorado, Beating His Way West, Sheriff Will Leave Today for Trinidad to Bring Him Back," *The Wichita Daily Eagle*, February 10, 1899.

40. "Talk with Tackett, Sheriff Simmons Visits Him in the Penitentiary, Tells Home He Escaped, Broke Jail in Oklahoma Since He Left Here," *The Wichita Daily Eagle*, October 15, 1899.

41. "Boys Attempt to Break Jail, Dug Hole Through North Wall of Prison, Used Handles of Spoons, When Discovered 20 Bricks Had Been Removed," *The Wichita Beacon*, October 24, 1902.

42. "Bold Attempt at Jail Breaking, Five Prisoners at County Jail Are Stopped by Prompt Action of Sheriff's Wife," *The Wichita Daily Eagle*, May 17, 1910.

43. "His Christmas in Jail," *The Wichita Beacon*, December 22, 1910.

44. "From the Halls of Justice, United States Circuit Court," *The Topeka Daily Capital*, November 13, 1889.

45. "Became Insane in Prison," *The Topeka Daily Capital*, August 30, 1889.

46. "Gus Nordmark Is Here, He Arrived Sunday Morning and Is Now Confined at the County Jail," *The Wichita Daily Eagle*, December 24, 1895.

47. "Kansas Notes," *The Leavenworth Weekly Times*, June 2, 1892.

48. "Must Pay the Penalty, Supreme Court Sustains the Decision in the Anderson Gray Case," *The Wichita Daily Eagle*, April 7, 1895.

49. "Kornstett Secreted in Jail, Sent Back Here and Held in a Mysterious Manner," *The Wichita Daily Eagle*, September 24, 1899.

50. "Kansas Items of Interest," *Garnett Journal*, May 17, 1901.

51. "In Sedgwick County Jail, Murderer Christy Is Brought Here From Wellington for Safe Keeping," *The Wichita Beacon*, June 22, 1903.

52. "Threatened Lynching, Three Wichita Negroes Hustled to County Jail Today," *Independence Daily Reporter*, May 23, 1906.

53. "Moore Taken to Winfield, No Danger of Mob Violence for the Arkansas City Wife Slayer," *The Salina Evening Journal*, October 24, 1906.

Chapter 15

1. https://en.wikipedia.org/wiki/Waxahachie,_Texas.

2. "The City," *Fort Worth Daily Gazette*, December 30, 1887.

3. "The Old Jail" The Rotary Jail Museum, Crawfordsville.

4. "Broke Jail, Nine White Men Escape from Ellis County Farm Prison," *Corsicana Daily Sun*, April 20, 1915.

5. "Humane Commissioners Buy Setee for Jail, Commissioners of Ellis County Introduce an Innovation—Welcomed by Prisoners," *The Waxahachie Daily Light*, April 11, 1911.

6. *Ibid.*

7. "Indicted for Murder," Grand Jury Bills Negro Who Is Alleged to Have Murdered J.H. Taylor," *The Waxahachie Daily Light*, October 14, 1905.

8. "Negroes Escaped, but They Were Recaptured in a Short Time," *The Houston Post*, January 13, 1906.

9. "Two Hangings in Texas Today, Tom Young of Georgetown and Albert Johnson of Waxahachie Paid Penalty," *Palestine Daily Herald*, March 30, 1906.

10. "Young Woman Attacked by Negro, Criminal Assault Near India Drives Neighbors into a Frenzy, Officers Catch Assailant, Man Is Hurried to Waxahachie and Place in Jail Under a Strong Guard; Rumors of Lynching Make Officers Uneasy," *Abilene Semi Weekly Farm Report*, November 21, 1908.

11. "To Hang After Seventh Trial, Burrell Oats to Pay Penalty at Waxahachie This Week," *Amarillo Daily News*, November 24, 1912.

12. Burrell Oates Was Executed: Remarkable Legal Fight Ended by Death on Eighth Anniversary of His Crime, *The Houston Post*, November 30, 1912.

13. "Murder at Millbrook, a White Bummer Kills a Black Peace Disturber," *Western Kansas World*, March 10, 1888.

14. "Negro Held Here Is Suspected of Murder of Lacy," *The Waxahachie Daily Light*, December 28, 1920.

15. *The Hamlin Herald*, February 2, 1917.

16. "Lou Sapp Is at Liberty After Years Behind Jail," *The Houston Post*, June 14, 1919.

17. "Escaped from Jail," *The Laredo Times*, November 10, 1891.

18. "Tom Varnell, Is Again Behind Bars of Waxahachie Jail, He Had Not Succeeded in

Getting Away from Town—Rejoicing Over Murderer's Recapture," *Fort Worth Daily Gazette*, May 14, 1893.

19. "Prisoners Break Jail," *The Houston Post*, December 22, 1896.

20. "City Officers Nab Swindler Who Broke Jail at Waxahachie," *Waco Morning News*, April 27, 1915.

21. "Corsicana Youth Arrested Trying to Saw Bars Through," *The Corsicana Semi-Weekly Light*, December 15, 1925.

22. "His Neck Saved, Governor Hogg Commutes Sentence of a Negro Rapist, the Man Being Isaac Bruce of Hill, and the Evidence Adduced at the Trial Not Being, in the Governor's Estimation, Sufficient to Warrant His Death," *The Austin Weekly Statesman*, May 18, 1893.

23. "Trial of Bartlett Is to Begin on the 19th of the Month," *The Houston Post*, June 12, 1899.

24. "The Case of Warren Bartlett May Be Appealed," *The Houston Post*, June 23, 1899.

25. "Warren Bartlett Convicted, Given a Life Term in the Penitentiary for Rape," *The Houston Post*, June 22, 1899.

26. "Held for Homicide," *The Galveston Daily News*, November 26, 1892.

27. "Removed to Another Jail," *El Paso Herald*, September 14, 1910.

28. "Petty Theft on Increase, These Crimes Chargeable to the Boys and Young Men of the Towns, Illegal Sale of Whiskey, Grand Jury Says in Final Report That Booze Is Being Sold in Waxahachie and in Ennis," *The Waxahachie Daily Light*, April 25, 1908.

29. "All Over Texas," *Nocona News*, November 29, 1906.

Chapter 16

1. *Gettysburg Adams Sentinel*, May 11, 1835.

2. "The Ku-Klux," *Boston Post*, March 10, 1870.

3. https://en.wikipedia.org/wiki/Charleston,_West_Virginia.

4. "General News of Interest," *Cumberland Daily Times*, April 15, 1887.

5. "Two Men in Kanawha County Jail Burned," *Raleigh Herald*, August 26, 1909.

6. "Two Thompson Girls, Recently Taken

to Salvation Army Rescue Home, Brought Back to Testify in Jail Investigation, Evidence More Damaging than Ella Clark's Story," *Bluefield Daily Telegraph*, December 23, 1909.

7. "Evidence Too Revolting for Publication, Kanawha Jail Investigating Committee Resumes Taking of Testimony, Jailor Accompanied Prisoners to Tenderloin," *Bluefield Daily Telegraph*, December 29, 1909.

8. "Jailor Is Scored in Report of Committee, Conduct of Kanawha Prison Merits Condemnation of All Who Stand for Law and Order," *Bluefield Daily Telegraph*, January 9, 1910.

9. "Jail Is Full, and Judge Black Has Only Begun Sentencing Bootleggers," *Charleston Mail*, December 15, 1914.

10. "Jail Is Full, and Judge Black Has Only Begun Sentencing Bootleggers," *Charleston Mail*, December 15, 1914.

11. "John Morgan Declines, Sheriff Still Huntington (Sic) Man for Night Jailor for Kanawha County," *Charleston Daily Mail*, April 6, 1918.

12. "At This Hour," *Charleston Mail*, October 19, 1918.

13. "New Jail Is Needed," *Charleston Mail*, March 8, 1919.

14. "Conditions in County Jail Described as 'Awful,'" *Charleston Daily Mail*, April 6, 1922.

15. www.rja.wv.gov.

16. *The Weekly Register*, July 29, 1887.

17. "Gave Himself Up, The Slayer of Henry Moore Delivers Himself to Charleston Authorities," *The Wheeling Daily Intelligencer*, February 14, 1888.

18. "Wouldn't Stand the Stones," *The Wheeling Daily Intelligencer*, September 13, 1892.

19. "Charged with Killing of Detective," *Beckley Raleigh Register*, July 20, 1911.

20. "Murder Charge Against Cook, Arrested on Warrant Issued for Killing Which Occurred About Two Years Ago," *Raleigh Herald*, April 4, 1918.

21. "Wife Kills Husband Because of Cruelty, Tragedy Occurs Among Colored People of Eskdale—Woman Admits Her Crime," *Charleston Mail*, August 13, 1918.

22. "Wife Slayer Committed Promptly to an Asylum, Fred Bailey Sent Away This Afternoon to the State Hospital at Spencer, He Is Pronounced Insane, Lunacy Commission

Disposes of Case of Kanawha Two Mile Murder Case," *Charleston Mail*, September 21, 1918.

23. "Tomes Held for Murder, Young Colored Man Held Without Bond for Grand Jury," *Charleston Mail*, September 24, 1918.

24. "Second Degree Murder Is Admitted by Davis," *Charleston Mail*, February 9, 1919.

25. "Fourteen Prisoners Sent to Moundsville, Transferred from the Kanawha County Jail to State Penitentiary," *Charleston Daily Mail*, June 24, 1922.

26. "Voiers Recaptured, Condemned Murderer, Sentenced to Be Hanged, and Who Escaped Jail, Caught at Charleston, W. Va.," *The Wheeling Daily Intelligencer*, September 10, 1897.

27. "Adams Captured, Fugitive Culprit from West Virginia Caught in New Mexico," *Raleigh Herald*, September 26, 1907.

28. "State News in Brief," *Raleigh Herald*, March 5, 1908.

29. "Third Escape Too Much for Relative, Herbert Wagner Drops Dead When He Hears of John Truslow Breaking Jail," *Bluefield Daily Telegraph*, April 5, 1914.

30. "Notorious Crook Breaks Jail and Two Go with Him," *Charleston Mail*, July 5, 1918.

31. "Two Escape from Jail," *Charleston Mail*, August 23, 1918.

32. "Big Jail Delivery Is Averted Sunday Morn, Fifty Prisoners Expected to Get away—Three Successful Deliveries Occur," *Charleston Mail*, February 3, 1919.

33. "Justice, Hot on the Trail, of the Roane and Jackson County Outlaws, an Organized Band of Conspirators Found, Who Have Perpetuated All Sorts of Crimes, Not Stopping at Murder, Round Together by an Oath to Kill and Plunder, a Story That Puts West Virginia to Shame, the *Wheeling Daily Intelligencer*, November 25, 1887.

34. "Reminder of the Hatfield-McCoy Feud," *The Wheeling Daily Intelligencer*, May 7, 1890.

35. "Escaped the Mob," *The Wheeling Daily Intelligencer*, July 20, 1899.

36. "A Game of Craps, Results in a Terrible Tragedy at St. Albans, Kanawha County, a Telegraph Operator Killed," *The Wheeling Daily Intelligencer*, July 16, 1892.

37. "Alleged Slayer Is Held, Isaiah Washington, Wanted in Ohio, Detained at the County Jail," *Charleston Mail*, December 30, 1914.

38. "Negro, Charged with Murder, Is in Kanawha County Jail, *Charleston Mail*, October 23, 1915.

39. *The Weekly Register*, December 3, 1890.

40. "A Female Moonshiner Jailed in West Virginia," *Covington Friend*, October 9, 1891.

41. "A Big Haul, of Moonshiners by Deputy Marshals—Lee Ward Killed in the Fight," *The Wheeling Daily Intelligencer*, May 1, 1895.

42. "Through the State, Accidents and Incidents in West Virginia and Vicinity," *The Wheeling Daily Intelligencer*, September 22, 1887.

43. "An Outrage, Perpetuated by Democratic Officials in Elkhorn Region, Scheme to Prevent Negroes from Voting by Arresting Them on False Charges," *The Wheeling Daily Intelligencer*, October 29, 1896.

44. "West Virginia Briefs," *The Wheeling Daily Intelligencer*, September 22, 1900.

45. "Use Bloodhounds to Trail Men Who Shoot at Militia, Company A., of Parkersburg, Fired on Above Eskdale Monday Night," *Bluefield Daily Telegraph*, September 18, 1912.

46. "End of Paint Creek Strike Is in Sight, Miners Win Many Points by Settlement and a State Strike Is Averted, Military Prisoners Released," *Beckley Raleigh Register*, March 27, 1913.

47. "Deserter Is Arrested and Held for Action, Harry Mooney Lodged in County Jail to Await Word from Government," *Charleston Mail*, July 20, 1918.

48. "Pardoned from Prison, Governor Acts on Four Recommendations of Pardon Attorney," *Charleston Mail*, March 15, 1919.

Chapter 17

1. https://en.wikipedia.org/wiki/Strafford_County,_New_Hampshire.

2. Robert Marston, Dover, N.H.; People, Businesses, and Organizations 1850–1950, *2004*.

3. *Ibid.*

4. *Ibid.*

5. "Eleven Years in Jail, Stubborn New Hampshire Man Won't Take Poor Debtors Oath," *The Bennington Evening Banner*, April 29, 1910.

6. "Riot in Dover Jail, Six Convicts in a Revolving Cell Start a Fire," *Essex County Herald*, April 5, 1895.

7. "Murderer Kelly's Return," *Evening Star*, April 22, 1897.

8. *Vermont Phoenix*, October 8, 1897.

9. "Pleaded Guilty, Joe Kelley Weepingly Admits Killing Cashier Stickney," *The United Opinion*, April 30, 1897.

10. "Defense Not Outlined, Alfred Jones to Be Tried Next Month," *Essex County Herald*, March 4, 1898.

11. "The Jury Disagreed, Alfred Jones Alleged Murderer, Out on Bail, *Essex County Herald,* April 15, 1898.

12. "A Murder Charge Abandoned," *The Baltimore Sun*, September 21, 1898.

13. "Begins Long Sentence, Mrs. Lizzie Provinchia Taken to State Prison at Concord, N.H.," *Boston Daily Globe*, October 15, 1899.

14. "Running Down Gang of Noted Criminals, Attempt to Break Dover Jail to Release Them Suspected by Authorities, Guard Have Been Doubled," *Boston Post*, August 13, 1900.

15. "New Charge May Be Made, Officer Joyce of Lynn Picks Out John Williams in Jail at Dover, N.H.," *Boston Daily Globe*, July 25, 1900.

16. "Ballard Charged with Murder, Shot Mrs. Jenkins of Lee Hook, N.H., Last Monday, He Says It Was Accidental," *Boston Post*, February 22, 1901.

17. "By an Expert, Glass Examined at the Dover, N.H., Jail, Purpose to Ascertain Mental Condition of Slayer of Brother, Prisoner's Mother Passes a Restless Night," *Boston Daily Globe*, July 1, 1902.

18. "Dr. Stackpole and Ryan Are Indicted," Dover, N.H., Grand Jury Finds True Bills for the Death of Katherine Ryan, *The Barre Daily Times*, Sept. 19, 1907.

19. "Drop Case Against Doctor, Prosecution of Stackpole, Indicted for Criminal Operation, Dropped," *The Barre Daily Times*, February 20, 1908.

20. *City of Dover, New Hampshire: Centennial Celebration 1855–1955.*

21. *Fitchburg Sentinel*, April 4, 1892.

22. "Jail Breaking Prevented by a Timely Discovery," *Boston Daily Globe*, June 23, 1895.

23. "Slipped His Handcuffs, but Was Recaptured," *The Portsmouth Herald*, February 16, 1900.

24. "Jump Dover Jail, Three Men Make Escape Quite Easily, One Is John Rogers of This City, Thirty-Two Others Might Have Gained Freedom, Why They Failed to Do So Remains a Deep Mystery," *The Portsmouth Herald*, January 22, 1906.

25. "In Police Court, Two Men Arraigned Monday Afternoon, Charged with Aiding John Rogers' Escape," *Portsmouth Herald*, January 23, 1906.

26. "Cummings Caught, Man Who Escaped From Dover Jail Captured in Railroad Station," *The Portsmouth Herald*, July 3, 1906.

27. "Mrs. Fredett's Case Continued, Woman Charged with Assault with Intent to Kill Babe, Held in $2000 at Dover," *Boston Daily Globe*, March 13, 1900.

28. "Harry Hough Begins the Second Term of His Penalty, No More Home Delights as in Dover Jail," reported the *Boston Daily Globe*, October 10, 1900.

29. "Harry Hough's Sentence," *the Portsmouth Herald*, October 10, 1900.

30. "Arrested Again, After Serving Two Terms in Prison, Lodged in Jail," *Portsmouth Herald*, May 3, 1907.

31. "Murderous Lover Forgiven by Girl, Arthur Marcoux, Who Cut Sweetheart's Throat, Weeps in Jail," *Boston Post*, June 17, 1907.

32. "Prisoner at Dover Commits Suicide," *Boston Daily Globe,* May 29, 1895.

33. "Was Arrested Here, Man Who Attempted Suicide in Dover Jail, the *Portsmouth Herald*, February 17, 1906.

Chapter 18

1. *A Visitor's Guide to Gallatin*, Gallatin Publishing Company, 1989.

2. David Stark, "*Gallatin*," October 1994.

3. Birdsall & Dean, *History of Daviess County*, 1882.

4. "Almost Ready, the Gathering at Gallatin to Witness the Frank James Trial, a Host of Legal Talent Engaged—Preliminary Law Skirmishes—Securing the Jury—The Defense an Alibi—The Murder of Sheets," *St. Louis Post-Dispatch*, August 23, 1883.

5. "Crittenden Shielded Him, the Reason Why the Cases Against Frank James Were Dismissed," *St. Louis Post-Dispatch*, February 12, 1884.

6. *Ibid.*

7. *Ibid.*

8. *Ibid.*

9. *Ibid.*

10. *Ibid.*

11. *Ibid.*

12. *Ibid.*

13. *Ibid.*

14. *Ibid.*

15. Jim McCarty, *Rural Missouri*, June 1987.

16. *Ibid.*

17. "County Jail Closed by Sheriff," *Gallatin North Missourian*, Nov. 6, 1975.

18. Joe Snyder, *County Seat Paper: A Glimpse into the Life and Times of a Small Town—Gallatin, Missouri*, 1991.

19. "The Squirrel Cage: Gallatin's Rotary Jail," *Rural Missouri, June* 1987.

20. "Daviess County's Circular Jail Offered as Museum," *The Chillicothe-Tribune*, May 28, 1986.

21. www.daviesscountyhistoricalsociety. com.

22. *Ibid.*

23. *Ibid.*

24. "A Negro Killed, a Mexican Greaser Kills a Negro with a Beer Bottle at Jamesport, Mo., the Deed Premeditated—The Bottle Loaded with Lead—Both 'Thoughts,'" *Chillicothe Constitution*, April 30, 1890.

25. "Boy Begs to Stay in Jail, Youthful Slayer Said He Could Not Remain Home," *St. Louis Post Dispatch*, February 11, 1908.

26. "Given 35 Years in Prison, Hugh Tarwater Convicted of Murder of Newspaper Editor," *The Salina Evening Journal*, October 14, 1920.

27. "3 Months for Stabbing," *Jefferson City Post-Tribune*, March 17, 1938.

28. "Ware Murder Case Set for Wednesday, to Be Heard in Daviess County—Slaying of Sonny Lewis Was in 1951," *The Chillicothe-Tribune*, May 11, 1953.

29. "Jury Finds Hampton Guilt of Murder, Penalty Is Set at 10 Years Imprisonment by Daviess County Men," *The Chillicothe-Tribune*, September 12, 1960.

30. "Whiteaker Found Guilty of White's Slaying," *Gallatin North Missourian*, February 4, 1971.

31. "Missouri State News," *The Chillicothe-Tribune*, February 16, 1890.

32. "Two Escape from Gallatin Jail," *The Hermitage Gazette*, August 24, 1898.

33. *Gallatin Democrat*, Jan. 12, 1899.

34. "Catch Lipps Again," *The Chillicothe-Tribune*, April 25, 1925.

35. "Reward of $50 Offered," *The Chillicothe-Tribune*, September 25, 1929.

36. "County Officers Arrest Two Men Who Broke Jail, Pair Who Fled from Gallatin Are Captured Near Parnell," *The Maryville Daily Forum*, January 29, 1931.

37. Poster at the Daviess County Historical Society Museum.

38. "Escapes from County Jail, but Freedom Short-Lived," *Gallatin North Missourian*, September 10, 1970.

39. "Prisoner Ends His Life by Taking Poison," *The Sedalia Democrat*, May 29, 1941.

40. "Everman Gets Jail Sentence, Gallatin Stockman Pleads Guilty to Fraudulent Use of the Mails in a Federal Court Monday," *Gallatin North Missourian*, September 23, 1920.

41. "Jamesport, Mo., Banker Is Rushed to Gallatin Jail, Crowd Severely Beats Him at Railroad Station When It Was Believed He Was Attempting Flight," *Joplin Globe*, February 25, 1925.

42. "Court Imposing Many Sentences, Man Convicted of Bootlegging and Grand Larceny Get Fines, Jail and Penitentiary Sentences," *The Chillicothe-Tribune*, May 11, 1923.

43. "Store Robbers Caught in Quick Time Monday," *Gallatin North Missourian*, February 27, 1975.

44. http://ddcrj.com/dd/.

Chapter 19

1. www.pueblo.us.

2. Clark, Ken, *Pueblo Lore*, May 2009.

3. "The Territories," *Morning Oregonian*, March 2, 1875.

4. https://en.wikipedia.org/wiki/ Colorado.

5. *Ibid.*

6. *Ibid.*

7. "Two Mexicans Lynched by Mob, Men Taken from Pueblo City Jail and Hanged to Bridge Girders," *The Oregon Statesman*, September 14, 1919.

8. "County Jail to House Prisoners," *Santa Ana Register*, May 12, 1927.

9. *Ibid.*

10. "Pueblo Jail Is for Sale," *Florence Morning News*, October 27, 1968.

11. "Pueblo's Old Jail Offered for Sale," *The Cincinnati Enquirer*, November 10, 1968.

12. *Ibid.*

13. "Killed at a Dance, Master of Cere-

monies Shot Two Men Who Attacked Him," *The Leavenworth Times*, November 24, 1901.

14. "A Pueblo Duel, One Principal Is Dead and the Other in Jail," *Arizona Republic*, October 21, 1902.

15. "A Tragedy at Trinidad, The Bloody Revenge of a Deputy Sheriff," reported the *Arizona Republic*, April 8, 1905.

16. "Found the Man, Mystery of Pueblo Jailer's Death Cleared Up, Circumstantial Evidence Points to the Guilt of the Negro Prisoner in the Jail," reported *The Evening Telegram*, April 17, 1908.

17. "Nunn Makes a Confession, Admits the Killing of Thurman Walker, Was Most Brutal Murder," *The Salina Daily Union,* November 9, 1908.

18. "Walker's Slayer Sentenced, Court Declares This the Most Cold Blooded Murder in History of Colorado," *The Valley Falls New Era*, January 21, 1909.

19. "Man Wanted for Murder Is Located," *The Oregon Daily Journal*, November 19, 1909.

20. "Gerbrick Goes to Pen for Life, Former Pawnee Co. Boy Plead Guilty to Colorado Train Wrecking, John H. Roddy Interviewed Gerbrick in Pueblo Jail and Got Interesting Story," *The Tiller and Toiler*, September 16, 1910.

21. "Commutes Two Condemned Prisoners in Colorado," *El Paso Herald*, July 24, 1919.

22. "Accused Man Arrested, Man Charged with Murder Found in Colorado," *The Junction City Daily Union*, August 11, 1919.

23. "Youthful Bandits, After Brief Career of Crime, Taken by Colorado Posse, One, 14 Years Old, Lies in Hospital at Point of Death, and the Other Is Held in County Jail at Pueblo—Both Charged with Murder," *Springfield Republican*, August 21, 1926.

24. "Baby Bandit Improves, Boy Sits Up in Bed and Jokes with Reporters, the *Emporia Gazette*, August 27, 1926.

25. *The Daily Morning Astorian*, July 29, 1888.

26. "Thirteen Colorado Prisoners Escape," *The Pantagraph*, May 6, 1889.

27. "Tries to Escape, Mrs. Garvin's Clever Coup Nipped in the Bud, Leaves Hospital in Disguise, Blacks Face and Masquerades as Negress, Arrested at Santa Fe Depot, Carried Dummy Baby in Arms to Aid in Concealing Identity—Her Sister, an Accomplice, Also in Custody—Had Ticket to Pueblo," *The Weekly Gazette*, December 6, 1906.

28. "Wounded Criminal Is Believed Beyond Hope," *Albuquerque Journal,* December 29, 1919.

29. "Prisoners Drill Through Pueblo Jail with Spoon," *Arizona Republic*, August 18, 1921.

30. "County Jail to House Prisoners," *Santa Ana Register*, May 12, 1927.

31. "Colorado Cullings," *The Salt Lake Tribune*, January 16, 1895.

32. "Fort Scott Man Drank Acid, M.B. Cart, Who Deserted His Wife, Grew Despondent in Jail and Attempted Suicide," *Fort Scott Weekly Monitor*, December 20, 1900.

33. "Scissors, Hatpin, Poison, Three Women Try Self-Murder in Pueblo Jail, Several Desperate Attempts Frustrated, Women Arrested on Charge of Shop-Lifting Feel Disgrace Keenly," *The Guthrie Daily Leader*, February 11, 1908.

34. "Turns On Foreign Husband: American Wife of Greek Tells Pueblo Police They Talked of 'Shaking Down' Wichita Banker, Quit First Spouse For Him, Following Her Arrest With Divorced Man She Comes to Wichita to Get Divorce," *The Wichita Daily Eagle*, August 8, 1913.

35. "Colorado Cattle Thieves, Arrest of a Gang That Has Operated for Twenty Years," *Estherville Daily News*, December 7, 1893.

36. "Preacher Sentenced, C.S. Rooks, Formerly of Kansas and Nebraska, Convicted in Pueblo, Colo.," *The Iola Register*, January 8, 1898.

37. "Confesses to Mail Theft, a Postmistress in Colorado Admits Robbing the Mail," *The Morning Times*, May 20, 1899.

38. "Drunken Indians Set Fire to Jail," *The Salt Lake Tribune*, March 9, 1908.

39. "Feared Attempt to Free I.W.W., Pueblo Jail Is Guarded by Fifty Armed Men, Unrest in Coal Fields, Surprise Attack Rumored, as Two Dozen Auto Loads of Strikers Left Walsenburg in Early Morning," *Lincoln Evening Journal*, November 8, 1927.

40. "Prisoners Released," *The Billings Gazette*, November 30, 1927.

41. "Pueblo Paper Publisher Will Pay Tax in Jail, the *Klamath News*, January 21, 1931.

42. "Colorado Cullings," *The Salt Lake Tribune*, January 14, 1891.

43. "To Prevent a Lynching," *The Marion Star*, May 10, 1895.

44. "Murder and Conspiracy, Information

Filed Against Cripple Creek Strikers," *The Salt Lake Herald*, December 4, 1903.

45. "Depositors Threaten, Ex-Banker Is Removed, Bond Fixed at $100,000; Schiffer Taken to Pueblo for Safe-Keeping," *The Salt Lake Tribune*, October 10, 1905.

46. "Robbed Mails, Alleged Murderer Held by Federal Officers, Wanted for Killing Night Marshal at Lamar—Think a Job Was a Put Up," *The Evening Telegram*, April 13, 1907.

47. "Plot to Release Starr, as a Result the Oklahoma Bandit Was Moved to the Pueblo Jail," *The Coffeyville Daily Journal*, June 10, 1909.

48. "Doomed Slayers Lose Hope of Escape and Turn to Religion," *The San Bernardino County Sun*, November 11, 1929.

49. "Doomed Pair Placed in Death Row Cell," reported *The Ogden Standard-Examiner*, November 29, 1929

50. "Ralph Fleagle Joins Mates in Condemned Row," *Arizona Republic*, December 12, 1929.

Bibliography

Published Sources

Birdsall & Dean, *History of Daviess County*, 1882.

Clark, Ken, *Pueblo Lore*, May 2009.

City of Dover, New Hampshire: Centennial Celebration 1855–1955.

Dodson, Kimberly D. "The Rotary Jail of Montgomery County, Indiana: An Early Experimental Penelogical Design." *Corrections Now*, Vol. 12, Issue 2, October 2010.

"History of DeKalb County Sheriff's Office," Office of Sheriff DeKalb County.

Hopkins, Arthur. *Prisons and Prison Buildings*. New York: Architectural Book Publishing, 1930.

Lunden, Walter A. "The Rotary Jail or Human Squirrel Cage," *Journal of the Society of Architectural Historians*. Vol. 18, No. 4, December 1959.

Marston, Robert. *Dover, N.H.: People, businesses, and organizations 1850–1950*, 2004.

McCarty, Jim. *Rural Missouri*, June 1987.

Miller, Douglas K. "The Salt Lake County Rotary Jail," *Utah Historical Quarterly* 75.4, Fall 2007.

Nodaway County Missouri, Vol. 1, B.F. Bowen & Company, 1916.

Pease, Theodore Calvin. *Collections of the Illinois State Historical Library*. The Laws of the Northwest Territory, 1788–1800 (1925).

Pevsner, Nicholas. *A History of Building Types*. Princeton: The Princeton University Press, 1976.

Randl, Chad. *Revolving Architecture*. New York: Princeton Architectural Press, 2008.

Roenfeld, Ryan, and Warner, Dr. Richard. *History of the Squirrel Cage Jail*, Undated.

Roenfeld, Ryan, and Warner, Dr. Richard. *Tales From The Squirrel Cage Jail*, Vol. 2, 2013.

Snyder, Joe. *County Seat Paper: A Glimpse into the Life and Times of a Small Town—Gallatin, Missouri*, 1991.

"'Squirrel Cage Jail' over 130 years old," *Historical Society of Pottawattami County Member*.

Stark, David, "*Gallatin*," October 1994.

A Visitor's Guide to Gallatin, Gallatin Publishing Company, 1989.

Newspapers

Abilene Semi Weekly Farm Report, 1908
Albuquerque Journal, 1919
Amarillo Daily News, 1912
Arizona Republic, 1902–1929
Attica Daily Tribune, 1915–1920
Barber County Index, 1897
Beckley Raleigh Register, 1911–1913
Bluefield Daily Telegraph, 1909–1914
Boston Daily Globe, 1895–1902
Boston Post, 1870–1901
Brazil Daily Times, 1913
Burlington Hawk Eye, 1890
Carrol Daily Times Herald, 1958
Charleston Mail, 1914–1922
Chillicothe Constitution, 1890–1923
Corsicana Daily Sun, 1915
Covington Friend, 1891
Creston News Advertiser, 1969
Cumberland Daily Times, 1887
El Paso Herald, 1910–1919
Elkhart Weekly Review, 1885
Essex County Herald, 1895–1898
Estherville Daily News, 1893
Evening Star, 1897

Fitchburg Sentinel, 1892
Florence Morning News, 1968
Fort Madison Evening Democrat, 1969
Fort Scott Daily Monitor, 1888–1896
Fort Scott Weekly Monitor, 1900
Fort Worth Daily Gazette, 1887–1893
Gallatin Democrat, 1899
Gallatin North Missourian, 1920–1975
Garnett Journal, May 17, 1901
Gettysburg Adams Sentinel, 1835
Great Clipper, 1933
Hammond Lake County Times, 1909–1928
Hopkinsville Kentuckian, 1915
Independence Daily Reporter, 1906
Iowa City Press-Citizen, 1948
Jefferson City Post-Tribune, 1930–1938
Joplin Globe, 1925
Kansas City Journal, 1897
Kentucky Advocate, 1934
Knox Stark County Democrat, 1900
Laurens Advertiser, 1888
Lincoln Evening Journal, 1927
Lincoln Semi Weekly State Journal, 1893
Lincoln Weekly Nebraska State Journal, 1891–1900
Logansport Journal, 1896
Logansport Pharos-Tribune, 1895
Macon Chronicle-Herald, 1953
Maryville Daily Democrat Forum, 1918–27
Maryville Daily Forum, 1930–1978
Maryville Republican, 1904
Mason City Globe-Gazette, 1962
Morning Oregonian, 1875
Newton Daily Republican, 1893
Nocona News, 1906
Omaha Daily Bee, 1885–1899
Palestine Daily Herald, 1906
Raleigh Herald, 1907–1918
Red Wing Daily Republican, 1886
Rock Valley Bee, 1906–1962
Rural Missouri, 1987
Rushville Republican, 1930
St. Joseph Gazette, 1938
St. Louis Post-Dispatch, 1883–1905
Santa Ana Register, 1927
Sedalia Weekly Sentinel, 1904
Shelbyville Daily Democrat, 1886–1917
Springfield Republican, August 21, 1926
The Alliance Herald, 1909
The Atchison Daily Champion, 1892
The Austin Weekly Statesman, 1893

The Baltimore Sun, 1898
The Barre Daily Times, 1907–1908
The Bennington Evening Banner, 1910
The Billings Gazette, 1927
The Call-Leader, 1927–1928
The Chillicothe-Tribune, 1890–1986
The Chillicothion-Tribune, 1907–1925
The Cincinnati Enquirer, 1929–1968
The Coffeyville Daily Journal, 1909
The Columbus Journal, 1907
The Corsicana Semi-Weekly Light, 1925
The Council Bluffs Nonpareil, 1888–1944
The Courier-Journal, 1881–1934
The Courier, 1901
The Daily Commonwealth, 1888
The Daily Morning Astorian, 1888
The Daily Reporter, 1938
The Des Moines Register, 1903–1952
The Emporia Gazette, 1926
The Evening Telegram, 1907
The Galveston Daily News, 1892
The Gazette Globe, 1916
The Guthrie Daily Leader, 1908
The Hamlin Herald, 1917
The Hermitage Gazette, 1898
The Hickman Courier, 1912
The Holt County Sentinel, 1900
The Houston Post, 1896–1912
The Huntington Press, 1918
The Indianapolis News, 1881–1932
The Indianapolis Star, 1916–1932
The Interior Journal, 1885
The Iola Register, 1898
The Jamestown Press, 1908
The Journal-Courier, 1919
The Junction City Daily Union, 1919
The Kearney Daily Hub, 1910
The Klamath News, 1931
The Laredo Times, 1891
The Leavenworth Times, 1901
The Leavenworth Weekly Times, 1892
The Macon Republican, 1889
The Marion Star, 1895
The Maryville Daily Forum, 1931
The Mason City Globe-Gazette, 1937–1942
The McCook Tribune, 1885
The McPherson Daily Republican, 1895
The Morning Times, 1899
The Nebraska State Journal, 1908
The Norfolk Weekly News, 1899
The North Platte Weekly Tribune, 1902

The Oregon Daily Journal, 1909
The Oregon Statesman, 1919
The Paducah Evening Sun, 1882–1910
The Paducah Evening Sun, 1906
The Palmyra Spectator, 1891
The Pantagraph, 1889
The Portsmouth Herald, 1900–1907
The Public Ledger, 1892
The Republic, 1892–1905
The Ripley County Journal, 1883
The St. Louis Republic, 1901–1902
The Saint Paul Globe, 1888
The Salina Daily Union, 1908
The Salina Evening Journal, 1906–1920
The Salt Lake Herald, 1903
The Salt Lake Tribune, 1891–1908
The San Bernardino County Sun, 1929
The Sedalia Democrat, 1898–1973
The Taney County Republican, 1901
The Tiller and Toiler, 1910
The Topeka Daily Capital, 1889–1908
The United Opinion, 1897
The Valley Falls New Era, 1909
The Walnut Valley Times, 1888
The Wanatah Mirror, 1917
The Waxahachie Daily Light, 1905–1920
The Weekly Gazette, 1906
The Weekly Register, 1887–1890
The Wheeling Daily Intelligencer, 1887–1900
The Wichita Beacon, 1893–1917
The Wichita Daily Eagle, 1887–1919
Union Record, 1887
Vermont Phoenix, 1897
Waco Morning News, 1915

Western Kansas World, 1888
Wichita Eagle, 1899
Winchester Journal, 1885

Unpublished Sources

Application for United States Patent No. 244,358, July 12, 1881.
"The Old Jail," the Rotary Jail Museum, Crawfordsville.
Signs at the Rotary Jail Museum, Crawfordsville, Indiana.

Internet

Cronk, Susan, "Nodaway County Jail," Blog
http://ddcrj.com
www.brainyquote.com
www.daviesscountyhistoricalsociety.com
www.ddcrj.com
www.hauntedhouses.com
www.insideprison.com
www.jailexchange.com
www.paducahky.gov
www.pottcounty.com
www.pueblo.us
www.rja.wv.gov
www.rotaryjailmuseum.org
www.thehistoricalsociety.org
www.weitz.com
www.westegg.com
wikipedia.org

Index

Numbers in **_bold italics_** indicate pages with photographs.

211